# Understanding Trauma

**Tavistock Clinic Series**
*Nick Temple, Margot Waddell (Series Editors)*
Published and distributed by Karnac Books

Other titles in the Tavistock Clinic Series:

Assessment in Child Psychotherapy
*Margaret Rustin and Emanuela Quagliata (editors)*

Facing It Out: Clinical Perspectives on Adolescent Disturbance
*Robin Anderson and Anna Dartington (editors)*

Inside Lives: Psychoanalysis and the Growth of the Personality
*Margot Waddell*

Internal Landscapes and Foreign Bodies:
Eating Disorders and Other Pathologies
*Gianna Williams*

Mirror to Nature: Drama, Psychoanalysis and Society
*Margaret Rustin and Michael Rustin*

Multiple Voices: Narrative in Systemic Family Psychotherapy
*Renos K. Papdopoulos and John Byng-Hall (editors)*

Psychoanalysis and Culture: A Kleinian Perspective
*David Bell (editor)*

Psychotic States in Children
*Margaret Rustin, Maria Rhode, Alex Dubisky,
Hélène Dubinsky (editors)*

Reason and Passion: A Celebration of the Work of Hanna Segal
*David Bell (editor)*

Surviving space: Papers on Infant Observation
*Andrew Briggs (editor)*

Therapeutic Care for Refugees: No Place Like Home
*Renos Papadopoulos (editor)*

Orders
Tel: +44 (0)20 8969 4454; Fax: +44 (0)20 8969 5585
Email: shop@karnacbooks.com
www.karnacbooks.com

# Understanding Trauma

## A Psychoanalytical Approach

Caroline Garland
Editor

KARNAC

LONDON          NEW YORK

First published in 1998 by
Gerald Duckworth & Co. Ltd.
Second impression 1999
This edition printed in 2002 by
H. Karnac (Books) Ltd
6 Pembroke Buildings, London NW10 6RE
Tel. (0)20 8969 4454
Fax. (0)20 8969 5585
Reprinted 2004

A catalogue record for this book is available
from the British Library

ISBN 1 85575 977 2

Edition amendments
by The Studio Publishing Services Ltd,
Exeter EX4 8JN

# Contents

# Series Editors' Preface

Since it was founded in 1920, the Tavistock Clinic has developed a wide range of therapeutic approaches to mental health which have been strongly influenced by the ideas of psychoanalysis. It has also adopted systemic family therapy as a theoretical model and a clinical approach to family problems. The Clinic is now the largest training institution in Britain for mental health, providing postgraduate and qualifying courses in social work, psychology, psychiatry, and child, adolescent, and adult psychotherapy, as well as in nursing and primary care. It trains about 1,400 students each year in over 45 courses.

The Clinic's philosophy aims at promoting therapeutic methods in mental health. Its work is founded on the clinical expertise that is also the basis of its consultancy and research activities. The aim of this Series is to make available to the reading public the clinical, theoretical, and research work that is most influential at the Tavistock Clinic. The Series sets out new approaches in the understanding and treatment of psychological disturbance in children, adolescents, and adults, both as individuals and in families.

This book describes the work of the Unit for the Study of Trauma and its Aftermath in the Adult Department of the Tavistock Clinic. This challenging and innovative work is rooted in psychoanalysis, both clinically and theoretically. The thoughtful and detailed account given here shows how much can be done for traumatised individuals, but also the complex and long-standing nature of their problems.

This book takes us back directly to the clinical experience of trauma which led to the founding of the Tavistock Clinic in 1920 by Crichton-Miller and his colleagues. These psychologically-informed physicians had had extensive experience of the treatment of traumatised soldiers in the First World War. The men had been psychologically damaged by their battlefield experience and showed many similar symptoms to the patients described in this book. The founding of the Tavistock came out of the physicians' determination to provide psychological treatment for traumatised people, not only in war but in everyday life. The knowledge that the Clinic had gained from this work was then applied in the Second World War, when the staff of the Clinic had a major involvement in army psychiatry, which had meanwhile developed a humane and thoughtful way of dealing with the problems of battle trauma and war neurosis. In turn, this war work led to many advances in psychiatry and psychological treatment which have since been drawn on more generally in the Tavistock. This strong reparative ambition or desire is at the heart of the ethos of the Tavistock Clinic and continues to inform its clinical and theoretical development.

This book revisits the whole field, but from the point of view of new psychoanalytic ideas which have been developed in recent years. The link between understanding trauma and the wider work of the Clinic is emphasised by Caroline Garland. She points out that the task of therapy is hard since the extent of human destructiveness has to be faced in both perpetrator and survivor. The place of this book in the series is particularly fitting when we consider that the Clinic began in 1920, having to face the destructiveness of the war and its sacrifice of young lives.

Nicholas Temple and Margot Waddell
Series Editors

And this I know: all these things that now, while we are still in the war, sink down in us like a stone, after the war shall waken again, and then shall begin the disentanglement of life and death.

*All Quiet on the Western Front*
Erich Maria Remarque (1929)

# Acknowledgements

Our most important acknowledgement is to the patients who agreed to take part in the work of the Trauma Unit and let us use some of their clinical material, appropriately disguised, as the basis for the findings set out in this book. I would also like to thank my colleagues in the Adult Department of the Tavistock Clinic, and Eleanor Morgan, who was the good-tempered mediator between the Editor, the typing services and Duckworth, for their unfailing support. All of us have also received invaluable help and practical assistance from our partners and families. In particular, David Taylor was a powerful source of encouragement and constructive comment throughout the putting together of this book. For all of this we are appreciative and grateful.

The quotation on page 18, from Chapter 22 in *A Textbook of Psychotherapy in Psychiatric Practice* (Editor J: Holmes), published by Churchill Livingstone in 1991, appears with the permission of the publisher. Random House kindly let me use the frontispiece quotation from Erich Remarque's *All Quiet on the Western Front*, which is now published under their Vintage imprint, London, 1996. USA rights: *Im Westen nichts neues*, copyright 1928 by Ullstein A.G.; Copyright renewed © 1956 by Erich Maria Remarque. *All Quiet on the Western Front* copyright 1929, 1930 by Little, Brown and Company; Copyright renewed © 1957, 1958 by Erich Maria Remarque. All Rights Reserved.

# Contributors

**David Bell** is a Consultant Psychotherapist and Psychiatrist in the Adult Department of the Tavistock Clinic. He is also a Member of the British Psychoanalytical Society.

**Caroline Garland** is a Consultant Clinical Psychologist in the Adult Department of the Tavistock Clinic, where she heads the Unit for the Study of Trauma and Its Aftermath. She is also a Member of the British Psychoanalytical Society.

**Elizabeth Gibb** was a Senior Registrar in the Tavistock Clinic Adult Department's Four-Year Training, and left to become a Consultant Psychotherapist and Psychiatrist in the Psychotherapy Unit at the Maudsley Hospital. She is currently a student at the Institute of Psycho-analysis.

**Graham Ingham** was a Senior Lecturer in Social Work in the Adult Department of the Tavistock Clinic. He is an Associate Member of the British Psychoanalytical Society and now works as a psychoanalyst in Leeds.

**Shankarnarayan Srinath** was a Senior Registrar in the Tavistock Clinic Adult Department's Four-Year Training, and left to become Consultant Psychotherapist and Psychiatrist at Addenbrooke's Hospital in Cambridge.

**David Taylor** is a Consultant Psychotherapist and Psychiatrist in the Adult Department of the Tavistock Clinic, and is Chairman of the Department. He is also a Member of the British Psychoanalytical Society.

**Nicholas Temple** is a Consultant Psychotherapist and Psychiatrist in the Adult Department of the Tavistock Clinic, where he is also Chair of the

Clinic's Professional Committee. He is a Member of the British Psycho-analytical Society.

**Linda Young** is a Consultant Clinical Psychologist, working in both the Adolescent and the Adult Departments of the Tavistock Clinic, where she is responsible for the training offered by the Unit for the Study of Trauma and Its Aftermath. She is an Associate Member of the British Psychoanalytical Society.

# Part One

# Introduction

# Introduction

# Why psychoanalysis?

*Caroline Garland*

Nearly a dozen years ago, in 1986, six students who were qualifying at the same time at the Institute of Psycho-Analysis were celebrating this event with a party. That same evening, the radio news and the television screens gradually filled up with the story and pictures of the sinking of the ferry, the Herald of Free Enterprise, off the coast of Belgium, with the loss under appalling circumstances of hundreds of lives. As the enormity of the disaster became apparent, it seemed increasingly important to us that our brand-new qualification in the field of mental health should be put to work outside as well as inside the consulting room; to have an direct application in the area of external relations as well as in the intrapsychic world of the individual. The next day, two of us travelled to Dover to offer whatever we could in the way of back-up, support, listening, expertise. What we saw and learned that day (including the blunt fact that 'helpers' arriving unasked at the scene of a catastrophe is by no means always helpful) was the first stage in the formation by one of us of what became, about eighteen months later, the Tavistock's Unit for the Study of Trauma and Its Aftermath.

This book collects together some of that Unit's subsequent work with a variety of cases. Its chapters are written by clinicians who share an interest in the understanding of trauma, all of whom work or have worked at the Tavistock, and been associated with the Unit's work in one way or another. What is distinctive about this book's approach, amongst the many that have been published on trauma and traumatic stress, is that it focusses upon a psychoanalytic approach to the treatment of traumatised states of mind. These are the mental states currently known in DSM-IV and ICD-10 as Post-Traumatic Stress Disorders, although they have had a long history under other names (Garland, 1993). Psychiatric and psychological advances in their treatment have played an important role in identifying and defining a typical clinical picture, making possible epidemiological research, and includ-

3

ing work on co-morbidity, as well as opening the way for studies of therapeutic effectiveness. These approaches have burgeoned, particularly in the United States and particularly since the extent and nature of the long-term damage to Vietnam veterans has become increasingly visible.

However, this work (which is looked at in more detail in Chapter 3), although providing part of the background to our own approach, is less central to it than is an understanding of psychoanalysis. Our own theoretical framework is grounded in the work of Freud and Klein, believing that the impact of traumatic events upon the human mind can only be understood and treated through achieving with the patient a deep knowledge of the particular meaning of those events for that individual. This means we pay detailed attention to the childhood and developmental history, since we regard as crucial the way in which the earliest relationships not only shape later mental (and thus character) structure but have a continuing and active influence in the internal world. These early experiences with others will inevitably influence the nature of the severe psychic wounding that may be received in the traumatic collision with the external world – in part through determining how those events will eventually come to be construed; in part through determining through those same internal structures the extent and nature of the recovery that is possible. The psychoanalytic approach therefore investigates, and tries to shift or modify, these internal object relations and the corresponding state of the internal world, rather than focussing primarily upon symptomatology and classifiable mental disorder.

It is central to the psychoanalytic view that to be caught up in a severely traumatic event stirs up without fail the unresolved pains and conflicts of childhood. When it comes to treatment, to attempt to understand the creature of the present without regard to his or her past may sometimes work, but for most patients it achieves at best a temporary and chronically unstable quiescence of the more acute after-effects of the immediate trauma. Increasingly, clinical findings indicate that events have to be remembered, rather than forgotten or put out of one's mind. This fact is becoming very clear, for example in the case of holocaust survivors (e.g. Jucovy, 1992; Wardi, 1992). In spite of their understandable wish to put the past behind them and to spare their loved ones the knowledge of the worst of what they have been through, it seems in many cases that areas of hidden or denied parental devastation becomes a burden that may have to be carried unconsciously by the children, even grandchildren of survivors.

4

This fact, and others like it, especially where unconscious mental processes are involved, are the outcome of the very structure of the human mind. They cannot be willed out of existence. Psychoanalysis tries to document and understand these phenomena. Thus we use a psychoanalytic approach to the understanding and treatment of trauma because it addresses directly what is felt to be most disturbing, intransigent and deeply-rooted in the individual's response. The trauma touches and disrupts the core of his identity; and to address that level of disturbance is not something that can be done quickly or lightly.

So, in our view, for traumatised individuals to get better, the knowledge and the memory of the events they have suffered may need to become part of, and integrated into, the individual's conscious existence, through being worked through instead of being walled-up in some avoided area of mental activity. Their meaning for the individual has to be discovered, even achieved, so that the individual's response makes sense to him or her, and can be thought about, rather than the trauma's being dismissed as bad luck, a meaningless 'accident', or fate. The task of therapy is hard, since the extent of human destructiveness has to be faced, in some instances in both perpetrator and survivor. Yet in the internal world there is no such thing as an accident; there is no such thing as forgetting; and there is no such thing as an absence of hatred, rage or destructiveness (as well as, of course, good and loving feelings), in spite of the urge in survivors to attribute all badness to the world outside them that caused their misfortune. These issues are what this approach, and this book, is about.

Each chapter is designed to be read separately, in that each draws upon, and spells out briefly, those elements of psychoanalytic theory that are relevant to its immediate clinical subject. However the book also has an overall structure. It is divided into five sections. The first contains an introduction to psychoanalytic thinking about trauma that I have written as Editor, describing some of the broad issues that are important in the understanding and treatment of survivors. It is followed by an essay by David Bell on the subject of the unconscious causation and meaning of the ostensibly accidental in everyday life. Accident investigators these days are more ready to pay attention to the state of mind of the pilot, the captain, the navigator, or the driver, in the hours before the fatal error. Was he stressed? Had he been drinking? Had he quarrelled with his crew? However, David Bell addresses how hard it remains to get the issue of unconscious motivation and, even more so, human destructiveness, into the public domain and into public consciousness. Many individuals expose themselves as well as others, to potentially traumatic situations – by tempting fate, by going too close to the edge – over and above the kind of everyday risks that are inevitable and desirable if one is to have a life at all. In our view, and in our Unit's by now considerable experience, unconscious factors are crucial when it comes to understanding why this decision was taken and not that one, or why this particular safety precaution was pushed aside or overlooked on this particular occasion.

The second section describes the opening moves in the therapeutic encounter. It contains a detailed account by David Taylor of two initial consultations in which he shows the significance of the psychoanalytic framework in establishing the fullest and deepest meaning of an event for a particular survivor. Linda Young then describes the four-session therapeutic consultation that is offered to all the Unit's referrals, through an account of the growing understanding achieved by both therapist and patient as the patient's reaction to a murderous assault upon him is described and elucidated.

At the end of the four-session consultation, most of those who come to the Unit are then offered the possibility of further treatment – for the individual, not for the trauma – and many accept it, recognising that the major upheaval provoked by the traumatic event in their internal, as well as external worlds, is not something that can be adjusted to quickly or easily if they are to make a good working recovery. Recovery is seen by the Unit as the capacity to *get on with it*, and in reasonably good spirits, rather than to *get over it*. The survivor can never be restored to his pre-trauma state (Garland, 1991). A traumatic event changes those who suffer it, and all change involves loss. As Isabel Menzies-Lyth (1989) points out, in the paper first given to the first of the Unit's termly conferences on trauma, survivors have much in common with the bereaved. 'He must mourn for something he has lost of himself. "I am not the person I was: I will never be the same again." The question, however, is whether in the end the survivor will be less of a person than before, a more disturbed person, or whether he can become more of a person, the disaster becoming a focus for growth.'

The third section of this book describes that very process, the struggle in once-weekly, psychoanalytically-informed treatment to become more, rather than less of a person, following a variety of extremely painful events. In Chapter 5, Linda Young and Elizabeth Gibb take up the difficult issue of grievance as it is encountered in certain survivors, often pre-dating the trauma developmentally, but equally often given fresh impetus by the trauma in the present. The consequences for treatment are serious, since the survivor's sense that his grievance (namely that his life has been altered in deeply unpleasant ways) can never satisfactorily be addressed or understood can be an overwhelming obstacle to change. Here, Graham Ingham's and Elizabeth Gibb's papers are central, since they describe through clinical material the work of mourning that has to be achieved if change and growth is to be set in motion. In my own chapter in this section I have addressed two further issues: first, the powerful adhesions that can develop between the trauma of the present and certain features of the individual's early history, particularly when the trauma is felt to provide confirmation of early phantasies; and second, the way in which these links can then be hard to shift because of the damage done by the traumatic event to the survivor's capacity to symbolise. Symbolisation is felt, following Segal (1957), to be the basis of a capacity for flexible thought, for the transformation of unassimilatable material into something more manageable, and ultimately for the capacity to mourn and move on. Finally in Chapter 9 Shankarnarayan Srinath describes, both through theory and through clinical illustration, the great significance of issues of identification for the understanding of the impact of trauma.

Two further papers by Nicholas Temple and David Bell form the fourth section of the book, both containing accounts of work with patients in five-times weekly analysis. Analysis offers a unique opportunity for study of the way in which traumatic early relationships affect the development of adult personality and vulnerabilities. Nicholas Temple's paper describes the treatment of a patient with many borderline features to her personality. He provides a detailed account of these processes in action, supplementing much of the recent work in psychiatry and forensic psychotherapy on the causal link between serious childhood traumata and the development of a borderline personality disorder. The final section broadens the picture, taking the Unit's work out into the community. I describe two pieces of work with entire groups that suffered traumatic events and subsequently asked for help. This work, a combination of an organisational and a group-therapeutic approach, is an important part of the Unit's work.

The book as a whole, as must be clear from this Introduction, is based upon the clinical therapeutic encounters that are the daily work of the Unit. Out of them has grown our understanding and respect for what has already been described by psychoanalytic writers of the past. To this body of work we have hoped to add our own clinical contributions, through careful and detailed attention to the stories that our patients have brought us, to the manner in which they have done so, and through our own thinking about the significance of what we have seen and heard, both for them as individuals and for the understanding of trauma in general.

# 1

# Thinking About Trauma

*Caroline Garland*

## What is a Trauma?

Trauma is a kind of wound. When we call an event *traumatic*, we are borrowing the word from the Greek where it refers to a piercing of the skin, a breaking of the bodily envelope. In physical medicine it denotes damage to tissue. Freud (1920) used the word metaphorically to emphasise how the mind too can be pierced and wounded by events, giving graphic force to his description of the way in which the mind can be thought of as being enveloped by a kind of skin, or protective shield. He described it as the outcome of the development in the brain (and therefore mind) of a highly selective sensitivity to external stimuli. This selectivity is crucial: shutting out excessive amounts and kinds of stimulation is even more important, in terms of maintaining a workable equilibrium, than is the capacity to receive or let in stimuli.

For infants and young children, when all goes well, that filtering function is largely served by the mother, or primary caretaker, through her sensitivity to what her baby is able to manage at any particular time. She acts to protect her baby from the extremes of experience, both environmental and emotional. Adults are in a different position. Some will have built up inside themselves, partly as the outcome of good parental provision, a capacity to take care of themselves in the best meaning of that phrase. Others will have been unable to achieve this degree of autonomy. Still others, for a variety of complex internal reasons, will actively seek out situations of risk, or extremes of stimulation, whether for positive or at least comprehensible reasons, or in more darkly self-destructive ways. Yet however well any individual feels he is normally able to take care of what he feels to be his own well-being, some events will overwhelm that capacity, will knock out ordinary functioning and throw the individual into extreme disarray. Much of the immediate disturbance and confusion is visible to the observer but

9

eventually it extends far beyond the visible, into the depths of the individual's identity, which is constituted by the nature of his internal objects – the figures that inhabit his internal world, and his unconscious beliefs about them and their ways of relating to each other.

Not all traumatic events of course are that devastating. Sometimes one can see the mind engaged in protecting itself from the potential rent in its own fabric by engaging in a variety of defensive strategies. A man who slipped and fell on some icy steps outside his own front door and broke his ankle clearly heard the radiologist say that it was broken, but he 'knew' the radiologist was mistaken: he 'knew' it was only a sprain. Half an hour later, when the shock of the event had somewhat subsided, he was able to acknowledge that it was indeed broken and that he would be spending Christmas with his foot in plaster. This man was *denying* the extent of the damage so that he could absorb the news more gradually, at a pace that he could manage without feeling overwhelmed.

Sometimes when a piece of reality is felt to be quite unmanageable, the defence is correspondingly extreme. Freud (1924), talking about the route into psychosis, describes the genesis of delusions: 'a fair number of analyses have taught us that the delusion is found applied like a patch over the place where originally a rent had appeared in the ego's relation to the external world.' In a vulnerable character, the delusional 'patch' is clung to and embroidered to avoid the breakdown that would follow if the reality were admitted. A woman who had always had some difficulty accepting the exigencies of reality learned of the death of the youngest of her five children abroad. She was unable to deal with this agonising fact. She believed that he was alive, and that she was the victim of a police conspiracy designed to prevent her from discovering the hospital he had been taken to. Gradually the patch came to take over her whole functioning. She was unable to maintain relations with her older children who were themselves desperately upset not only by the loss of their brother, but also by what effectively became the loss of their mother. Thus the fear of one kind of breakdown, with which she could in time have been helped, was replaced by a more severe and more intractable breakdown in her functioning, in which all help was rejected – to accept it would have been to acknowledge the delusional nature of her belief that the boy was still alive.

So a traumatic event is one which, for a particular individual, breaks through or overrides the discriminatory, filtering process, and overrides any temporary denial or patch-up of the damage. The mind is flooded with a kind and degree of stimulation that is far more than it can make sense of or manage. Something very violent feels as though it has happened internally, and this mirrors the violence that is felt to have happened, or indeed has actually happened, in the external world. There is a massive disruption in functioning, amounting to a kind of breakdown. It is a breakdown of an established way of going about one's life, of established beliefs about the predictability of the world, of established mental structures, of an *established defensive organisation*. It leaves the individual vulnerable to intense and overwhelming anxieties from internal sources as well as from the actual external events. Primitive fears, impulses and anxieties are all given fresh life. Trust in the fundamental goodness of one's objects, that is to say the world itself, is shattered – who after all let this terrible event happen? Failed to protect you from it? Worse, might even have wished for or provoked it? Loss of a belief in the predictability of the world, and in the protective function of one's good objects, both internal and external, will inevitably mean a resurgence of fears about the cruelty and strength of bad objects. There is a rapid slide into primitive paranoid beliefs about one's status in the world. Crucially, the anxieties coincide: the external event is perceived as confirming the worst of the internal fears and phantasies – in particular the reality and imminence of death, or personal annihilation, through the failure of those good objects (internal and external) to provide protection from the worst.

Thus a trauma is an event which does precisely this: *overwhelms existing defences against anxiety in a form which also provides confirmation of those deepest universal anxieties*. The damage done, more often than not, is neither trivial nor temporary. Some kind of help is therefore important, whether arrived at fortuitously or sought out, intentional and organised.

Although Freud's description of the way in which such events breach the protective shield is an important, indeed necessary, part of understanding trauma, it is not on its own, as I have already suggested, sufficient. It still has a mechanistic quality. It describes the breakdown in the smooth running of the machinery of mind, but not the collapse of meaning: the failure of belief in the protection afforded by good objects, and from that point onwards the longer-term consequences for the entire personality.

In the Trauma Unit's Workshop, we have come to think of the ensuing processes as the transformation of the traumatic event, whatever it might have been, into a shape that is recognisable as an existing form of internal object relationship. Since an object-relations perspective in psychoanalysis believes that all events are attributable to some notion of an agent held to be responsible for them, for both good and

11

ill, a traumatic event, not surprisingly, is attributed to some very noxious agent indeed. As I have said, the event provides *confirmation* of the most persecutory of unconscious phantasies about one's objects, even the world itself. The internal good object that one believed one might turn to for protection or for help has been revealed to be careless, or unconcerned, or worse, malignant. Bion (1962) points out how a hunger pain is interpreted by the infant not as the absence of a feeding object, but as the presence of an attacking object. The implication is that as trust in the goodness and strength of one's internal objects is undone, the power and malevolence of bad internal objects increases. It was Melanie Klein's view (1940) that if the loss of the good object, around which the ego has organised itself from the beginning of life, cannot be mourned then the outcome can be a progressive deterioration in the personality. In the Unit, we hear this at almost every consultation: *I'm not what I was. My life has just gone to pieces. I used to get a lot of pleasure from my kids, but nowadays they just drive me mad. I don't care about anything these days.*

Interestingly, whatever the nature of the event, whether an act of God, or man-made, or an intentional personal assault, the outcome is the same: although the individual may struggle to defend himself against this process, eventually he comes to make sense of the event in terms of the most troubled and troubling of the relationships between the objects that are felt to inhabit his internal world. That way the survivor is at least making something recognisable and familiar out of the extraordinary, giving it meaning. Not surprisingly, the internal object relationships that give most immediate sense and meaning to the traumatic event will be those that resemble it, both structurally and in terms of associations. The sunken ship full of dead babies is the mother who struggled and failed to keep herself and her children afloat. The smoke that is heard choking someone to death recalls the loss of a young sibling to muscular dystrophy, similarly choking for air. Yet in a psychoanalytic way of thinking, the most telling of these links will be made less with remembered events than with the non-verbal or pre-verbal registers of experience, which link with primitive notions of the earliest failures of the primary object, and with the unconscious yet annihilating impulses and phantasies that these provoked.

These primitive fears and phantasies, up to the point of impact with the traumatic event, may have been invisible because accommodated to and managed, more or less successfully. From the point of impact, they seem to take on increasing significance. The process of making sense of the senseless, while in some ways recreating order and meaning in the internal world, will inevitably imbue the event in the present with disturbing meaning from the past; and it is this connection of past with present that is part of what makes the after-effects of trauma so hard to undo.

## Freud and Trauma

It is beyond the scope of this chapter to trace in detail the evolution of Freud's thinking on trauma, and its development in the work of later analysts. I am instead going to pick out certain of Freud's ideas which, when put together, seem to offer a sound working basis for the clinician. Later theoretical and clinical developments add to, deepen and enrich this three-dimensional structure, but do not contradict it. It is clear that the history of psychoanalysis and the development of Freud's under- standing of trauma are linked. Hysterics, he said in 1893, repress the memory of certain very intense or painful experiences, as well as cutting off the feeling associated with those experiences, preserving it in a 'strangulated' state (i.e. bottling it up). The feeling then makes itself visible via 'hysterical symptoms' (i.e. symptoms for which there is no detectable organic cause), which also manage to be symbolic of the repressed memory. The conclusion he reached is that *catharsis cures*: once the original events are brought into consciousness, most impor- tantly along with all the original intense feeling that accompanied it, the symptoms will disappear. Until that point, 'the psychical trauma – or more precisely the memory of the trauma – acts like a foreign body which long after its entry must continue to be regarded as an agent which is still at work ...'

Modern clinicians may still find something useful in this early attempt to understand trauma, disturbance, and its treatment. Certain thoughts or feelings can from a functional point of view become 'forgotten', or sealed-off, existing as foreign bodies within the rest of that mind's functioning until released intact, perhaps by treatment, perhaps by particular events, or by time itself, years later. Moreover, the obsessional preoccupations which are such a feature of the thought processes of the traumatised may represent continuing attempts to process ('discharge' in Freud's language) the intense affect surrounding certain painful experiences. They are perhaps only a short step further on from the flashback itself, the sudden sense of being caught up once more in the overwhelmingly painful events (see Chapter 8) instead of being able to think back on them from the position of the present.

As an example, a successful young Consultant Anaesthetist was referred to the Unit following a motorway crash, in which he had been severely injured. He was recovering from his injuries, but found himself depressed, brooding over the events of the accident, unwilling to drive, feeling nothing for his girlfriend, and worse, unable to work. He had taken sick leave and stayed at home, but he was aware even after three months that he felt in no state to take up his job again. He was irritable in the consultation, wanting to know where 'the treatment' was, and why I was making no helpful suggestions. I pointed out to him that as he worked in the Health Service he must have been aware that the Tavistock Clinic offered psychological help, a 'talking cure.' I said to him that I thought he must have come here because he had something he wanted to talk about. I wondered what it was. Full of the same irritable scepticism he began, somewhat watchfully, to tell me about himself. It seemed that during his childhood – he came from a Welsh farming family that had struggled endlessly to make ends meet – he had never had a holiday. He had always worked for his parents on the farm, and they had paid him for this work, putting it into a savings account to pay for him to have a good education – to go to University, which would have been a first for his family. He did in fact go to Medical School and was clearly doing well, and had been enjoying his life and although he recognised that his parents' motives had been good, he had nursed a considerable grievance towards them for depriving him of his childhood, as he saw it. During the accident, when he was lying severely injured with a punctured lung in Casualty, he managed to get on the bad side of the Ward Sister, who told him injured doctors always made more of a fuss than anyone else, then mishandled his treatment and left him in a great deal of pain. He found himself frightened, helpless and enraged. He thought to himself that if ever he had to give her an anaesthetic he would make sure that it was light enough for her to suffer deeply. In fact, he wished her dead. The analysis of his history, and his thoughts and feelings about the accident – why had his girl-friend travelling in the car behind not flashed her lights to warn him of the impending disaster since she said she'd seen it coming? – left neither of us in any doubts that he had had quite murderously retaliatory impulses toward the Ward Sister and to the girl-friend, and behind them in the distant past the mother, all of whom should have taken proper care of him, just as my waiting and listening stance in the consultation felt like yet another failure of 'proper' care. These thoughts had frightened him, since an anaesthetist in a very real way controls not just pain but also life and death. He had suppressed the memory of those murderous impulses (i.e. split off the affect) but produced a symptom (being unable

14

to work) which carried some considerable symbolic significance – he was avoiding putting himself in a position where he could have someone's life in his hands. Three meetings later, relieved by our discoveries, and even amused by the recognition that he too had an unconscious – he had thought it was a 'symptom' that belonged only to neurotics – he went back to work. He also went back to driving a car and he and his girl-friend began to talk of planning a family. In the short term at least, it seemed as though the problems had resolved enough for movement to occur. (I was rather taken by the fact that when his way of dealing with pain, namely through unconsciousness, was inadequate for his own mental pain, he should have turned to someone who increases, rather than reduces consciousness ...)

Freud's original paradigm for a traumatic event was sexual seduction, and his original understanding of anxiety was that it consisted of undischarged libidinal excitation. However, we read of his frustration and puzzlement in 1914(a) on learning that many of the seductions his patients had described had been products of phantasy rather than fact. Yet this same disappointment made possible his momentous recognition of the importance of infantile phantasy – 'this psychical reality requires to be taken into account alongside practical reality' – freeing him from having to remain wedded to the notion of infantile trauma as the sole basis of neurosis.

Yet even in 1893 he had been clear that the trauma was produced by the *effect* of the event upon the mind. 'Any experience which calls up distressing affects – such as those of fright, anxiety, shame or physical pain – may operate as a trauma of this kind.' Repression is then called into play when the feelings provoked by an experience are felt to be too intense to be accommodated by a mind concerned with keeping the level of excitation or feeling within certain limits.

The shift of emphasis from fact to phantasy marked a fork in the development of Freud's thinking about trauma. Recognising that although phantasies of seduction were universal, actual experiences of seduction were not, Freud's primary interest branched off from the path it was following, concerning the pathogenic nature of the external experience – 'practical reality'– towards a detailed and revolutionary exploration of the unconscious – the 'psychic reality'. Traumatic situations were now seen primarily in terms of unconscious phantasy and the internal world, and this remained his central preoccupation. However, he picked up again later on his original interest in the significance of the external event, possibly stimulated by the appalling legacy of the battlefields of World War One, when he began to speculate upon the significance of repetitive traumatic dreams, and the repetition compulsion. These phenomena had obliged him, for instance, to rethink the role of the Pleasure Principle as the only determining factor in the formation of dreams.

Two later developments then add significantly to our modern understanding of trauma. First, by 1923 Freud had arrived at a final formulation of his model of the mind. In 'The Ego and the Id' he describes mental structure as consisting of relations between three agencies, three modes of mental functioning, namely the id, the ego (the organised and conscious part of the id), and the superego – that part of the ego that sits in judgement on all its own activities. Correspondingly, Freud now viewed mental activity as the constant relations, negotiations and equilibrations that went on between these parts of the mind; and in this he began to come close to the more modern concept of an internal world consisting of dynamic relations between internalised objects.

Second, by 1926, Freud had also reworked his understanding of the origins of anxiety. This development provides a crucial piece in the three dimensional structure that composes our modern understanding of the effects of trauma. When a sufficiently extreme external event impacts on the mental organisation, its effect is to obliterate all defences against anxiety. The anxiety that then overwhelms the mind comes from *internal* sources, although the anxiety– provoking event is external. Freud lists five primary anxieties, felt to be both universal and potentially traumatic for anyone. They are birth; castration anxiety; loss of the loved object; loss of the object's love and, finally and overwhelmingly, annihilation anxiety. I think these anxieties have a single crucial feature in common: they consist of the separation from, or the loss of, *anything that is felt to be essential to life*, including life itself. They therefore bring the individual closer to a psychic recognition of death (see Freud, 1915a).

Once Freud had moved away from the notion that all anxiety derived from undischarged libidinal excitement, he relocated anxiety firmly within the ego, using his new structural model of the mind. The ego can tell the difference between anxiety experienced in an *actual* situation of danger (automatic anxiety) and that anxiety experienced when danger *threatens* – which he called signal anxiety (1926). Signal anxiety warns of an impending situation of helplessness. This distinction continues to hold good in most lives, but once the threat of annihilation has been encountered face to face, something changes. My own view is that *the ego, once traumatised, can no longer afford to believe in signal anxiety*

16

*in any situation resembling the life-threatening trauma: it behaves as if it were flooded with automatic anxiety*. This is a crucial factor in the loss of symbolic thinking, at any rate in the area of the trauma, which is such a marked feature of the behaviour of survivors. Certain smells, sounds, sights, situations, even words connected with the traumatic events all produce states of immense anxiety, and the mental state known as the flashback. There is no capacity and no place for belief in 'signals' or 'warnings': *this is it*.

The devastation of World War One stimulated in Freud the short paper, 'Thoughts for the Times on War and Death' (1915a), which is also one of his richest. It suggests a rekindling of his interest in the traumatic neurosis, predating by five years the culmination of that original line of thought in 'Beyond the Pleasure Principle'. This earlier paper addresses the subject of death itself, and man's attitudes to it, giving flesh and blood to the statement that annihilation is man's most fundamental anxiety. Amongst much else, Freud recognised not only that 'in the unconscious every one of us is convinced of his own immortality,' – that is to say, to conceive of a personal death is virtually impossible until we meet it face to face – but that in the death of an other, even when it is someone we love, there is something of triumph for the survivor, since 'in each of the loved persons there was also something of the stranger', and hence the rival. Ambivalence, which 'governs our emotional relations with those whom we love most', means that even our loved ones can arouse in us some degree of hostile feeling, and unconsciously we feel satisfaction that we are still alive when our rival is not. This paper has not only great theoretical significance, but also considerable clinical usefulness. Survivors of traumatic events have often witnessed the death of others, even relatives and loved ones. Added to the impact of the traumatic event is the task of mourning the death of others important in one's life – difficult under any circumstances, but made more so by the guilt evoked by having survived – perhaps particularly when the relationship was troubled or deeply ambivalent. Mourning is always immensely hard work, even when the relationship was relatively straightforward. The individual may feel he simply does not have the internal resources to do this work in the context of feeling that his own personal world is in pieces. Some of that mourning, as has often been pointed out, must be for himself – for his own lost world, his own pre-trauma life and identity.

Rather than face the guilt of survival, and the rage at being abandoned by those who have died, some survivors may unconsciously choose a path of lesser resistance. The task of mourning for both the pre-traumatised self and the other, the lost object, particularly in a world that seems irrevocably damaged, is felt to be unmanageable. Some survivors turn away from this task, and instead, make an identification with the dead object. Rather than mourn the dead, or mourn the loss of their own earlier undamaged identity, they will descend into a pathological substitution for mourning – melancholia. Freud's great paper, 'Mourning and Melancholia' (1915b) spells out these processes in detail. Although 'Mourning and Melancholia' is not in fact about trauma, this paper, together with 'Beyond the Pleasure Principle' (1920), and the revised view of the nature of anxiety, provide the basis for all later psychoanalytic developments in the field of trauma. They also incidentally add considerable richness to much of the psychiatric understanding of the impact and after-effects of trauma.

At the beginning of this chapter, I described one of the central passages in 'Beyond the Pleasure Principle' – Freud's theory of the way certain events actually achieve their traumatising effect upon the mind, after which the personality begins to take account of and adapt to these changed internal conditions. A significant element in this rapidly developing process is what Freud, still in the 1920 paper, called 'binding.' It is hard to be sure what precisely he meant by 'binding' since he used it at different stages of his work in slightly different ways (Laplanche et al., 1973) . However, by 1920, it has taken on the general meaning of a defensive operation that restricts free-flowing 'excitation', and this is its particular significance for the understanding of the longer-term effects of trauma. Once the catastrophic breach in the protective shield has taken place, and mental functioning is in turmoil and disarray, the problem is one of 'mastering the amounts of stimulus which have broken in and of binding them, in the psychical sense, so that they can then be disposed of.'

I described some aspects of this process in an earlier paper:

> By creating links with what is already there , by joining up what pours in with an existing feature or function of the mind, the ego is attempting to create once more structures of some permanence in which ego functioning is possible ... The central difficulty with a disaster lies, I believe, right here: the very intensity of the struggle to deal with the flood of unmanageable material *in the absence of the apparatus for thinking itself* locks that material powerfully and precisely to whatever has been released by the breaking down of internal barriers and structures. (Garland, 1991)

In other words, the traumatic influx of stimulation from the present stirs up the early phantasies of devastation and cruelty, and paranoid views of relations between objects, which then get bound up with the present events in a way which is hard to undo. It seems that the more intense and long-lasting the traumatic event, the greater and more lasting the emotional loading that it carries, which makes it still harder to disengage from the newly-released and highly charged material to which it gets attached.

Sometimes events in the present have a specific meaning for those who endure them, certainly when they seem to confirm the worst of those early phantasies and object relationships (see Chapter 8). In such cases, what Freud might have called *binding* seems to intensify and become a kind of fusion. The past and the present become indistinguishable: each not only makes sense of the other, but each seems to confirm the most pathological features of the other. Segal's (1957) description of uneven development in the personality offers a clear way of understanding this phenomenon. She shows how where there is only a partial attainment of the depressive position (Klein, 1952) the result can be a situation in which earlier, unintegrated ego experiences are retained in a split-off, sealed pocket of vulnerability whose existence forms 'a constant threat to stability. At worst, a mental breakdown occurs and earlier anxieties and split-off symbolic equations invade the ego.' The experience of an external traumatic event will open up such pockets of disturbance, and through the process of binding, keep them open, giving their contents fresh life and imbuing the present with the significance of the past.

Although 'Mourning and Melancholia' predated 'Beyond the Pleasure Principle' by five years, it laid the foundations for modern psychoanalysis. The recognition that the ego could, by dividing itself into parts, take a part of itself as its own object, opened up the possibility of an internal world populated by objects in dynamic relations with each other. Moreover, understanding that parts of the ego could become identified with objects was revelatory when it came to recognising what was happening when mourning went wrong. The processes of mourning, and its pathological counterpart, melancholia, have particular significance for the final outcome of trauma for the individual. So often the long-term outcome presents as a state of chronic melancholia. In this case, the identification with the lost object becomes a way of avoiding unbearable guilt – ultimately the guilt of having survived at all, sometimes compounded by the survivor's feeling in some way responsible for the deaths.

As a clinical example, I saw a 16-year old survivor of the Hillsborough tragedy, at the request of the team responsible for treating him.

They were worried by his state and contemplating giving him ECT for his suicidal depression. He had been lifted out over the heads of the crowd 18 months earlier in the disaster in the football stadium, when a sudden rush of spectators pouring in at the back of the standing area meant that nearly 100 fans at the front were crushed to death against the barriers. Although this boy had been treated for depression, he had not responded, and worried about his failure to recover, his local psychiatrists had sent him away from his home town to a major psychiatric institution in the South. There, by now away from home for over a year, he had been exposed to systematic 'desensitisation'. The walls of his room were papered with newspaper photographs of agonised faces crushed against the wire and daily he was required to watch television newsreels of the catastrophe. He had become suicidally depressed, curled up in his room, crying out in pain, and whimpering for his mother. For a long time in the consultation he was unable to speak to or look at me. He began to uncurl mentally, as it were, as I asked him about his mum and dad, his little brother, and his early life in a rather ordinary way. My feeling was he was immensely relieved he was not going to be put through a rehearsal once again of the events in the stadium. As this ordinary conversation progressed, and he told me a bit about his parents and his home life, I began to get a picture of a boy with a fiercely Catholic mother, who had taken in from her and identified with some quite strong ideas about good and bad. Although he had just reached the age of puberty, with all its resurgence of Oedipal interest in the mother, this boy had not yet taken the step of going out with girls. Instead he was at a transitional state, allying himself with the definitively masculine world of football, and projecting the fierce Oedipal rivalries he felt with his father out on to the football field, where the battles could be enacted by the opposing teams on his behalf. In this way, he could enjoy the area in which he and his father were on the same side, and avoid the area in which they were rivals. However, when the symbolic battle went horribly wrong and the violent and symbiotically-shared crowd emotions resulted in death, the boy was faced with something he felt deeply implicated in, identified with through a massive pre-existing projection. In order to avoid the truly unbearable guilt of feeling responsible for the opposing team's supporters' deaths, he entered into a state of identification with the dead, thus avoiding the cruelly violent and persecuting superego which told another part of him that he was a murderer, a worthless criminal. I suspected that the reason the densitisation treatments could not help is that they coincided with deadly accuracy with the state of affairs in his internal world. The

20

treatments were perceived to be both a confirmation of his irredeemable guilt and also a torture rightfully and justly inflicted upon him as a worthless criminal. Anything good or lively in him he had projected into (attributed to) certain of his doctors and caretakers, where it could not be contaminated by his own terrible badness. He was, I felt, dominated internally by a very pure culture of deathliness. What was significant for his treatment was that this state of identification with the dead had for him a distinct survival value, because it saved him from the unbearable guilt which made him feel most like killing himself.

There was a point in the interview in which this became poignantly and painfully clear. For a short while he became free of the crying and persistent nose-blowing and nose-bleeding (I felt he was perpetually engaged in trying to empty his head of the torturing feelings) and appeared to become more alive and even quite interested in some of the things we were talking about. He looked up from his collapsed position, made eye contact and even smiled. But then, as though he had suddenly caught himself in a forbidden activity, he cried out in a renewed agony that he could not get better (i.e. less depressed) because then his body would be in such pain again and he would feel so guilty. I felt during the interview that I could see his identifications shifting between the dead, the criminally worthless him, and the cruelly harsh judge; and I could also feel the sense of his pushing me into becoming identified with his own capacity for life, as well as the more loving and kindly aspects of the maternal object – manifested as the wish in me to urge him not to think so harshly of himself, to treat himself more benignly. Some of this process I tried to describe to him, particularly the way in which he attacked his own capacity to cheer up, as well as the reasons for it, since I knew I would only be given the opportunity to see him once.

How does one help someone in this state? I recommended to the team that the idea of ECT, and the densitisation treatments be ended, for the reasons I have outlined above. I thought that the events of the disaster should no longer be the focus of his treatment, because they were not in fact the problem: the problem was the shape and form that those events had taken up in his internal world and the meaning he had given them. In fact, I thought, given his youth, he should be helped by stages to go back home, go back to school, be given some once-weekly psychotherapy, plus medication at night to help with the bad dreams. (I never heard what if any of these recommendations the team accepted, but six months later I did hear, to my great relief, that he was back at home and attending school.)

21

In any traumatic event it is possible that particular external events and certain aspects of psychic reality will fuse in an intractable way, and will need treatment. The point about this particular case is that it bore out so precisely the clinical picture Freud presented in 'Mourning and Melancholia.' It is not hard to see in the clinical picture arrived at in 'chronic PTSD', or more recently, 'complex PTSD', what we in other circumstances might call melancholia.

Since an object relations perspective on human development and emotional functioning developed out of Freud's, Klein's and others' work on identification, it has become increasingly possible to understand in detail the effects of traumatic events on the personality. Much of this is contained in the chapters in this book, each of which focusses upon that aspect of theory that is felt to be most helpful to the author's understanding of the clinical material. I have already touched on Freud's major contribution to the understanding of the damage to the personality that is done by a traumatic event. Segal's work on the breakdown in symbolisation when there is a loss of the containing object is crucial, as is Bion's later development of this concept of containment. Bion described the process of the transformation of unassimilatable raw material ('beta elements') into something that can be processed mentally ('alpha functioning') and this is felt to be highly important to the outcome of treatment. Again, I have described this in detail in the earlier paper (Garland, 1991), and its particular significance is touched on in the present volume in Chapters 3 and 7, as well as others.

This chapter has followed one particular line of conceptual development. There are other significant contributions by major authors, each with their own particular contribution to the understanding of object relations and the impact of trauma on the human mind (Abraham, 1907; Ferenczi, 1933; Greenacre, 1953; Winnicott, 1958; Balint, 1969; Khan, 1963, 1964; Furst (Ed.), 1967; Yorke, 1986; and others). The reader who wants to investigate further the background to this book might begin by exploring the section in the Bibliography called *Suggestions for Further Reading*. But for the time being, I want to go back to the practical issues that face the clinician.

## The Individual and the Event

So far I have been writing as though two things were always the case: that individuals are the same when it comes to the response to a traumatic event, and that getting caught up in such an event was an involuntary matter, just sheer bad luck. Yet clearly individual differences, or individual vulnerabilities are immensely important. However precisely we might be able to identify and quantify the nature of the stressor, it is not sufficient as a way of understanding the impact on the individual. The individual has a constitution and a history which have shaped his internal world; hence a character and personality. He also has a culture. So he is someone who is more or less vulnerable to that particular event at that particular moment in his developmental history. That vulnerability is a function of the inevitable interplay between objective and subjective, external and internal reality. In practice it is a complex business.

As far as bad luck is concerned in the collision of individual and event, sometimes this is indeed the case. To have a life worth the name will inevitably involve some risk. We leave the home in the morning, cross the road, take public transport, go to the bank, go for walks along cliff-paths, eat unpasteurised cheese because it tastes nice, even steak, put cars on ferries, holiday in countries where there have been earthquakes or hijacks, decide to go skiing or hot-air ballooning. Any of these activities could land us in a crisis, but still we think they are worth the candle.

More complicated are those activities that involve a disavowed risk, the turning of a blind eye to carelessness or a wilful disregard for known hazards. These might include smoking, or the use of drugs, or – these days – casual sex, or not bothering to wear a seat belt for a short journey. Here there may be many factors at work. There may be a kind of defiance or challenge to an object who is perceived as restricting or depriving or judgemental. There may be an omnipotent identification with a careless (carefree?) object who is felt to take insufficient care of the well-being of the baby, and this may involve a corresponding contempt for the feelings of that frightened infant. There may be a wish to provoke an external crisis, with all its drama and its heightened emotional concomitants, in order to avoid having to address some feared internal state, such as conflict, or loss, or emptiness. Whatever the detailed analysis of a particular event turns up, it has to be faced that human beings sometimes have immense potential for self-destructive behaviour without, perhaps, quite recognising what the impact of that same destructiveness on their lives will turn out to be.

I include here a simple diagram that we have used in the Tavistock's Unit for the Study of Trauma in order to orientate ourselves when first contemplating the conjunction of a particular event with a particular psychopathology. Could this have been foreseen or was it an act of

God? How much has this individual brought this event on himself? How aware is he of some process of destructiveness in himself? Is he fascinated by it? Does he indulge it?

INDIVIDUAL AXIS

Not sought out

e.g.
earthquakes
floods

e.g.
war, torture,
major transport
accidents

Acts of God      NEGLECT      Man-made

EVENT
AXIS               AND

Accidental      CARELESSNESS      Intentional
e.g.
hijack

e.g.
high risk
sports

e.g.
bomb disposal work
high wire artists
smoking cigarettes
not wearing seat belts

Sought out

The two axes represent the individual and the event. Events are categorised along the horizontal axis, moving from so-called acts of God (earthquakes, floods), through the ambiguous area of the man-made but still accidental (for example, major transport disasters, or collapsing buildings) to the man-made and frankly intentional – hi-jacks, wars, robberies, muggings, torture. The vertical axis that represents the individual's motivation travels from the unsought-out (the mugging, the bank robbery, the train crash), through the area of ambiguity (falling off ladders, road traffic accidents) to those events that are frankly sought-out. It is important to recognise that an event may be no less traumatic because it was sought out. The test pilot, the demolition expert, the high-wire artist, the man who visits a club designated for those who seek out sado-masochistic sex are no less traumatised when they crash, are blown up, fall, or are beaten-up and raped (all of these cases were seen in the Unit) than those who were caught in transport disasters, or trapped in fires. The reality for each of them turned out to be very different from the phantasy. We are constantly reminded of Freud's statement that in the unconscious there is no such thing as death. If the actual reality of the outcome of their self-destructive activities can be faced, there is the possibility of improvement. However, the treatment of these patients is complicated and lengthened by those personality factors that originally led them into their high-risk activities, and by the fact that they now have to face their own complicity in the tragedy. The unconscious sense of guilt that may have contributed to the tragedy might have been assuaged by the ensuing damage, but that damage then has to be faced and lived with; and this fact has not been anticipated by the unconscious, which sought only relief from the torment of guilt. Treatment may only be able to make the best of a bad job. Thus for every survivor mapped onto this grid, the encounter with death is still powerfully traumatising because somehow still unanticipated. As Freud says in 'Thoughts for the Times on War and Death', in our unconscious there exist two opposing attitudes towards death: 'the one which acknowledges it as the annihilation of life and the other which denies it …' They come face to face when the reality of death is encountered, either one's own or that of a loved object, who is, by virtue of that love, also 'an inner possession', a 'component of our own ego.'

## The Death Drive

In studying the effects of traumatic events on the human personality, or in attempting to mitigate those effects through treatment, sooner or later one has to confront the clinical expression of what Freud (1920) called the death instinct. In 'Beyond the Pleasure Principle' he makes explicit his carefully arrived-at belief that all human activity can, broadly speaking, be placed into two categories: that which pushes in the direction of constructiveness, connectedness and life, and that which pulls in the opposite direction, towards destructiveness, disintegration and ultimately, death. 'All pain comes from living,' Hanna Segal (1993) points out. The wish to avoid that pain, to end the struggle, can become very powerful. 'Life itself', Freud writes in 'The Ego and the Id' (1923), is 'a conflict and compromise between these two trends.'

Freud pointed out how these two great opposing forces stimulate each other, provoke each other into renewed activity. Perhaps the battle with the environment pursued in the proper practice of certain kinds of sporting activity – sailing, skiing, or mountaineering for example – is one way of representing externally and enacting this internal struggle, so that death can be confronted and evaded positively, enjoyably and even creatively. Yet one behaviour that appears regularly in those who have been traumatised is the apparent compulsion to repeat the events, either in a directly recognisable form, or symbolically, and sometimes in a way that is less than positive or creative. This repetition is a sign that, at the very least, something is stuck and has not been worked through.

Freud (1920) gives a nice example of a symbolic reenactment in his description of the little boy's game with the cotton-reel following his much-loved mother's sorties from the house. He repeatedly throws a cotton-reel out over the edge of his cot, saying mournfully to himself as he does it, 'Gone!' Then he hauls it in again on its piece of string, saying joyfully as it bobs back into sight, 'There!' Why, Freud asks himself, should the little boy repeat a distressing experience in this way? He sees part of its function as converting a painful passive experience (being left) into an active game, and so through practice achieving an inner mastery of those feelings. Yet this is not the whole story. The wish for revenge may come into it, enacted on the symbolic substitute for the mother rather than on mother herself. The trauma, however minor, is reversed, and the other is vengefully made the passive recipient of the unpleasant experience.

However innocent this particular instance of repetition, reversal and the wish for revenge, such impulses play a major role in attempts to work through more seriously traumatising experiences. The literature is full of accounts of the painful counter-transference experiences that may have to be lived through by therapists treating traumatised patients. (See Chapters 4 and 8) The reversal of the trauma may not simply be an expression of revenge on a substitute, nor simply the wish to evacuate the mental turmoil and distress into an object that he hopes can manage it. It may be the only way the survivor has available of *communicating* some of the intensity of his distress and pain, which are outside the compass of words. Projective identification, our most primitive and powerfully effective means of communication, may be the best a patient can do when *in extremis*, and before a therapist can help him find words that do justice to his state of mind.

Thus when a survivor of traumatic events contrives to repeat them in one form or another during his lifetime, actively or passively – and it is astonishing how often they manage it – the understanding of this phenomenon is not a simple matter. It may be, as it was with the little boy, the conversion of passive into active, in an attempt at mastery of the feelings evoked. It may be, in the passive form, the repetition of something that has not yet been remembered or understood, in an unconscious attempt to get the original event into conscious mental life, as Freud describes in 'Remembering, Repeating and Working Through' (1914b). When this occurs in symbolic form in the treatment setting we think of it as part of the transference, an opportunity to enlist the therapist's understanding of the past, and thus an expression of life. On the other hand it may be a pull to something more destructive, whether to others in the form of a reversal of the trauma (what has been called an *identification with the aggressor* – Anna Freud, 1946), or to the self, where it can emerge as an expression of masochism and hence of a deathly drive. These are the kinds of questions that emerge, and can only truly be approached, in the clinical setting.

Freud's formulation of the conflict between life and death helps to make sense of many observable phenomena, as Segal (1993) has made clear with her clinical examples. In everyday life, the same things can be seen: for example, risk-taking in certain sports can be a finely-honed expression of that very conflict. To exert one's physical and mental mastery over the obstacles afforded by the environment refuels a pleasure in actually being alive, keeps in good shape the skills required for doing so. This might be an expression of that fundamental conflict in which the balance is tipped in favour of life.

Sometimes the balance is more evenly weighted. One of the survivors of a major fire, a man who enjoyed his life, described his struggle to go on making the very painful effort to escape and survive while he was trapped underground. The temptation was to let go, to give up and relinquish his burned body, his pain, and his life, consigning them and the effort to oblivion. He described being overcome by an immense lethargy, wanting simply to close his eyes and submit to the fire. Only the thought of his children, who would be fatherless without him, drove him into continuing the immense effort to go on fighting to stay alive and to reach help. As he talked, it seemed as though he was describing a force that had almost seductive powers, soothing and cajoling him to give in, to end the pain and the struggle. He survived, but he knew that the narrowness of the achievement had been an act of will on behalf of his objects rather than himself. Here we can see how love, itself an expression of life and connectedness, only just succeeded in outweighing the negativity and the dissolution of death, which would have ended his own pain.

At other times, the balance tips more frankly in favour of death. The young woman who answers advertisements in the back-pages of certain magazines for sado-masochistic sex with strangers, or the climber who tackles ever more fearsome and isolated mountains under chancy conditions and with inadequate equipment, or the compulsive smoker, seem to the ordinary eye to be courting death. Some of the factors that drive this kind of behaviour can eventually be understood if the risk-taker is willing and able to engage in and sustain the process of enquiry. However, enquiry pre-supposes curiosity, and one of the striking features of the repetitive urge towards potentially deathly situations is the marked absence of a wish to know, of self-scrutiny, of more than a superficial curiosity. Any of these might take the enquirer too far in the direction of recognising the existence of desires, preferences, needs, feelings – in other words towards life.

Yet however far we take the investigation, there is a deep core of this apparent negativity which remains enigmatic, even mystifying: where the investigator seems to reach a brick wall, the survivor turns away from the process of investigation, and the room and both people in it can seem suffused with a deadly despair. We can assume that our methods of enquiry are still too crude to take things further, or that we ourselves are not up to using them adequately. We can assume that there may be constitutional factors at work, something taken seriously by both Freud and Klein. Yet when a patient who has ostensibly come for treatment repeatedly turns away from enquiry and from the struggle to make things better, who undoes the progress that was hard-won in the preceding session, who slides away from attempts to understand, it is hard not to feel you are up against something impenetrably negative that may be beyond both of you. Segal (op. cit.) points out how 'the wish to annihilate is directed both at the perceiving self and the object perceived,' or in this case at both the patient-self and the analyst-other, 'hardly distinguishable from one another.' It is in grim reality a conflict between the forces of life and the forces of death.

Yet for those patients in whom the drive for life just outweighs that pull towards death, treatment has much to offer. Treatment is, at its best, about connectedness, about emotional contact, about making sense of the apparently meaningless, and of refinding one's good objects, however long and difficult and bloody the process on the way to those goals.

28

## 1. Thinking About Trauma

### Treatment

Clinical experience and knowledge inform and illuminate theory; but the theory is necessary if therapists are to understand and account for the effect that violent and unanticipated events have on those who suffer them. We need theory behind us for at least two reasons. First, we know that when survivors come for treatment it is because the sympathy and support of family or friends or neighbours or colleagues has not, on its own, been enough to help repair the damage. Instead of getting gradually better they find themselves getting gradually worse, and that is when they may find themselves turning to professionals. Professionals use theories to *organise* their knowledge and often wide experience, and to *account* to themselves for why this is happening and not that, why this person is reacting in this way and not that. Second, when we listen to someone in deep distress because terrible things have happened to them, it can also be very distressing for the listener. Real listening involves, in part, making an imaginative identification with the speaker, and with his or her experience. We need to be able to listen without being so overwhelmed by the raw intensity of our patients' experiences that we retreat from the emotional impact of what they are saying, shut down so that we don't really take it in. If we retreat in this way then we confirm the survivor's view that what happened to them, and is still happening inside them, is indeed unbearable. There is no-one who can help them with it, help them see it through to the point of having a life once more.

Yet it is the essence of trauma that it is overwhelming – that it knocks out ordinary thinking and behaviour, the capacity to think straight or act sensibly. The survivor is looking for help to regain his or her equilibrium. If we want to understand this process in a way that is helpful, we must not be overwhelmed ourselves. We have to sustain a complicated balance: to be open enough to the survivor's experience to take in a real way his or her state, but steady enough not to be knocked off balance by it. In psychoanalytic therapy, the capacity to do this thing (containment) is felt to be centrally important and very difficult. *Important* because without a renewed experience of containment there is no real treatment; *difficult* because it may involve our being feared and hated for long periods until the survivor can begin to trust us in a realistic way as reliable and humane – neither ideal or omniscient, nor dangerous and malignant. A theory then acts as an important container for the therapist, a supporting structure that helps

29

the therapist keep his own equilibrium. (These are the positive uses of theory; it can of course also be used defensively, to act as a barrier to emotional contact under the guise of 'professionalism.')

The treatment we offer, as with all psychoanalytically informed treatment, follows rather than leads the patient. Most importantly, it is not 'focal', in the sense of concentrating on the traumatic event. Instead it takes the transference – the progressive unfolding of the relationship between therapist and patient – as its basis, although of course not exclusively so. This attention to the transference is because, as I have outlined in this chapter, the event has become translated into a relationship, or several kinds of relationship, all of which eventually become visible and alive in the room between the patient and the therapist.

What is offered by the therapist is that particular way of understanding, in a setting that offers a new experience of containment. Attention to the transference will, bit by bit, help re-establish the capacity to think about the traumatic events and their significance without the patient's being overwhelmed by flashbacks. At the same time it offers the opportunity for the gradual amelioration of the damage to the internal world brought about by the longer-term impact of the trauma. Containment is hard work. It involves a reworking of the traumatic experience with all its emotional impact, and all the guilt, fear and hatred released by the original event, with someone who can, in spite of the severe internal buffetings of the counter-transference, provide for the survivor something of what the mother (or primary caretaker) unconsciously offered her very young baby when it was overwhelmed by anxieties. This is not an easy or simple task. Not all traumatised individuals can be helped. Some, particularly those who were severely ill-treated in a brutal and sustained way in childhood, cannot tolerate the constraints and the demands of the one-to-one treatment setting, which may stir up intense claustrophobic or paranoid anxieties (Garland, 1997). These patients are often those most in need of treatment. Here, group therapy, or the loose but stable containment offered by a district's psychiatric or forensic service can be very helpful.

However, the rest of this book is about our attempts to get to grips with the task of individual treatment for those patients who recognise that they need help, and are able to tolerate what it may stir up along the way towards what they hope for and expect – namely to feel better about themselves. Those who manage it may eventually even find that their lives have in some ways improved. Matters shift internally, sometimes profoundly and constructively. Knowledge about oneself deepens; priorities become clearer. Above all the significance and pleasure of being alive can more keenly be appreciated and fought for.

# 2

# Human Error

## David Bell

At the beginning of this century the scientific imagination lagged significantly behind the literary imagination. The success of Franken-stein and then Dr Jekyll and Mr Hyde attested to a popular cultural interest in forces beyond ordinary awareness that could wreak havoc on so-called civilised values. It was Freud who brought together the many different observations of unconscious mental life and constructed a theory that could do justice to the facts. It has often been said that, in doing this, he joined the line of 'the great de-centrers' – namely Copernicus, who de-centred man from his position as centre of the universe, Darwin, who removed him from the centre and zenith of creation, and Marx, who de-centred him from being able consciously to determine his own history. Freud perhaps dealt the biggest blow of all to our narcissism – and one which despite the overwhelming evi-dence in his favour is still resisted. Following Freud, Man can no longer even see himself as consciously and rationally in control of his own mind, but ruled by forces often totally beyond awareness.

The purpose of this chapter is to show that no explanation of errors and accidents can exclude the understanding of the role of unconscious forces and conflicts. We cannot afford to evade awareness of those aspects of all of us that have a vested interest in making things go wrong. This is not to say that other types of explanation can be excluded (e.g. the sociological, or those deriving from decision theory). However, there is something about the psychoanalytic point of view which, because of the very nature of the issues it investigates, makes it less easy to accept.

Human error is part of the almost unremarkable daily commonplace of the errors, slips of the tongue, accidental actions and lapses of memory, which Freud grouped together under the heading of 'parapraxes'. It is here that we find strong and clear evidence for the existence of unconscious mental life, available for all of us to examine

32

from our own experience. Freud was particularly fond of using such apparently trivial phenomena to launch his theory of unconscious mental life when addressing lay audiences.

Freud published 'The Psychopathology of Everyday Life' in 1901, the year after 'The Interpretation of Dreams'. I will illustrate the main argument with one or two ordinary and familiar errors. You have an appointment and you forget. One person may say quite openly, 'I didn't want to go and I expect that's why I forgot', although this was not deliberate in the ordinary (conscious) meaning of the word. Another may not think this consciously, putting his lapse down to 'simple oversight' but, on being questioned, may agree that it was an appointment he didn't want to keep, he hadn't checked his diary that day for reasons he cannot account for, though he dimly remembers intending to look at his diary and somehow feeling drawn from doing so – something, in this imaginary example, that was most unusual for this man to do. He may now accept on balance that the best explanation is that a part of him beyond ordinary awareness prevented him from keeping the appointment. But now we come to a third case which is at one and the same time the most problematic and the most interesting: the man forgets the appointment and, on its being suggested that maybe he did not want to keep it or at least felt in conflict about it, he violently repudiates this, claiming that it was just 'an accident and that's that'. He is particularly critical of any suggestion that there is any part of him, beyond his awareness, that might have facilitated this accident. This hypothetical man may strike us as rather unreasonable in that he does not even seem the slightest bit interested in the possibility we are suggesting. 'He shows', as Freud (1915c) said, 'a strong personal interest in demonstrating that his parapraxis does not have sense'.

Central to this view of slips is the notion that all human action and thought *has a sense*, and is a communication. Let us look briefly at the counter arguments: firstly the idea of 'pure' accident, a random event. In other words, something just happens and that is it. This argument, often strongly maintained, if examined closely is a most strange argument. It claims that there are 'certain occurrences however small, which drop out of the universal concatenation of events; occurrences which might as well not happen as happen. If anyone makes a breach in the determinism of natural events at a single point it means that he has thrown overboard the whole *Weltanschauung* of science' (Freud, 1915c). Simple observation shows how difficult it is for anything in mental life to be random. It is for example impossible to think of a name at random: the name one chooses will inevitably have significance. It is also impossible to conjure up a nonsensical sentence. Secondly, why put forward a view that can lead nowhere in furthering understanding? Surrendering to chance is like surrendering to the gods. Is it not more fruitful, as in all scientific enquiry, to start off not by assuming blind chance but instead by assuming that a given phenomenon may by careful study become explicable. Insistence on 'chance' suggests a vested interest. The next argument is this: mistakes and errors are to be explained only by factors outside mental life, such as physiological disturbances, that interfere with attention. We might say that Mr A forgot the appointment because he was tired: there is no need to invoke an inner opposing intention beyond awareness. Slips do occur with more frequency when we are tense or tired, but is this adequate as an explanation? We can leave aside the obvious counter-instances of parapraxes occurring in the absence of fatigue or when they are repetitive, or when the mistake occurs in the context *not* of a lapse of attention, but of attention assiduously applied. Some tasks are executed easily with almost complete lack of conscious attention. But apart from this there is something wrong with the argument itself, as Freud demonstrated. It is certainly true that physiological disturbances such as fatigue increase the frequency of errors and slips of the tongue, but this argument has no specificity and so cannot be a sufficient explanation. It explains the increased frequency but not why one particular slip occurs rather than another. Freud illustrates the weakness of this argument in the following way.

> Suppose one dark night I went to a lonely spot and was there attacked by a rough who took away my watch and purse. Since I did not see the robber's face clearly, I laid my complaint at the nearest police station with the words: 'Loneliness and darkness have just robbed me of my valuables'. The police officer might say to me: 'In what you say you seem to be unjustifiably adopting an extreme mechanistic view. It would be better to represent the facts in this way – under the shield of darkness and favoured by loneliness, an unknown thief robbed me of my valuables. In your case the essential task seems to be that we should find the thief'. (Freud, 1915c)

In other words a physiological disturbance, such as fatigue etc. cannot be the culprit but only the 'shield' which provides the conditions under which the unconscious intention does its work.

Let us now return to the example of the man who vigorously repudiates any suggestion that his accidental parapraxis has any meaning, as we need to anticipate the argument that would run as follows:

## 2. Human Error

'Some science, this science of yours, that accommodates any facts to its theory! One man agrees that his forgetting is easily explained by his not wishing to keep his appointment. The other finds this explanation satisfactory after some introspection and taking other evidence into consideration. These you take as supporting the thesis that the error resulted from the action of forces which had a sense, and were not consciously available to the man at the time and which acted against his conscious intentions. But in the third case the man actively repudiates everything you say, finds no trace in himself of such intention – and you take this as further evidence to support your theory. Why, it's no better than saying that when your patient brings material that confirms your theory you are satisfied and when he doesn't you are equally satisfied'.

There is a point here, of course, in that anything we say about the man who repudiates the claims remains speculative – unless he happens to be our patient, in which case the matter can be more carefully studied. More important is the general context; what evidence can be brought to bear from a thorough knowledge of the man and his circumstances? Whilst in this third case the thesis cannot be taken as proven, there is little ground to exclude it out of hand. Often those close to us are more able to see intentions in our actions than we ourselves are. Also, however, as already stated, to assert that any aspect of psychic life is without meaning or determination is to make an extraordinarily strong claim on weak evidence and to ditch the enquiry before it has started.

So far we have only examined the simplest phenomena, those that might appear, at least on initial inspection, to be understandable within the context of a surface psychology without the need for suggesting hidden deeper intentions. However, there is a whole class of phenomena which cannot even be approached from such a superficial perspective.

I am referring to that class of errors which are repetitive and it is here that some of the strongest evidence for underlying motives is to be found. Some people for example habitually lose things. Such repetitions could be called characterological errors; namely, those types of mistakes which are repeated and have a particularly symbolic meaning concerning deep preoccupations. They are part of character. There are those who habitually make mistakes concerning appointments which on a conscious level they have actually been *looking forward to* and for which they have assiduously taken every precaution to keep, and yet still repetitively miss. So explanations in terms of what is *consciously* desired flounder immediately.

I will now give two examples of 'errors' to illustrate further both the phenomena and the way that psychoanalytic explanation 'works'. Mrs H was deeply distressed by the fact that her mother was dying and became preoccupied that the hospital should not lose the medallion which her mother wore around her neck. She removed the medallion to keep it safe. The following day she could not find it anywhere. After searching she became quite desperate. She felt convinced she'd given it to her father and angrily blamed him for losing it, saying that 'when she dies it would be important to have it'. Her father became angry and said to her, 'She's not dead yet, you know'. The following day Mrs H went into the lounge and turned to the mirror, as she said 'in just the way my mother always did', to look at herself before going out. As she gazed at her reflection she saw the medallion around her own neck. This disturbing event showed how she identified with her mother – in a sense 'became' her – in order to preserve her and not to lose her. It also revealed, more disturbingly for her, the presence of an infantile death wish against her mother (which is what her father had responded to) in order to rob her of her valued possessions and to take them for herself.

Mr K, a patient of mine, habitually loses documents that are of great importance. When he loses such a document he becomes desperate, persecutes himself as he searches wildly for it, feeling himself to be guilty of terrible crimes, worthless and deserving to be punished. However, as a result of some insight gained in his analysis he became more able to attend to what went on in his mind during these episodes and also to observe the context in which they occurred. He discovered the following: first, he often lost documents that were particularly important to his progress in his career; second, he felt intensely guilty about success – as he put it, 'I manage to snatch failure from the jaws of success'. This was related to his guilt concerning his wish to triumph over his dead father and be more successful than him; third, whenever he found the missing document this was accompanied not by a sense of relief and pleasure but by disappointment. This latter was made up of at least two components. His wild searching exactly relived the state of agitated searching he experienced after the death of his father, desperate to find him in the external world. So the finding was accompanied by the disappointment of not finding what he had *unconsciously* been looking for (i.e. his father). Also that aspect of him, largely unconscious, but revealed frequently in dreams, which persecuted him if he was successful, and made him feel worthless, was placated by failure. He was safer if he failed. It was as if he was saying 'Look father, I have failed so you have no need to punish me for triumphing over you'. Finding the documents meant success and therefore fear of further persecution. It was only when he was able to accept his death wishes against his father, as well as his more conscious wishes for his father to live, and to bear the guilt of these impulses, that he was freed from the persecution and was able to pursue his career without seeking out situations in which he could be further punished.

With these examples we enter new territory. It serves to illustrate the complexity of even ordinary errors, their relation to an inner world and the far-reaching influences of this inner world on that which we call character.

So far I have used the most ordinary everyday accidents that occur in normal people and have sought to demonstrate that a necessary part of their explanation is contained in the idea of these accidents and errors *having a sense, and intention*. Careful study of these phenomena leads one to the conclusion that there are intentions which are beyond conscious awareness, intentions which are in conflict with those that are conscious and which form an inner life which has powerful effects on our behaviour.

When a patient comes for analytic treatment we are afforded an ideal opportunity for the careful study of human motivation and of the link between the inner and outer worlds. A psychoanalytic treatment is at once a therapy and a research exercise. This careful study of individuals can yield much information in regard to our understanding of accidents. Accidents that occur during an analytic treatment provide an opportunity to study in detail the relevance of various internal and external factors. In some cases the accident is entirely independent of the individual (for example where the train he regularly travels on crashes). Others are less independent, such as, I suspect, many car crashes. Others seem to be almost entirely dependent on the individual and to be independent of external sources. In the latter category is a patient who after bringing some very disturbing material in connection with his fear of sexuality – quite literally a terror of his penis being damaged – felt relieved and hopeful that he might soon feel able to have a sexual experience. During the weekend however, he sustained a deep cut to his finger whilst doing some cooking, a resurgence over the weekend of his terror symbolically expressed.

Other patients bring to attention their need to sustain a multitude of different accidents – those who are 'accident prone' – and this seems to be of as much importance as the particular symbolic meaning of any particular accident. In some patients it may be a way of being punished; indeed some people seem only able to live if they are continually punished. They suffer from what Freud termed 'an unconscious sense of guilt' and, it is interesting to note in passing that being punished is often a way of avoiding the pain of guilt. This particularly appears to be the case in some compulsive recidivist criminals who seem to pay little attention to preventing the discovery of their crimes and obtain relief when they are revealed. The real source of guilt in these cases is usually quite unknown to the individual, harking back to earlier life situations which continue to be a source of unconscious guilt (see Freud 'Criminals from a sense of guilt', 1916a).

An example of an 'accident' brought about by an unconscious sense of guilt is given by the psychoanalyst Marie Langer (1989). She tells of a Nicaraguan psychologist she trained, who worked with Sandinista soldiers at the front. He gave a report of a 'comrade' just out of hospital who had been wounded in a 'moment of clumsiness', which could have cost him his life. The psychologist discovered that a very admired and envied brother had been killed in action, and this had caused a deep unconscious sense of guilt, as it made a reality of his hidden murderous wishes directed towards the envied brother. To placate this sense of guilt he had put himself in a very dangerous situation. The psychologist after discussing this with him said to him that although it was admirable that he was prepared to die at the front 'this did not mean he had to make the enemy a present of his corpse'.

Mrs X, a middle-aged woman of Russian parentage had a particular detestation of parapraxes, especially those that occurred within the setting of her analysis. If she made any mistakes concerning her analytic appointments, or in things she said or did during her session, these were not seen as episodes which may have a sense and therefore whose understanding might be potentially enriching. She instead regarded any attempt to understand an error beyond its being a 'simple accident' as an insult to her integrity, a deep narcissistic wound. She invoked 'simple accident' rather than face the possibility that she could not be master of everything that went on in her mind; in other words that certain acts and thoughts could have a sense beyond that which she attributed to them.

Mrs X's inner world was dominated by cruel forces that treated all human vulnerability with contempt. One day she came to analysis and placed a book on the couch. It was placed in such a way that I could not see the title. When I wondered what she may be communicating by placing the book on the couch, she exploded with fury: 'Where do you expect me to put it, I'll put it on the floor next time!'. She seemed to have taken my interest in the meaning of her act as an attack on her belief that she was in complete control. She denied with violence that putting the book on the couch had *any* meaning. It later transpired that the book contained accounts of the horror of living under Stalinist persecution, a very accurate description of her own inner world which she, on one level, did want to 'put on the couch', literally to bring into the analysis. Though in Mrs X's case the reaction is quite extreme, I believe all of us have some level of dislike of our parapraxes being noticed. We experience it as a wound and humiliation. This results in a reluctance to go beyond fairly superficial explanations when examining accidents and disasters. We avoid explanations that suggest there may be an intentional aspect to certain disasters, even though one that may be beyond conscious control. In the case of accidents some of the reasons for this resistance are obvious: it might appear that unconscious intentions imply a clear and straightforward relation to issues of responsibility and blame. This is clearly not the case (I will return to this point).

As a psychoanalyst one cannot but fail to be impressed not only with the evidence of the unconscious meaning of errors and accidents, but also with the precision of the unconscious in bringing about situations in the external world which can so accurately express inner situations. By forgetting to pay bills, for example, we bring about externally a constant source of persecution which threatens to cut us off from essential supplies and communication. The presence of destructive forces within us is distressing to face – we naturally prefer to locate these things in others and do so through projecting these destructive forces outside of ourselves. The denial of these forces however, means that no aversive action can be taken. We all have particular accidents to which we turn a blind eye: one person may be especially assiduous about avoiding a fire at home, but not at the office, another may have the most up-to-date car security but never checks his tyres. In a general way we all thus demonstrate the silent activity of destructive forces which pull us away from ordinary caution and towards accidents of our own particular predilection, which will have their specific symbolic meaning.

A most vivid demonstration of the presence of these destructive forces may be seen in driving a car. Psychoanalysts are familiar with the deep symbolic meanings people attach to their cars. Many patients will talk about cars and their relation to them as ways of expressing their relation to their own bodies, and also to their own ego or self. It is for this reason that even minor car accidents can have at least temporarily quite devastating effects. For a moment the assault on the car is experienced as an assault on the integrity of the self. A colleague of mine recently pointed out to me that a number of cars have more than one dent on them in the same area of the car. Since then I have noticed that when someone pulls out and nearly hits you, they quite often already have a dent on that part of the car that would have been involved in the collision. Some seem to have a special predilection for bumping their fronts, others their backs; I leave it to the reader to speculate as to the possible meanings of this!

The picture, however, becomes more disturbing when we see just how rapidly a personality changes when getting behind the wheel. A patient of mine is normally a confident and considerate man; polite, as he puts it, to a fault. He has underachieved in life and feels constantly aware of others who seem to fly by and get what they want. When he drives he rapidly becomes aggressive and impatient. He returned from his summer holidays and told me about a number of near-accidents whilst driving. On one occasion, on a three lane road, a faster and larger car came up behind him, flashing its lights to overtake. He held him up and found himself saying, 'Just because you have got a big one I'm not going to let you get in front of me'. The other driver pulled out and commenced overtaking. Mr X pressed his accelerator, thus closing the gap in front of him and also delaying the other driver in overtaking. A car could be seen coming the other way down the third middle lane which Mr X noticed with an increasing sensation of triumph. Suddenly he realised what might happen and he emerged, as he put it, 'as if from a dream', released the accelerator and, pressing the brake, allowed the bigger car into the gap. This latter was associated with a sudden rush of a mixture of angry and also affectionate feelings towards the driver of the bigger car. One does not have to be a psychoanalyst to appreciate the meaning of some of the imagery contained in the language used by Mr X. It suggests quite ordinary oedipal rivalry, namely the little boy's competitiveness and death wishes against the father who 'has a bigger one' and by virtue of his superior status is entitled to occupy a position, enter a particular gap which is denied the small boy. It is worth adding that Mr X's 'politeness to a fault' was particularly directed towards men in authority. It was his inability to be rivalrous with men that led to his underachieving, and in this material one can see that the inhibition is probably related to a fear of facing the real violence of his competitive impulses.

The temptation to delinquency is ever present. A colleague of mine recently qualified as a pilot, and took me up in a small plane. Shortly after we took off, the weather conditions worsened and he became anxious. He was indecisive and toyed with the idea of continuing, though with unease, feeling it too humiliating to turn back. He did turn back, however, and when we were having a drink in the lounge he saw that the weather had completely cleared and felt stupid and small for having turned back. At this point an experienced flying instructor, who had overheard the conversation, joined us and said, 'I would much rather be down here wishing I was up there, than up there wishing I was down here' – a very sane and balanced position.

These examples show how easy it is for an individual to surrender his hard won capacities for thought and give way to dangerously delinquent impulses often related to fear of humiliation. This tendency becomes even more marked in group situations.

A few years ago I participated in the first Tavistock conference on disasters. After the first paper, when we were looking forward to coffee, a member of the conference stood up and drew the chairman's attention to the lack of adequate safety conditions in the conference. He pointed out that there were no aisles between the chairs and, in the event of a fire, people would not be able to get out easily. The reaction of the conference was to view this man as some sort of crank. People exchanged glances which conveyed a sense of 'Oh God, there's always one at any conference'. The chairman of the conference at first got caught up in this atmosphere and did not take the intervention seriously.

It later transpired that the man who had made the intervention was a permanent worker from the Bradford fire disaster. Later we were able to examine this sequence of behaviour and come to understand its great significance. Johns (1989) has written a most helpful paper elucidating this event. The conference as a whole had got caught up in a type of delinquency that in fact makes an important contribution to the causal chain that leads to many disasters. It had the same quality as adolescents in a classroom who, when a fire bell goes, think it is big to ignore it, and mock the entreaties of peers to vacate the building as the words of 'goody goodies'. They thus mock ordinary human concern and thoughtful action in just the way that it occurred at the conference.

Many accidents occur as a result of quite ordinary safety precautions being ignored. This results partly, I think, from this idealisation of the delinquent position. Often those who warn of danger are mocked and ignored like the prophets of doom in Greek tragedies.

Quite recently I had some correspondence with a prestigious psychotherapy clinic concerning the lack of proper fire precautions. I had suggested there should be occasional fire drills. There was great concern by the authorities at that clinic that fire drills would disrupt the psychotherapeutic treatment of patients. It would be awkward for the therapists who normally took a neutral stance to have to leave the building hurriedly with their patients and so on. It was even seriously suggested that fire drills could perhaps take place when there were no patients being treated in the building. It did not seem to occur to these authorities that an actual fire, for which there had been no adequate preparation, would cause far more disruption to the psychotherapeutic treatments than any fire drill.

It is because people get so easily drawn into turning a blind eye, projecting responsibility into others that, so often, ordinary precautions are not taken. This creates situations in which there is quite literally an accident waiting to happen. I am also suggesting, however, that these errors and oversights have a sense and give expression to deeply unconscious destructive wishes. How do we contemplate the state of mind of those who build slag heaps above Welsh villages, or of those who continue to live in such a village? It is almost as if there is a dicing with death, something we commonly see in more disturbed patients.

Some patients who make frequent suicide attempts, have, consciously, no intention of dying but achieve an excitement by gambling with death. There is a near delusional conviction: 'I can't really die'. Every time they are rescued their sense of omnipotence is increased. When such a patient eventually takes a massive overdose and is not found in time, it would appear to be a deliberate and planned suicide. However, I believe that paradoxically such situations are also accidents; the patient has so come to believe in his own omnipotence that he has completely lost touch with the realities of death.

This dicing with death is commoner than I think is often realised; for example in those who drive cars dangerously, or drink whilst driving. It is as if they say to themselves in a depressed and violent mood, 'I'll give death a chance'. Others in a state of excitement and almost complete dissociation, lose touch with the reality of death. It calls to mind the game of 'chicken' on three-lane highways as depicted in 'Rebel Without a Cause'. Some apparently accidental deaths on the roads are also masked suicides. It is one thing if it is an individual in a car, but what if someone in this state of mind is a bus driver or an engineer doing the final checks on aeroplanes? The situation is made considerably worse if the person works in an atmosphere dominated by that type of excitement and bravado which generates contempt for those who say, 'I can't cope'?

I am here emphasising the dangers of a delinquent turning of a blind eye but also its very seductiveness. Yesterday's marginal 'weirdos', the 'Cassandras' warning of disaster, such as the Friends of the Earth, or the Greens, often become accepted as today's orthodoxy.

## 2. *Human Error*

In this chapter I have attempted to demonstrate the importance of unconscious factors in the causation of errors and accidents. I hope to have shown that no theory of the causation of accidents can afford to exclude this perspective, though I think there are always forces operating which seek to do so. I have particularly emphasised the importance of appreciating that errors and accidents always have a sense, a meaning, and are indicative of largely unconscious destructive forces common to all of us. It is important to recognise this in order to avoid the usual witch hunts that follow disasters – namely the seeking of an individual to blame – which serve to project and deny personal responsibility. It is also essential to differentiate between understanding the cause of a disaster and attributing blame for it. This confusion is often evident in the types of discussion that take place following urban riots. Those who seek to understand the causes and name, for example, unemployment, social alienation and poverty are treated as if they are justifying the violence rather than attempting to understand its causes.

For any situation there can be no 'right' level of risk to accept. The level that is tolerated will depend on the balance between those forces which seek to protect from and avert accidents (whilst not omnipotently demanding no risk at all) and those forces present in all of us which seek to give expression to our own most destructive impulses whilst at the same time trying to evade their reality.

# Part Two

# Assessment and Consultation

*Henry Percy (Hotspur), Son of the Earl of Northumberland, has decided
to go to war against the King. His wife comes into the room while he is
reading the letter that has provoked him to action ...*

Hotspur:     How now, Kate, I must leave you within these two hours.

Lady Percy:  O my good lord, why are you thus alone?
             For what offence I have I this fortnight been
             a banished woman from my Harry's bed?
             Tell me sweet lord, what is't that takes from thee
             thy stomach, pleasure, and thy golden sleep?
             Why dost thou bend thine eyes upon the earth,
             and start so often when thou sit'st alone?
             Why has thou lost the fresh blood in thy cheek,
             and given my treasures and my rights of thee
             to thick-eyed musing, and curst melancholy?
             In thy faint slumbers I by thee have watched,
             and heared thee murmur tales of iron wars,
             speak terms of manage to thy bounding steed,
             cry courage to the field! And thou hast talked
             of sallies and retires, of trenches, tents,
             of palisadoes, frontiers, parapets,
             of basilisks, of cannon, culverin,
             of prisoners' ransom, and of solders slain,
             and all the currents of a heady fight.
             Thy spirit within thee hath been so at war,
             and thus hath so bestirred thee in thy sleep,
             that beads of sweat have stood upon thy brow
             like bubbles in a late-disturbed stream,
             and in thy face strange motions have appeared,
             such as we see when men restrain their breath
             on some great sudden hest. O what portents are these?
             Some heavy business hath my lord in hand,
             and I must know it or he loves me not.

William Shakespeare, *Henry IV* Part 1 (1596)

# The Psychodynamic Assessment of Post-Traumatic States

## David Taylor

In this chapter I want to describe how psychoanalytically-informed assessment interviews can be used to get a sense of the impact of traumatic events and an idea of the individual they have affected. Whatever its particular nature, the interaction between the event and the individual is always complex and getting a view of the ensuing psychological configurations is the basis for reasoning out subsequent therapies. The process of the assessment itself may free up some inherent processes of recovery, although the disturbance these interviews can induce sometimes leads to a temporary worsening.

In the interview, getting this kind of psychological perspective is entirely dependent upon arriving at a point of meaningful contact within the transaction between the patient and interviewer. The interviewer seeks to respond to some relevant, non-trivial aspect of the patient and his presentation and to use this understanding in his communications to the patient. Where this is successful, some aspect of the patient's way of relating to others, to the interviewer, to himself and his experiences, including the traumatic event, becomes alive and vivid. This point of contact may then broaden so that the interviewer and/or the patient are able eventually to form a more meaningful view of the patient's life and the events within it.

In the interview, the choice of the particular point of contact and the network of connections that spreads from it is based, of course, upon the content of patients' material, as well as upon the many non-verbal cues and communications which emanate from both parties in the opening minutes of an interview. However, the substance of this contact is not solely determined by what the patient brings. The interviewer is selective according to his prior clinical knowledge and theoretical approach. This framework is an amalgam of empirical knowledge, theory and clinical methods, used in an unconscious or pre-conscious way. Two of the most important contributions to this framework will be described, followed by clinical illustrations of the assessment process.

## The Contribution From Nosology and Epidemiology

In recent times much work has been devoted to making diagnostic categories more reliable so that they can be used in epidemiological and therapeutic research. One drawback of this work has been a tendency in modern psychiatry to lose contact with the many other essential components of making a psychiatric diagnostic statement, which were described, for instance, by Menninger (1959). This traditional case-study method with its careful understanding of the patient, his environmental and social context, developmental history, the formulation of individual personality, of strengths and weaknesses, the rate of developing illness, the lifetime patterns, and their eventual synthesising in both longitudinal and cross-sectional views of a person is a crucial foundation for subsequent clinical management. Whatever explicit disclaimers there are to the contrary, the price paid for the apparent neatness of research diagnoses is the loss of an overall clinical perspective. Itemised solutions are adopted for itemised problems. In contrast, the psychodynamic assessment shares many of the aims of the case-study method, but because of its additional ambitions, the techniques and methods it employs differ from those of psychiatric history-taking and mental state examination.

However, research diagnoses do permit comparisons between different studies and patient groups. General common sense impressions can be checked. Individuals and events can be placed within a known range. For instance, depending upon our life-experience and cast of mind we may think of life as safe and secure, or predictable in the sense that we expect it to be full of woe. The 'facts', such as they are, will not tell us which view is 'correct' but will provide another finding to be taken on board. So, Kessler et al. (1995) report that 60% of men and 50% of women of a sample representative of the USA's general population will experience at least one significant traumatic event in their lifetimes (defined as rape, natural disaster, combat, accident, etc.).

Whilst only a proportion of these will go on to develop a PTSD syndrome, PTSD is not a rare disorder. The same authors found an estimated lifetime prevalence of 7.8% in a representative sample of the general USA population. More than one third of these had failed to recover even after many years. As might be expected, surveys of groups at higher risk showed correspondingly higher prevalence rates. Kulka (1990) reported lifetime rates amongst Vietnam veterans of 31%, and the disorder persists for many years. Engdahl et al. (1991) reported a lifetime rate of PTSD of 50% amongst W.W.II POWs. Over fifty years on, 29% of this sample still suffered from PTSD. A similar picture of prevalence, severity and chronicity emerges in relation to non-combat stressors such as natural disasters (Green, et al. 1992).

Just as PTSD is not rare, nor short-lived, neither is it the clear-cut diagnostic entity it was sometimes wished to be. A whole batch of studies has reported high rates of what is described as 'co-morbidity'. For example, Breslau (1991) reported that 80% had other disorders, including depression, anxiety states, conduct disorder, substance and alcohol abuse. Kessler's general population study confirmed that PTSD occurs more often in those who have had a previous psychiatric disorder. Even more often, PTSD precedes other psychiatric episodes. Current findings indicate that PTSD as a disorder evolves over time, sometimes with substance abuse or serious depression developing after a while.

Interpretation of these findings is complicated, for the diagnostic differentiation of these different conditions is not clear-cut. Some of the symptoms of depression overlap with those of the PTSD syndrome, others with anxiety states. Furthermore, 'pre-morbid' motivations clearly influence the rate of self-exposure to traumatic events and the vulnerability to PTSD.

As would be expected, patients referred to specialist PTSD services are a heterogeneous group. Keane & Wolfe (1990) found that a random sample of patients referred to a PTSD centre consisted of 70% patients with alcohol dependence, 42% drug dependence. The lifetime prevalence of depression was 68% and 25% suffered from at least one personality disorder. Patients referred as suffering from the after-effects of traumatic events present a range of symptomatology, of which DSM-IV PTSD is only one type.

## The Contribution From Psychoanalytic Findings and Technique

The technical procedure of trying to establish a point of contact within the patient-interviewer transaction is based generally upon guidelines provided by the psychoanalytic method. Close attention to the often-subtle features of the analytic relationship, and knowledge of the transference, is used by the psychoanalytically informed assessor to facilitate the deepening contact characteristic of the successful assessment interview. Clearly the interviewer will be helped by already knowing the typical effects on the personality of any serious traumatic event.

Ever since post-traumatic states were first described, observers have been struck with the way the sufferer and his mental apparatus appears to have been overwhelmed by impressions derived from the shocking or violent event. For the sufferer, the subjective experience is often of feeling the mind as invaded by a kind of 'stuff', almost like a physical blow. For Freud (1920), it was the existence of this sort of unprocessed stuff within the mind which led to the repetitive dreams which characteristically follow a traumatic event, as the mind seeks to work through the almost physical 'excitation' it contains by repeatedly representing the apparently indelible event.

Some of our more modern psychoanalytic theories of development contain something of the same basic notion as these early ideas. Bion (1962), building upon the ideas of Klein (1975), suggested a way in which infantile emotional development is dependent upon the mother's psychological help. He considered that aspects of the infant's raw experience are intolerable to it. Unaided, the infantile psyche is only able to deal with these states by wishing them out of awareness, sometimes through phantasies of being able to evacuate this indigestible matter as if it were a physical product like faeces or urine. The mother's involvement with her child enables her to process these mental states through the way she manages and looks after the child as well as through her relationships with others.

As far as we can tell, the infant's raw experiences can take on fearful or malign qualities. In my view, the feelings that fill the traumatised ego are similar. They present the traumatised ego with a task of working through similar to that which faces the infantile ego in its development. At first this vague yet powerful 'stuff' is without content but it has a great potential for turning into persecuted states of mind and for generating subsequent disturbance and upheaval. It is very difficult for the traumatised and disrupted individual to return to the pre-traumatic adjustment and identity. The choice is either to work through to a different organisation or for some personality deterioration to take place.

As is described in Chapters 1, 6 and 8, there are many connections and similarities between post-traumatic states, object loss and grief. However, the process of working through post-traumatic states, al-

50

though in some ways similar to those in bereavement, may be considerably more difficult. The ego may be less able or less prepared to deal with the problems posed by damage to the fabric of the whole world than with object loss. The violence of certain traumatic situations can make it very difficult to regain a sense of equilibrium. Another problem repeatedly emphasised by Klein is that certain states which she termed internal persecution – an early form of guilt – are particularly unbearable to the ego, which is usually driven to rid itself of these states rather than to know them. One way of doing this is to project the situation by involving the external world and its figures.

These various features mean that it is difficult to deal directly with the internal world. Its object relationships have to be externalised. The concept of the internal world is based upon observations of the patterns of inter-relationships that exist between states of mind, external object relations and the world of dreams, memories and fantasies. The experiencing subject has only small glimpses of it, for we are comprised of our internal world rather than merely containing it. These processes of externalisation can miscarry and then what must be reintrojected are situations that have worsened. However, in favourable circumstance these same processes can be a means of working through disturbance. Internal figures and anxieties can be modified beneficially by encountering situations or objects which permit the gradual metabolising of the anxieties which cannot immediately be dealt with symbolically. Things, sometimes seemingly inexplicably, may begin to go wrong after a trauma. These are the reverberations of the effects upon the sufferer's ego and internal world of a serious accident.

## The Assessment Interview – Two Case Illustrations

To illustrate something of the technique of the psychodynamic assessment, as well as the impact upon a relatively healthy personality who had suffered a chance traumatic event, a first interview will be described in detail. Following this, some other types of patient will be summarised to give some impression of the range of possible situations. One aim of this type of interview is to locate the clinical picture presented by the patient in relation to the field markings provided by existing knowledge. Having made the right kind of contact with the patient it becomes possible to gauge his or her symptomatic state and internal world. His relationships, which may be viewed as carriers of the processes of working-through, can then be understood and some appreciation of the personal task confronting the patient will be formed.

51

The patient, a young man in his early twenties, had been on holiday in Mexico, when he was caught in a serious fire in which several people had died, including some of his friends and acquaintances. The patient had made a safe escape from the hotel but he knew that he had been extremely fortunate, escaping death by a matter of minutes. Some dangerous wiring had caused the fire. Fire escapes were blocked, there had been a delay in calling the fire services, and the fire had got out of hand.

In the year before the incident, the patient had also suffered a succession of major bereavements, chiefly the death of his father. The fire had occurred three months before the consultation, when he was in a state of just-contained grief. He was missing his father and had begun to have very intense wishes to be a child, still looked after by his father. He hadn't been feeling too good before the fire but following it he felt depressed, pressurised at work, easily threatened and quick to take offence.

At the start of the interview, this tall, good-looking young lawyer said a number of things which I thought revealed his state of anxiety. First, he asked if X, another member of the Department with whom he'd had some contact, was around. Accepting politely yet somewhat reluctantly that he was instead with me, someone unknown to him, he described himself, as, 'wondering where it was going to come from next'. This anxious anticipation of what the future might bring extended beyond negative *ideas* about the future. He was as well continually in a state of bodily preparedness and experienced many ordinary environmental events as invasive and alarming. In the few hours after the fire he'd had to make some journeys in ambulances. Of these he said, 'There was so much traffic and the cars coming at you from every direction and although not fast it's like being bombarded. So I think that left me very nervous'.

This hyperarousal characterises post-traumatic states. The state is threatening, but otherwise largely without obvious meaningful content. The patient is afraid – a paranoid-schizoid state. Later in the consultation, Mr J described himself as feeling like a zombie when he'd finished some demanding work immediately after the fire. He felt lifeless, cut off, and then more open and cut-up. By and large, this was his condition at the time of the interview. In addition, Mr J felt intensely the need for mental time and space to process these events and recover his balance.

The next part of the interview with Mr J illustrates one way in which the processing of these events takes place, namely through the external-isation of what has become, as a result of the effects of the trauma, a difficult internal situation. As I have indicated, this can miscarry but it also can be an essential part of the process of recovery. When he returned to work a few weeks after the fire he went through a very testing time. Mr J told me that, at first, the senior partner had been sympathetic and supportive, but then began to express doubts about the patient's capabilities. Things came to a head with the partner's giving him a kind of 'pull yourself together talk'. The implication of the interview was, 'Do you think this is the job for you?'. Although Mr J knew intellectually that his senior partner was panicking at this time because of difficulties with a worrying case, and consequently scapegoating him, he still felt very shaky about himself.

This was a critical point. He was at his lowest ebb and thought it would have ruined his morale to leave in this way. For the next month, he threw himself into work. 'I just became two people. That was the only way. Just go into work and work. Any pain I kept completely for home,' he said. The strategy worked. He was involved in cases which were successful, and when the senior partner congratulated him Mr J responded with exhaustion, saying, 'Well, to be honest, I am thinking of leaving'. To me he said, 'Outside, I was doing fine but it was taking such a toll upon me privately'.

Mr J was aware that the effort to prove himself at work was, as he put it, symbolic. He commented that he was a conscientious person who'd not been doing things up to his usual standard. By coming through this difficult period, he was able to restore his belief in his capacities and prove things to his senior partner. His success allowed him to restore his pride in himself and his reputation with some of his objects, external in the case of the senior partner. However, the restoration achieved by this period was limited, for he had not succeeded in restoring his internal world, because he didn't feel much better, he still felt like a zombie.

I had no doubt that all this happened just as described by the patient. In all probability, the senior partner did off-load his insecurity in this way. However, I thought this sequence was an enactment of an internal drama that had taken place within the patient. From this perspective, the senior partner with his doubts, demandingness and lack of sympathy gained his influence over the patient because he was enacting the role of an object possessing these qualities in the patient himself.

I thought that a very similar sort of relationship was being relived in the interview itself, and the next stage of the consultation involved my taking up some aspects of Mr J's relationship to me as it had evolved over these first 20 or 25 minutes. Thus far, Mr J had seemed reserved and ill at ease. I mentioned above how at the beginning of the interview he'd asked for X, one of the other members of the team whom he'd previously met and with whom he felt comfortable. He had several times seemed on the edge of tears but on each occasion had fought them off, regaining his self-possession. He was helpful and co-operative with the aims of the interview but only so far. He was not deeply involved nor did he seem to be fully open with me. The interview was being tape-recorded (his permission for this had been asked in advance) but at the beginning of the interview I had felt that the recording might be one reason for his discomfort. This he denied, saying that he accepted it, as it would be helpful in the research. I felt unconvinced by his disclaimer, for he did seem to be disturbed by the tape-recording, amongst other things.

It was at this point that Mr J had gone on to say that in order to cope he had become like two people: one who worked and got on with the job; the other kept for home, the one who was feeling pain or anything at all. I then said to him that he may have felt that there had been a near-catastrophe inside him and that this had made him feel shaky and incapable. His way of managing that situation was to become, in a manner of speaking, like two people. So, also, I continued, he was managing here today to tell me all about the losses but in a professional way; the other kind of feelings, I thought, were kept for elsewhere, just as he'd kept them at home instead of at work.

Mr J was defensive about this point of mine, I think finding my phrase a 'near-catastrophe' especially difficult. He replied that it wasn't very easy to come here and bare your soul. I said that I wondered if he felt that *he* had been saying that there had been a collapse, not externally but internally. Again, he was defensive; perhaps, feeling that I was making out there had been a failure on his part or a situation which would damn him as a collapsed person, a state which he very much feared. When I clarified that I was talking about how he *felt* rather than how in fact he was, he told me in a very different tone of voice, in a serious and bleak way, that he felt terrible. He then became tearful and he told me a little bit of how he was 'actually feeling'.

He said he felt like an experimental animal. To put this remark in context, I should mention that this interview took place only a few days after some animal rights protesters had put a bomb under the car of a scientist involved in animal testing. This reference of the patient's along with some non-verbal cues made me more convinced that amongst other things Mr J was also angry; his actual feelings about seeing me and the nature of the consultation included resentment, a feeling that he was being tested, something like an experimental animal. At this point I said that the example he had chosen, of feeling like an experimental animal, was connected very directly with something violent. It wasn't too safe to be an experimenter upon animals at the moment.

Mr J responded, saying he'd come to the research with the idea that it would be helpful to others who might have to go through some difficult events in the future. That was how he felt, he said, in principle, and in principle it was great. But in practice, he continued, it was difficult for he actually felt embarrassed and observed. After a short slightly tense pause, I suggested that he was furious and he agreed, saying, 'I am pretty cross'. Becoming upset again, he said that everything that had happened to him had left him in the end feeling as if he had to apologise for them, and for his reactions, to pay for it. Again he referred back to the situation with the senior partner. I suggested that at this moment that the problem with the partner was the more familiar, the more easily explicable situation than the one here. I said that he was angry, feeling here that I was exposing him, bringing to mind uncomfortable things, making him feel distressed and embarrassed and feeling furthermore that I might complain at these needs and reactions of his, and all this was felt by him as making him pay.

Mr J seemed relieved and agreed with these comments and said that he thought that this was because, 'It's not anything that shows, so it's not the kind of injury that people can be sympathetic about, it is something that you hide inside you'. Mr J then went on to say that generally he is, at the moment, 'sensitive'. He compared himself unfavourably to his girlfriend, 'Like we might come away from dinner and I might say, "You know, they were a bit off, weren't they?" but she won't have noticed'.

I think this material shows that Mr J is carrying a tendency to feel that someone, 'they', are a bit off. Sometimes, 'they' are more than a bit off. I think 'they' are felt to be the cruel testers of animals, watching and inducing suffering, and then blaming the sufferer for it. 'They', are feared by him at some level and a violent explosion is not far off. He makes the point that the injury is not something that shows. It is an injury not only in the realm of his conscious feelings but an injury to the state of his internal world; while he can sense the effects of this he cannot directly perceive or describe it. Since it is an injury that doesn't show, the grievance against the felt neglect by his internal objects is all the greater because he feels he has to make efforts to convey it and then feels awkward having done so.

We can see a continual interplay between Mr J's internal state, his expectations of his objects and people actually in the outside world. Mr J talks about this when describing the work situation with his senior partner, but it also is lived out in relation to myself as the person interviewing him. There is yet another version, with 'they' as the people at the dinner. Mr J's senior partner and I were, I think, potentially bad, dangerous objects for him. It is easy to imagine how finding a bad object in the external world can come as a kind of relief. It's finding a familiar face in a crowd; one you can recognise as responsible for your ills. This may be easier for the ego than tolerating an uneasy feeling of unidentifiable persecution. It also offers an opportunity for re-working internal anxieties and their being modified by experience.

The recognition of his potentially explosive fear and resentment, of a less 'correct' view of the interview, freed him up. He now had a temporarily better relationship with the interviewer. In this better climate, he was able to engage more freely and began to speak of the fire and the events around it with more feeling. His account was now graphic and it was in this phase of the interview that personal biographical details emerged in a way that made it possible to make meaningful links.

Mr J was rendered shocked, incredulous and angry by the negligence and carelessness surrounding the fire. The delays of the fire brigade and the inexperience of the medical staff especially dismayed him. These things were like blows to his view of the proper order of the world he felt he'd previously lived in. When he'd got back to this country he'd sought out a fire officer and found his practical, as well as expert, approach helpful. The fire officer had particularly helped by being *really* realistic about the actually very limited opportunities to save those who had perished, for Mr J felt guilty about not having done more to save them. He'd functioned too, I think, as an important general proof of the existence of safe and competent persons. At one or two points when Mr J was describing the death of those who had been physically very near to him, he was acutely overcome by the realisation, and not for the first time, of how close he had come to losing his own life.

It emerged too that Mr J's escape was not as fortuitous as it appeared at first sight. Some weeks after the fire he'd been minutely interviewed by a forensic investigator. In the course of this he had realised that when he had walked through the lobby to go to another part of the hotel, a fire hose was lying unwound across the lobby. In the assessment interview, he said, 'I remember seeing fire hoses as well, which I didn't take in at the time'. When Mr J got upstairs to his room, untypically for

56

him, he'd looked at the fire escape map and traced the lefts and rights of the escape route with his finger. So when the fire alarm went, half an hour later, it was like, 'OK, now, do it! This is so weird'. He spoke again of the long interview with the forensic investigator and how some time after it, in a mood of preoccupation, there had been, 'this kind of blinding flash of what had happened', and with that flash he remembered there were several lines of hose across the lobby floor and, 'I can remember joking with the others and saying, "Oh, you know, this is funny, what is going on here?".' And thinking then to himself that 'they have some problem with the drains or, you know, it's a funny time to do the hoovering and, you know, no more significance than that, and then all that had completely gone from my mind'.

I suggested to Mr J that his experience of the fire may have seemed to him like being exposed to negligent parents, and that his seeking out of the fire safety officer when he returned to this country was to try and find again someone like a good parent. Mr J replied that this must obviously link with his feelings following his father's death. I now summarise greatly the many things Mr J next spoke of. He'd missed his father terribly and felt he was a kind of protector whom, as I said, I had compared to the fire officer. It then emerged that father had been himself very safety-conscious, that he'd always insisted upon safety rules, care with fire, matches, do-it-yourself procedures. This was tedious when they were children. Unselfconsciously he told me, 'I'd never really been frightened, always actually been fascinated by fire, certainly by fires in films, and fires, you know, and candles and matches. In Mexico it was the first time, you know, that I saw how it eats things up, how quickly it can consume'.

At this point in the consultation Mr J again became more suspicious of my search for connections. His previous detachment and watchfulness of me returned. He now told me, too, that one could go too far in looking for the meaning of things. He said, 'What is the deep significance of this for me? Maybe there isn't any'. At this point, Mr J seemed not to want to know. I pressed him, why was his dad involved in safety so much? Mr J tried a variety of obvious answers, most which were, I think, designed not to take us any further. Eventually, I brought up a fact that I knew from other information, that his father had had a depression. This reliable, deeply important but anxious father had become depressed and had developed the worry that he'd harmed some people. He'd been treated with medication and had made a good recovery. The patient felt that his father who was a straightforward, relatively unsophisticated man had felt belligerent and didn't know what to do with it.

In the final part of this long interview Mr J indicated that he felt that he was over the worst, that the interview had churned him up and that he had some doubts about the necessity or helpfulness of knowing more. Mr J decided not to proceed with getting any further treatment. He had sufficient ego capacities to continue the processing of what the events of the previous years had stirred up in him and may have been right in taking this decision.

What role had self-destructiveness played in his apparently ignoring the warnings of danger displayed in the lobby? Again, my impression was that this had not been a major factor, nor did self-destructiveness play a significant part in his make-up for it had been counterbalanced by his tracing the fire escape. Amongst other things this meant that his dealing with the impact of the fire was relatively uncomplicated, just as the basically good tenor of his feelings about his lost objects made his mourning of his father a painful but constructive process.

With Mr J the trauma had called into being the disturbance, whereas in other cases the disturbance has summoned the trauma. Such situations are not at all uncommon. They obviously complicate for the personality the task of working through the ensuing consequences. As with any traumatic event, the individual has to deal with the losses, with other directly damaging effects of the traumatic events, and to re-orientate a personal history now containing events outside the common stream – but it also has the difficult task of facing guilt and responsibility for having sought or caused the trauma. As well, the original internal situation to which the sought trauma may have been a hoped-for solution or evacuation usually remains unchanged, sometimes worsened.

These situations as they unfold can come to seem like modern versions of Greek tragedies, driven by the merciless gods. They caused Freud, as he came across them again and again in his patients, to experience an awed dismay. It was to account for these powerful, unlooked-for connections and motivations that he adduced the notions of an unconscious sense of guilt, a need for punishment and the workings of a compulsion to repeat. Tolerating certain types of anxieties within the ego may be very difficult. Seeking out some terrible damage may arise from the need to put outside what is inside, by provoking or enacting it so that it becomes an event, something that has really happened.

The position with the patient whom I will describe as Mr G was an instance of this type. At the time of his consultation, Mr G was a single man in his late 30s, highly intelligent and thoughtful. Since his early 20s Mr G had been involved in highly dangerous activities, although always of a controlled premeditated sort. He had been a professional soldier, carrying out repeatedly very difficult missions. Subsequently, he'd taken up a very dangerous high-speed sport and after a number of close shaves he'd eventually suffered a terrible accident in which there had been a crash and a fire. In the accident he'd sustained serious burns, had lost the sight of both eyes and had as well a number of other disabling injuries. He was mobile but only with difficulty. Before this accident he had realised that he was driven internally to seek out more and more challenging and dangerous situations. He knew, he said, that sooner or later it would come to this. 'I feel as if I had a death wish only I wasn't so lucky, if you see what I mean.'

At the start of the consultation he appeared to be remarkably at ease in a place that was completely strange to him, given the extent of his physical vulnerability. After a while I came to think that this invulnerable, bold stance was meant to leave his interlocutor wondering at him, admiring perhaps the absence of more usual reactions of anxiety or fear. There was also in his intelligent, often wry, attitudes a strangely reassuring and sometimes fascinating quality.

An attitude of courageous realism was important to him. 'If you can't pay the price you don't play the game. Don't you agree?' It was clear that any expression of regret or frailty was a threat to his understandably precarious ability to tolerate his difficult position. When I suggested to him that he might be frightened in this unfamiliar situation he smiled. He thought the world used the word 'frightened' too easily. He knew what it was to be frightened and by comparison being blind in an unknown street was as nothing. For what could happen? What bothered him was the feeling of frustration, which was like being a child again; also the way people treated him, like a child. After a while I pointed out that there was much more to being a child than merely being frustrated; for most children being lost is terrifying. Mr G quickly latched on and asked if I meant he might be scared of being scared. Becoming more alert and engaged in the interview he began to speak of his background.

As he began, he said that although he now did not feel any pain he 'felt that kind of nervousness you have before an injection'. Mr G was born and brought up in Southern Australia, by a mother who had devoted herself to looking after him and his two older sibs – a sister and a brother. His father, of whom he had little knowledge, left home in the final stages of the mother's pregnancy with Mr G. The children were sent to boarding school in North Australia and family life was restricted to the three holidays of the year. Mr G had one strong memory from when he was about ten years old. He was playing soldiers, dreaming of being a soldier, when his mother got upset, saying anxiously that he didn't wish to be a soldier, did he? 'They'll take you away and you'll get hurt.' A few years later his older brother was killed in a road traffic accident. Mr G became even more important to his mother. He did well at school and by his early twenties had become a civil engineer with a promising career ahead of him. At this time his mother developed a serious illness and after a few months died. It was in the months following her death that Mr G remembers himself becoming 'bored', feeling that the future was a pointless prospect and now that his mother was no longer alive there was nothing to keep him from soldiering. As the years went by he sought out situations of greater and greater risk.

Mr G conveyed vividly the feelings occasioned by his mother's illness and death. He recalled being tall and upright. Although she was so proud of him, he was unable to save her. While Mr G emphasised her pain and suffering, I was more struck by the difficulty he had in being aware of his own feelings of loss and his anger at her departure. After all, subsequently in his life he had exposed this tall, upright person to repeated, calculated gambles with death or serious injury. I wondered too about the effect of his father's departure upon Mr G's attitude to his own manhood. The father left him to what may have felt like sole possession of mother but with its unfortunate concomitant, sole responsibility. Certainly, Mr G had an unrealistic belief in his own psychological invulnerability, a belief that I thought was probably reinforced as a solution by the long boarding-school periods cut off from what family life there was. One effect of the brother's death was to cut off a possible co-bearer of these burdens.

I came to think that Mr G had reacted to some powerful internal childhood anxieties linked with a fear and hatred of his own and his mother's depressive anxieties. He had massively brought himself down, by literally turning himself from the powerful adult figure he appeared to be into someone with many of the physical limitations and needs of a child. Although it is possible to read this account of Mr G's motivation and nature as merely plausible or fanciful reconstruction I think this would be mistaken. Mr G himself knew that he had reacted to events in his life, although he didn't know the full extent of it. Interestingly, he was not, on this showing, against insight, responsibility or self-knowledge. However, the side of his personality which had made him repeatedly expose himself to potentially mutilating situations was motivated by a violent fear and hatred of what he might come to feel. A talion law had ruled the main parts of his life and most of the insight he had was like that possessed by a powerless witness.

Many other types of people and problems will be encountered in an assessment service. A traumatic event may possess some especial significance for the person who has suffered it. Many people possess areas of their personality partially quiescent, partially split-off from the mainstream of their life. Some kind of fit between the nature of the traumatic event and split-off aspects of the personality will often mean that the individual can find no new adjustment without the re-working of the anxieties that have previously been sidelined. These will need identifying in the assessment process.

Other patients present with a sense of injury, a feeling of being ill-treated. Even when the ill-treatment is real it is often difficult to feel real or spontaneous sympathy. Instead there is an atmosphere of coercion in which the interviewer senses that failure to respond in the 'right' way will produce a much more persecuted or paranoid response. Others are recruited to agree that the patient has been badly treated, that all men, for instance, are bad or that with different less 'traumatising' treatment, either now or in the past, the patient would not be so difficult or so upset. The feeling of being guided, pressurised or subtly intimidated to take up a position either for or against something is often diagnostic of these situations. They are complex and require a difficult mix of permeability, openness, tolerance and firmness from the interviewer if the clinical encounter is to have a productive outcome. Many of these processes are discussed further in Chapter 5.

## Conclusions

The psychoanalytically-informed assessment of patients suffering from the after-effects of seriously traumatic events has some of the aims of the traditional case-study approach of the best of general psychiatry. Added to this is a distinctive attempt to understand at a deeper level the event, its occurrence, its impact and the patient's internal situation. This includes knowledge of the significance of unconscious phantasy and the importance of childhood. To reach an understanding of this sort, it is necessary to engage with the patient around a meaningful point of contact and to trace its development throughout the interview.

In this chapter, I have implied rather than spelled out the techniques involved in a psychodynamic assessment, including enquiries about dreams and early memories, and other ways of building up a picture of the patient's personality, difficulties and relationships. Milton (1997) outlines a more detailed approach to the general psychodynamic assessment interview, and of course, many of these same aims and techniques are relevant in the specialised assessment of patients who are referred as suffering from the after-effects of trauma. However, there are also some distinguishing features. The traumatised individual may not consider himself to be a 'patient' (See Chapter 4). Also, one of the effects of significant trauma upon the ego is the loss of a capacity to process meaningful events, which is of course one of the emotional tasks most necessary if the traumatised ego is to begin to recover. There is then a need for a new orientation in life, one which can include the significance and impact of the disturbance. Some of the working-through necessary following a traumatic episode will take place through the externalisation of disturbed internal object relationships and the subsequent reintrojection of the constructive responses of external objects. When this happens, more symbolic functioning can develop, more benign internal objects can be established and eventually these developments are connected with the emergence of personal meaning. In the assessment interview, one of the key judgements concerns the individual's capacity for processing the disturbance in this way – for this is how ghosts may be laid to rest.

# 4

# Preliminary Interventions

## The Four-Session Therapeutic Consultation

### *Linda Young*

### Introduction

In this chapter I relate one man's story, as it emerged in the course of his meetings with me, following referral to the Trauma Unit by his GP. The consultation as a whole consisted of four sessions, spaced either two or three weeks apart, covering a period of three months. Each session was one and a half hours long, apart from the first which was deliberately slightly longer. Most individuals referred to the Unit are offered a four session consultation as an initial intervention. In this chapter I shall be giving a picture of this kind of consultation. The case I have chosen is one in which the consultation seemed to have some beneficial impact. Of course not all the cases we see are quite like this; some patients are more broken down, inarticulate, do not attend, act out and so on. However, essentially what we are trying to do in every consultation remains the same and it is this that I want to describe.

The experience of being alive is an ambivalent one, a mixture of good and bad. By and large most people manage the difficulties, drawing on the kinds of support normally available to them – their social and family networks, and their own internal resources. Our consultation is offered only when the individual requests it, perhaps via a professional referrer, rather than as a standard intervention following a traumatic event; not everybody will need professional help. When someone comes to us it is because their capacity to manage has broken down. Some are able to re-establish their capacity to cope with a time-limited intervention because it is possible for the therapist to mobilise the individual's *own* resources, which previously sustained them, so that they can then function independently. Others, perhaps with less in the way of pre-existing internal and external resources, or

63

who have experienced particularly devastating external events, need longer-term help.

It is because it is overwhelming and incapacitating, and *cannot be managed* psychically, that an event can be defined as traumatic. Flexible and creative thought is replaced by nightmares, flashbacks and at times unconsciously driven re-enactments of the event. The experience cannot, in the usual way, be *contained* in the mind through thought. (In Bion's terms (1967) there is a breakdown in the capacity to transform beta into alpha elements). It is possible to conceptualise the impact also in terms of the psychoanalytic model of an internal world of object relationships. Melanie Klein (1929a, 1929b,1945) described the mind as an internal world populated from the beginning of life, via primitive unconscious phantasies, with figures she called internal objects. These were variously deemed to be benign and helpful or malevolent and dangerous. In Klein's descriptions all events are, in phantasy, felt to be *caused* either by good or bad objects, dependent on the nature of the event. One can think then that the internal experience of a traumatic event is an experience of being abandoned by loving good internal objects which protect and contain, and instead left to the mercy of hateful and hating objects, felt to have *caused* the trauma. This is especially the case when there has been a real external disaster, since it is to be protected from these extreme experiences, involving the death of someone and/or the possibility of dying oneself, that one *most* expects from one's good object. If the attempt in the consultation to make contact is successful, then the individual is provided with an experience of being understood, of a good experience of containment. In this way, the therapist may help, within the confines of a brief intervention, to begin to re-establish an internal good object, necessary for healthy psychic functioning.

A brief intervention of this kind is consistent with the exigencies of a busy NHS Clinic receiving many referrals. But this is not the only consideration. People like Mr A who are referred to the Trauma Unit do not come wanting psychotherapy. They come wanting help with an overwhelming external event and wanting things to be restored to how they were before the event happened. It is not, we think, the most helpful thing then at that point to be offering a one or two session assessment for psychotherapy. The consultation is therefore *not* an assessment alone, but a therapeutic intervention. Nor, *at the outset*, would it be helpful to offer a more long term ongoing psychoanalytic intervention. At the outset of the consultation it is the *external event* of the trauma that is being brought, and the capacity for meaningful thought about the event which has broken down, and it will be necessary in the consultation to spend some time talking and thinking about the detail of the external event itself, coming to include in that the internal meaning of the event and its aftermath for the particular individual. The individual needs help to be able to begin to think about what has happened to him or her from this other perspective, and to relinquish and mourn the wish to 'recover', to be as if the event had never happened. As with all psychoanalytic clinical work, the consultation is not structured by the therapist's providing directions and themes, and there is an emphasis on the therapist's following rather than leading, allowing for the emergence of transference and countertransference. The work of the consultation may lead the individual to go on to think of ongoing psychotherapy, or it may in itself have been of sufficient help.

## Clinical Example

Mr A came to England from Ireland in his early 20s. He was just over 40 at the time he came to the Clinic. He immediately struck me as a pleasant-looking man, with evident natural gifts, but I soon became aware that this feature of his presentation was overwhelmed by an attitude of utter despair and defeat. In bare detail, his story was as follows. Mr A had trained as a Probation Officer many years ago, and reached the top of his field. Three years before I saw him he had been involved in a very serious incident whilst visiting a client in a prison hospital. Whilst talking to his client, Mr A was suddenly approached from behind by another patient who had a history of violent assaults on others. The patient launched a vicious attack on Mr A, beating him about the head and face, until he eventually fell to the ground bleeding heavily from wounds caused by a chair leg the man was using to hit him with. When he fell, his assailant stood on his neck, pressing down forcefully so that Mr A blacked out. His last memory was of great physical pain and the terrifying conviction that he was going to die. It took several minutes before anyone came to his assistance, and the first to do so was in fact another client. Other staff then came, and his assailant was dragged from him, struggling and shouting. Mr A was taken to casualty with concussion, a severely bruised face, and a gaping head wound which required dozens of stitches. He was away from work for several weeks before he was sufficiently recovered physically to return.

Not long after the incident itself he was visited at home by two of the senior staff at the prison hospital, whom he had known and worked with for some time. They told him that when the inevitable enquiry took place, he should not say exactly what had happened and they suggested an alternative version of the events. Mr A thought that this was because they were worried about being seen as having been negligent. He was threatened with being accused of fault himself if he reported the truth of what had taken place. Mr A, however, wrote a report which described accurately what had happened during the incident. The senior colleagues acted as they had indicated, and Mr A was made the subject of a disciplinary hearing. It was not until two and a half years later that its conclusion was finally reached, during which time Mr A was moved to a less responsible post. The outcome was that the seniors were themselves made the subject of a disciplinary investigation, and Mr A was exonerated.

However, in spite of the acquittal, three years after the incident, when he was referred to the Trauma Unit, he told me that his life had lost much of its meaning and he could no longer think of the future with any optimism. He was now not working at all, was afraid indeed of even going outside the front door, and was suffering from chronic anxiety and a sense of dread. He was troubled by nightmares and flashbacks; his relationships were in difficulty, particularly his marriage, and his self esteem had gone. He displayed, in a horribly vivid way, the classic symptoms of Post Traumatic Stress Disorder – anxiety, sleeplessness, guilt, depression, flashbacks and nightmares, low self confidence and the breakdown of relationships. He felt that his world had collapsed, and this included his mental world.

### The First Session

The man I first met appeared physically and mentally crushed. Although his cuts and bruises had long healed, his whole demeanour conveyed collapse and despair; his shoulders drooped and his eyes remained cast to the ground. He began with a question – asking me to tell him what I needed to know. He wanted to be co-operative, and do all he could to provide the information that might be of help to *me*. I felt that he was letting me know right away about the passivity and submissiveness which now typified a man who had formerly been successful and ambitious. In this first meeting I was not surprised to hear of the various doctors who had helped him in some way. Whilst undoubtedly this assistance was of great value, I was aware that this also told me how dependent he was now feeling, compared with his prior capacity to, as

66

he put it, 'sort things out himself'. 'I was reporting all this to the occupational health manager and the occupational health doctor, Dr X at the Y Clinic, she was helping me, with Dr W and so on, and in fact they intervened on my behalf. Dr W organised psychiatric help for me, I was on anti-depressants and sedation. I've stopped seeing Dr W, and I am not sorted out.' I felt a pressure to do better, and thought that Mr A was now bringing to me, as he had to Dr W and Dr X, his hope for an ideal and therefore magical object, on whom he could depend to sort things out on his behalf. I said something like this to A, who then commented, 'Yes, I'm in your hands', confirming my impression and underlining how much he wished to be gathered up by me, looked after and made better.

Therapists of course do not do magic. Fortunately so, because for Mr A to re-establish some kind of life for himself he was going to have to regain something of his former capacities to cope, and relinquish being totally dependent on someone else to look after him. However, his wish for this was strong, and understandable. Whilst the assault was happening, Mr A's colleagues had at first run away. It took several minutes before two of them regained their courage and came to help, so that Mr A's fear of being abandoned and left without any support was particularly strong. I felt that his desire for me not to do this was very urgent. He needed me to be a powerfully helpful figure, to counteract feelings of persecution inside from bad, malevolent, abandoning internal objects. I addressed again his wish to be in my hands, to be looked after, and he agreed. He said that he did hope I could sort things out, then sat back, eyes cast down, passively waiting for me to 'do whatever I would to make him better'. His agreement with my comments was a feature of the four meetings I had with Mr A, and a further indication of his passivity. I was aware at times of feeling irritation with Mr A, wanting to shake some life back into him. Mr A could no longer take action for himself (other than to protect himself by staying ensconced in his house with the curtains drawn, because the street felt too dangerous to risk going out) and in our first meeting this was very evident with me too – he would go along with whatever I or any of the other doctors advised.

In the session, Mr A now remained silent. I commented on this, and on the way in which he seemed unable to decide himself what he wanted to tell me. He agreed, and then said that he wanted to tell me about the assault. For a brief moment Mr A had again been able to think for himself, rather than believe all the thinking had to be done for him. He then spoke without pause for around 20 minutes, slowly, painstakingly, telling me in a quiet, hopeless voice the details of the incident and its aftermath.

He told me that the event continued to flash into his mind with extraordinary vividness. He said: 'It's as if it happened yesterday. I can see the man who attacked me, I can describe him. I can see the number of rings on his fingers and what he was saying. What he was doing. That's the worst part of my problem. I can't push it out of my mind'. He was steadily becoming more and more depressed and anxious. He fell asleep at night with great difficulty and would suddenly wake, bathed in sweat, from a nightmare repetition of the attack. He had continued to work for some months, but having to struggle with a dreadful panic that would descend upon him whenever there was any threat of anger or violence amongst the clients with whom he was working. Shortly before my first meeting with him the panic had become too much and he had stopped working.

His marriage too was in difficulties. He said to me: 'The sexual relationship with my wife is nil at the moment and this is from after the assault. There hasn't been the threat of divorcing, but we have started sleeping in separate rooms, and one thing leads to another'. I thought that Mr A was telling me that with his wife too he could not risk engaging actively and potently; they slept apart and he avoided trying love-making. I said to Mr A that I thought he was letting me know how difficult it was for him now to take any action, to be potent himself, so that I had to be felt to be the one carrying that on his behalf. Mr A then said that he felt very helpless but did not know how to be different. He had been helpless during the assault, he said, and did not know how to regain his capacity to be effective. He added that a particularly distressing moment during the assault was when he had been lying on the floor, believing that he was going to die but unable to do anything about it. He went on to say that at that moment, lying on the ground bleeding heavily, he had seen an image of his son telling him to stand up and run, but he had not been able to do so. It seemed as if all the *life* had been projected into his son at that moment. He then continued that it had also been deeply distressing when his seniors had come to visit him at home and whilst there, had threatened him in front of his wife and child. I thought that both of these experiences felt particularly humiliating to Mr A. They robbed him of his manliness, and filled him with shame. On both occasions he told me that he felt that he had let his family down. 'Here I was the husband, the head of the family and I couldn't do anything. I let these people intimidate my wife, my son and

I did nothing. And I've cried in front of my family, which I would never have done before. To me, crying is a sign of weakness.'

At this point in our meeting I said to him that I thought that *he was telling me* something about why he was like he was now: that the idea of himself as capable and strong, and always able to cope was extremely important to him, something that he was proud of, and which was very much part of his image of himself. Mr A agreed, and told me that after the incident, when he was waiting for the disciplinary action and had been moved to a different job he had thought of suicide. He felt he had lost everything – 'I lost my wife, my children, everything I had, and I couldn't cope'. In fact his wife had stayed with him and offered much support, but I think he felt that he had lost his image of himself as the one who looked after and protected her. This was the first time he had not coped. He had felt betrayed, but also felt that he had betrayed his wife and his image of himself as a potent protector. I said to him that it seemed as though before the assault the thought that he might not be able to cope with something just hadn't entered his head, as if he had felt that he had a kind of invulnerability. Mr A agreed that this was so. It seemed that the kind of infallibility he wished I had (the ability to restore him to health) was the picture he had had of himself before the assault, and contributed to the devastating effect it had had on him. Having 'failed', Mr A felt that he had therefore *become* a failure, entirely helpless and weak. I wondered if the fact I could not make everything better would leave Mr A feeling I had failed, or whether it would be possible for me to be both less than perfect but also able to be of some help. If so, this might also offer Mr A an alternative to identify with, other than either perfect and omnipotent on the one hand, or utterly helpless on the other.

### The Second Session

Mr A came to the second meeting with me, as downcast as before. He started by commenting that things were the same, perhaps worse. I said that I thought that he felt disappointed by this. Mr A agreed, and then said that he had always had great faith in therapy, but he wondered if anyone could help him with this.

In the immediate aftermath Mr A had certainly not felt helped by those he thought he could depend on for help. In this way his experience had been particularly shattering because those he had thought of as good and trustworthy, had twice betrayed him – not only during the assault itself, but also during the aftermath, when his seniors had tried to have him found to blame. In his internal world, good objects were left in pieces, bad objects had taken over and were felt, through processes of projection, to populate the external world too. Because of this, feelings of anger and mistrust continued to dominate, particularly importantly towards those who offered to help, whether professionals, friends or family members, especially if they proved, as I had, to be unable to make everything all right again.

In the consultation I felt drawn to reassure Mr A, perhaps particularly because the terrible events he had experienced had been at the hands of another person. There can be quite a pressure on the consultant to dis-identify explicitly from the perpetrator, and to convey 'I am not like that, I am here to make things better for you, not to betray you or let you down'. One consequence can be that this places the patient's anger about what has happened *outside* the consulting room. Although I felt the wish to reassure Mr A, I think to do so would have left him feeling that I could not bear to be the target of his anger and his mistrust. I thought that this would not be helpful to Mr A, particularly since, like most survivors of traumatic events, mistrust of others is a dominant and insistent feeling. The reality anyway is that any therapist will sooner or later in some way let the patient down, because he or she cannot make everything all right again, and moreover cannot guarantee no further awful events in the future.

I said to Mr A that I thought he felt disappointed in me and was left uncertain as to how much he could trust me to be of help to him. Mr A replied that he was sorry to appear suspicious, but he also felt worried that I would have contact with his Occupational Health Department, which might jeopardise his future employment. I said to him that when he did think of me as powerful, it was also in a worrying way – that I would use my power against him and in this I thought he felt I might be like the colleagues who could not be trusted. Mr A agreed, but as he did I was aware of his hesitant and apologetic manner. It seemed that if I was felt to be powerful in a malign way, I was also to be placated – Mr A was not angry, and not able it seemed to stand up to the me whom he feared would betray him in this way, any more than he had been able to with his senior colleagues 3 years ago. I said this to Mr A, who told me that in his family anger was not something to be proud of. This was the first time he had mentioned his family of origin, and I commented that it seemed he still felt this now. Mr A agreed. He told me that his father had been a firm man, strong but also fair, but never someone he had seen distressed or angry. He added that his father had brought him up to believe that men did not show their emotions, certainly did not

70

cry, and did not show uncontrolled aggression. He wondered whether this was why he now found it so difficult to accept any such feeling in himself. He went over the detail of the assault and the disciplinary hearings again. This time he also commented on how striking it was that he had not ever been angry – just afraid.

## The Third Session

I met with Mr A again three weeks later. He was dressed this time rather smartly, with jacket and tie. The impression he gave via this clothing was different – he seemed more confident, more in control of himself. However, he began the meeting by telling me, his voice still soft, but conveying slight impatience, that he did not see how talking here for two more sessions was going to help. He then looked straight at me, waiting for an answer, before again looking down at the floor. Feeling somewhat on the spot, but not at that moment as irritated with Mr A as I had previously been at times, I could only think to comment that I thought he was disappointed and perhaps angry about this. Mr A looked up at me and agreed he was disappointed.

He then looked down at the floor again, a stance in which I was more used to seeing him. He told me that he couldn't concentrate on anything, and so could not drive. In a shop he had been charged too much and just handed over the money. He was afraid of people and mostly tried to avoid them. I said that Mr A was now emphasising how fearful and impotent he was, perhaps to get away from the moment of irritation and disappointment with me. I thought to myself that for a moment Mr A had been able to feel angry himself rather than having to project it all into the outside world and other people. When I at times had felt irritation in response to his passivity, I think it was at least partly a result of his disowned, that is, projected, aggression.

In the session Mr A said that he was afraid of his anger now. I said that it was perhaps because his anger now felt like the mad violence of the man who had attacked him. Mr A responded by saying the man often came to his mind. I thought that this was a particular issue for Mr A, as it frequently is following a violent traumatic event – the fear of one's own aggressive feelings when there has been actual external violence and destruction. It becomes difficult to distinguish powerful internal feelings from actual violent behaviour. Some manage the experience of being attacked by identifying with the aggressor, but Mr A, because of aspects of his personality and history, did not. As well, if Mr A were to start to function successfully and to believe in himself

71

once more as an effective man this laid him open to the possibility that he would be attacked again, and to further betrayal. It was better in this sense for him to remain passive, humiliated, than to risk another violent assault.

Mr A then said he had gone on thinking about the way his father had disapproved of anger when he was a child, and about how he had never seen him angry. He thought this may have affected how he felt about anger. I thought that he was also saying that there was an internal father whose wrath he feared were he, Mr A, to be angry. Also, Mr A explained, in his job, anger was something that he had been taught to contain within himself – it was important, particularly when having to manage potentially aggressive clients, to remain calm and unprovoked. It was hard therefore to react differently this time. I felt however that Mr A was beginning to show a different sort of reaction. I was very struck that he was now himself thinking about the question he had first rather helplessly posed to me – *why he was now the way he was?* He was beginning, through thought, to make some sense of his experience as opposed to being passively overwhelmed by it. In the session, I said to Mr A that I thought he was saying now that he felt that his previous experience was relevant to how things were now. Mr A said that he had not particularly thought it before, but it was maybe so.

I asked Mr A to tell me more about his background. This is not an invariable point of technique, but it seemed to me that at this point it made sense for us to look at this. Indeed in the course of any consultation I would hope to get details of a person's background and history. Mr A told me that he was the youngest of 8 children from a poor Irish family. Both his parents were now dead, his mother 15 and his father 18 years ago. His father had worked as a customs officer, and was hard working, having to provide for 8 children. He told me that his mother was extremely ill in the months before she died, and, as he spoke of her weakness and vulnerability in the last months of her life, tears filled his eyes. His mother seemed very alive for him still. She was described as utterly devoted to the family and when I asked him for an early memory, he told me about an incident as a child when he had been playing on land near where they lived in a quite isolated spot. He was playing barefoot, and had trodden on some broken glass, leaving his foot badly cut and bleeding. He was in some pain but mostly very frightened, and anxious that no-one would come. He began to limp painfully homewards, bleeding from his wound, when his mother appeared, looking for him. She gathered him up, carried him to the house and phoned for an ambulance to take him to hospital. This was

72

a picture of a helpful parent (internal object in the internal world) who did not let you down, who came to your aid and did not let you bleed to death. I thought this picture of his mother linked with his wish for me too to 'gather him up' in the first session, to be like this helpful parent of his childhood memory.

Like his father, when he left school Mr A became a customs officer. Unlike his father though, after a year and a half, he left, in order to train instead as a probation officer. It seemed to me that his chosen profession was a combination of an identification with his caring, devoted mother, and his powerful, strong vigilant father – Mr A did not just catch wrong-doers, but worked in a 'caring' capacity, and, like his father, with people who were involved in crime. His own sense of strength and confidence seemed very much tied up with these parental identifications, leaving him striving to be a highly successful professional, sometimes managing violent criminals, and also a devoted family man. In both areas he believed himself to be invulnerable, which was also how he saw his parents. It seemed that this was an image of himself he had held from childhood, when it had had a particular significance for the son who was the youngest and thus potentially the weakest and most vulnerable in the family. It was all this that Mr A felt he had lost when he first came to see me. Mr A told me that something acutely embarrassing and humiliating had happened since the attacks – that he occasionally wet the bed. He commented: 'It's odd I didn't recall this before, but I did for a while as a child and felt then so pathetic, helpless and small'. In this session I said that I thought that the attack had had this particular meaning for him, that it had left him feeling suddenly robbed of all his capacities as an adult male and identified instead with the vulnerable mother he particularly remembered from his later life, and the helpless child who wets the bed or injures his foot. This for him was terribly humiliating. He felt he had lost everything – internally, he had lost contact with his early good objects, his dependable, invulnerable mother and his father. In fact I think Mr A had always managed anxieties about his own and his objects' vulnerabilities by holding rigidly onto a sense of their and his own omnipotence. It was this psychic defence against real-life human frailty that had been shattered by the assault. Mr A commented that he had been dreaming of his mother since the assault, and longed for her to be still alive. He felt he could trust her, and it was difficult trusting strangers (like me) with his life story. He added that although he still didn't feel entirely sure he could trust me, he felt less anxious about saying that to me than he had at first, and perhaps that meant he did feel more at ease with me than he had quite realised. He then went on: 'What you said, about a grown up like me who saw myself as capable and strong, is very difficult – I find myself now unable to hold my emotions, I tend to cry a lot. I was thinking that I was still strong and could manage, but I knew inside that things were wrong. I tried to hide it from people and from myself and told myself it was a passing phase. Now I know that it is not, and I hope that the Clinic will be able to offer me more help. If you can't then I will find it somewhere else. I know though that I do not need more medication. I need to talk about what has happened to me'.

## The Fourth Meeting

Mr A began speaking, saying that he did not know what was best for him now; what did I think? After a short pause he continued that he was finding himself in the last couple of days constantly thinking of the worst, and was withdrawing more within himself. I said that I thought perhaps he withdrew from something more assertive and capable in himself which we had seen last time, when he had told me something of what he did and did not want to happen now. I thought he may be withdrawing because he knew that this was our last meeting. His withdrawal protected him from any feeling of upset about that, but perhaps also protected me from any anger he may have. 'I don't know what I feel', said Mr A. 'I think it isn't enough. I don't know how to cope.' I said that I thought he may feel that all he could do at the moment was to convey to me how awful things are, in the hope that I might do something. Mr A smiled, 'I don't want to stop talking about this; it helps me understand and think about it'.

He then told me that he had had another dream about his mother since he had last seen me. He could not remember much of the detail, but recalled feeling sad when he woke from the dream. I said that I thought that he did feel very sad that his mother was no longer alive and so was not there for him to talk to about all the things that had been so troubling to him in the last years, and that he felt that I too was now leaving him without me to talk to either. Mr A said that at first he had felt pleased about being offered as much as four sessions. Then when he began to feel that everything was not going to be better within four sessions he had thought that he might be to blame for that, and that perhaps he was letting me down. However he had just begun to think that four sessions really wasn't very much. I said he seemed to be experimenting with the possibility of being able to assert his wishes and needs rather than blaming himself. Mr A replied that from 'day one' he had blamed himself for all that had gone wrong. Now he thought that was a mistake: after all, he was not responsible for what had happened, and the official investigation had proved that; it had always seemed so hard to believe in the conclusions though. 'When I was vindicated I thought it should make me happy, but it didn't, there were no celebrations. I thought why did I let it happen in the first place? I do think it was difficult for me because I have been taught by my father and in my job not to be blaming of others or angry. And my own family upbringing meant it was so humiliating to lose my sense of confidence and capability. And I'd never not coped before.'

I commented to Mr A that some of the work which we had done seemed to enable him to make some sense of his situation. Mr A agreed; 'I do think this has helped', he said. I wondered then if this positive comment by Mr A was part of his feeling that he needed to please and placate me. I put this to him and although I couldn't be quite sure what this meant, he disagreed. It had been evident particularly when we first met that he had, for defensive reasons, tried to idealise me; I was wondering if this was becoming stronger again now that our contact was coming to an end, and he needed to get rid of more difficult feelings about the ways I had not helped him, or had not helped him enough. This was one of the themes of our last meeting.

By the end of this fourth meeting I did think that the picture I had and that Mr A had of himself had changed. He no longer thought of himself simply as a man suffering the consequences of a violent assault; he was an individual with a particular history which contributed to his having been the kind of person he was, very identified with strong, devoted parental figures, and determined to be a successful professional and a successful family man. It was the importance of this to him, and the consequences of the loss of this, of his internal objects and identifications, that helped to make sense of the specific impact of the assault and its aftermath. By the end of the consultation I think Mr A had been able to make some sense of the impact on him of the traumatic event and of the place that it had taken up in his internal world and in the context of existing internal object relationships.

As I have been trying to show, it is making sense in this way that begins the process of assimilating what has happened into the mind, so that it can be thought about and understood, rather than simply repeated in nightmares or repetitive behaviours. Making sense with someone else is also the beginning of rebuilding an internal object world in which good objects feel more stable and trustworthy. This in turn allows the external world to be evaluated in a more realistic way. It also begins the process of reintegrating aspects of the self that have been projected into the external world, which in Mr A's case were particularly feelings of aggression, activity and potency.

Towards the end of our last meeting I spoke with Mr A about possibilities for ongoing help. He could see the sense, he said, of psychotherapy, because he thought he needed to understand more about the way the event had affected *him*. This seemed the outcome – that during the consultation the event had come to be linked up with his past and current situations, and thereby had become available for *thought*. By the end of the consultation Mr A was considering ongoing psychotherapy that could potentially further address wider issues as well as those evoked by the assault. He was no longer specifically looking for the services of our specialist Unit, since he no longer saw his situation only in terms of a response to an external traumatic event.

## Postscript

Mr A was offered and accepted a place in an ongoing general psychotherapy group in the Department, which he attended for four years. After several months in the group he reported being able to stand up to someone for the first time since the assault, when a bullying relative had wanted him to give up his rights to some family property and he had been able to say no. More recently he described being involved in a coach crash; he had been able to remain clear headed and help those who were injured until the emergency services arrived. Although Mr A continues to experience serious difficulties with his passivity and with anger (in himself and others) which continue to undermine his capacity to manage life (and he has not yet returned to full-time work) there are indications of his beginning to rediscover his competencies. He describes himself as less depressed, and, with considerable relief, that, contrary to his expectation, his marriage and family life have survived.

## Conclusion

Some of those who come to the Unit go on following the four-session consultation to further general psychotherapy, as did Mr A. As in his case, the consultation can help this development. Others do not want more; some do not need more. Four sessions of course is not very much; for some there will certainly be much that remains to be addressed. But for those who go on for more help, they are now doing so for themselves, not because of the trauma. This is an important function of the four sessions: it can help with the important process of disengaging from a central preoccupation with the trauma itself, and reconnecting with past life and personality, and with disowned aspects of the self, especially destructiveness. Instead there develops the capacity to formulate and to think about what has happened and continues to happen, and through this process to contain it within the mind.

The limited number of sessions also introduces from the very beginning the inevitability of ending, and thus facing loss. The ability to mourn the loss of the pre-disaster self is central to working through a traumatic event as well as mourning those who may have died (both internal and external objects), and mourning lost omnipotence. There is no magic of course about the number four. It is what we are able to offer to the many referred to us within the context of limited resources. However, it allows for greater depth than is possible in one session, for going back to issues raised at the beginning, but which may be returned to later in a way that suggests they are being viewed and experienced in a rather different way. Four sessions also allows for a beginning, a middle and an end, also in terms of the relationship with the therapist.

I hope I have given a picture of this kind of preliminary brief intervention. It focuses on exploring and understanding the impact of the trauma in terms of the loss of the capacity of the mind to manage experience through thought, and the loss of an internal object relationship in which experience is managed through containment. I hope I have also given some flavour of the way in which the attempt to make sense of and think about what has happened can also be of help in getting back into and on with life after the experience of a traumatic event.

# Part Three

# Treatment in Psychoanalytic Psychotherapy

# Trauma and Grievance

*Linda Young and Elizabeth Gibb*

It is not uncommon for people who have experienced a traumatic event to show intense anger about what has happened to them. However, there are patients who, for a variety of reasons, need to defend themselves against knowledge of their anger. This may be because the violence of the disaster in which they have been involved arouses unmanageable anxiety about any further violence, including that which is related to their own destructiveness. Those people who are left too afraid of their own anger to do other than defend against it may remain crippled by the trauma for a considerable time. One such defence involves denial and projection – that is, getting rid of feelings by, in phantasy, locating them in the outside world and other people (Freud, 1926; Klein, 1946). In consequence the world around is experienced as suffused with danger. While there is no longer the threat from destructive feelings located inside, the individual is left feeling surrounded by hostile and threatening forces. One patient seen within the Tavistock Unit for the Study of Trauma and Its Aftermath was subjected to a very violent attack in which he nearly died. For a number of reasons, he could not tolerate the violent anger which the assault aroused in him. This included childhood and professional prohibitions against his becoming angry himself, as well as a new sense of anxiety about violence, having experienced such a violent and potentially lethal attack. Unconsciously he dealt, in part, with his own feelings of rage through projection. When seen he was submissive and compliant, but terrified of leaving his home, even of a knock at the front door; this knock represented to him a violent return of his projected anger, and therefore a considerable threat. He had to ignore it, and leave the door closed. As can be seen from this example, the inability to experience and express anger after a traumatic event can lead to chronic anxiety and phobic symptoms.

It is, we think, important and indeed necessary for the traumatised adult to be aware of his or her own aggression, since this helps to re-establish a realistic perception of the dangers of the world following a traumatic experience. Knowing about and taking back inside (re-introjecting) your own anger allows it to be disentangled and differentiated from the actual dangers of the world, which can then be experienced and dealt with in a modified and more realistic way: the knock at the door is, more than likely, innocuous. Anger is also a potent form of assertiveness, enabling the determination to rebuild one's life after something devastating has happened. It is allied to potency and agency; without any anger all that remains may be passivity and a sense of defeat.

In some people, however, a sense of grievance may accompany or replace feelings of anger. In this chapter we intend to explore the nature of grievance, as it arises in victims of trauma. We shall begin by outlining what we understand to be the essence of grievance, as distinct from other related emotions, such as anger.

Distinctively, grievance involves a feeling of being the victim of an injustice. Because of this, there is little sense of personal responsibility or guilt. Injustice involves a sense of unfairness, and potentially can be relieved by the injustices being seen to be put right, or at least acknowledged and apologised for, with perhaps an attempt at reparation. For some, there is a sense of injustice which cannot be assuaged until revenge has taken place, some kind of attack seen to be equal in weight to the original injury ('an eye for an eye'). For others, the need for revenge is not so assuaged and acts of violence are extreme and unending. Steiner (1996) described grievance arising when such acts of revenge – whether in phantasy or reality – are felt to be unacceptable. Later in this chapter we shall go on to explore this in more detail.

Freud (1932) suggests that it is inevitable in infancy that feelings of being unfairly treated by the mother arise, together with feelings of hostility and wishes for revenge.

> The reproach against the mother which goes back furthest is that she gave the child too little milk – which is construed against her as lack of love ... whatever the true state of affairs may have been it is impossible that the child's reproach can be justified as often as it is met with. It seems rather that the child's avidity for its earliest nourishment is altogether insatiable, that it never gets over the pain of losing its mother's breast ... Nor does it make much difference if the child happens to remain the mother's preferred favourite. A child's demands for love are immoderate, they make exclusive claims and tolerate no sharing.

82

## 5. Trauma and Grievance

Steiner (op. cit.) and Feldman (1995) extend Freud's ideas, believing that the original resentment can be understood as related to the mother's being part of a parental couple, rather than belonging exclusively to the child. Britton (1989) addresses a similar theme:

> Later, the oedipal encounter also involves recognition of the difference between the relationship between the parents as distinct from the relationship between parent and child: the parents' relationship is genital and procreative; the parent-child relationship is not. This recognition produces a sense of loss and envy, which, if not tolerated, may become a sense of grievance and self denigration.

The latter is evident, for instance, in melancholic states, also vividly described by Freud (1915b). For all of us, therefore, it is a struggle to overcome feelings of early unfairness. Doing so requires facing the wish for revenge against the object which is so depriving, with all the destructiveness this entails. Only then can sorrow, forgiveness and reparation become possibilities (Steiner, op. cit.). Whilst for some this seems possible following unfairness in adult life, for others grievance remains insidiously prominent. The influence of these earlier situations of injustice and the manner in which they were or were not overcome are relevant here, and we will go on to describe clinical material which explores these themes further.

Understandably, a traumatic event in adult life can be experienced as deeply unfair. Attempts to have acknowledged or made better the injustice of the situation may involve pursuing those seen as responsible through the court system. Some people, if they are successful in their attempts at litigation, find this helpful and enabling in moving on in their lives. For them, the acknowledgement of wrong doing and an apology is sufficient; others may also require compensation as a reparative action. However, there are individuals who remain stuck in an aggrieved state whatever the outcome, needing to pursue their claims of being treated unjustly in one form or other, in a way that seems driven and unassailable. Although this is not a simple, clear-cut clinical distinction, it does seem to be the first process that is more in evidence in the following case.

### Clinical Illustrations

#### Ms A: *a legitimate grievance*

Ms A was a woman in her 30s when referred to the Trauma Unit by her GP. She described remaining depressed and fearful following an operation which had gone wrong, with near-fatal consequences. She was experiencing hypochondriacal symptoms, nightmares and flashbacks to the events around her hospitalisation and operation. She was offered and accepted a four session consultation with one of the team in the Trauma Unit. During the first of the four meetings the patient appeared anxious and tearful, but determined to detail the events of her hospital stay clearly and forcefully. She was certain that it was negligence on the part of the hospital staff that had led to some near-fatal errors, and equally concerned as to whether the therapist would believe her evaluation of what had taken place. Now physically well, she nevertheless remained preoccupied with her ordeal, and particularly embittered that the hospital had not acknowledged what she judged to have been their mistakes, or then apologised to her. She felt that this would have made all the difference to her recovery, and thought that she had not received any official explanation of the events or an apology because the hospital staff were trying to cover up their own errors and wanting to protect themselves. The patient felt extremely bitter about this, and was determined to bring the hospital to justice through the courts. What was most important to her, however, was that the notes from her hospitalisation should be made public, so that she and others would know the truth of what had happened. Legal proceedings were going ahead, and the notes were to be subpoenaed as part of this. The patient clearly felt that she had been wrongly treated and it seemed that her distress was caused not so much over the medical errors, but in the subsequent cover-up. She felt that she wanted justice to be done. She was in no doubt that she had a real cause for complaint and vividly conveyed her distress over what had happened to her.

## Mr F: an unconscious grievance structure

For other people litigation is more clearly a part of maintaining rather than relinquishing a feeling of grievance, and a way of remaining stuck with the identity of 'victim' rather than moving on from it. It is an avoidance of external and internal 'truth' rather than a part of seeking after it. These individuals display an often unconscious attempt in various ways to embrace, or cling tenaciously to this state of affairs, to the identity of victim. It is as if their own psychic survival is based on its maintenance. This stance may not include and of course does not require litigation, but it is always ultimately detrimental to the ability to engage successfully with real life. Together with the identity of victim, the sense of grievance and of being ill-treated persists, along with a focus on the event, or an aspect of the event and its aftermath at the cost of a future with other preoccupations and other people. This is illustrated by the example of Mr F.

He was 55 years old when he was referred to the Unit for a consultation. Although he had to come from Bristol in order to see us, he particularly wished to come to our Unit in spite of the geographical distance involved, having heard about the Unit from a friend who was working locally as a professional in the mental health field. At the time we thought it reasonable to offer him at least a preliminary consultation. His story was a particularly tragic one. Seventeen years before, he had been involved with his family in a train crash whilst travelling on holiday abroad. His wife and one of his children had been killed; two other children survived. He had battled to free these two children from the wreckage, and having managed this turned to help his next child and then his wife, but they were both already dead. In completing our standard initial questionnaire Mr F wrote of his continuing feeling of guilt that he had not attended more quickly to his wife and to the child who had died. As it was, he and the two surviving children were themselves seriously injured in the accident and were in hospital for many months as a consequence, at first abroad and then in England. When he was well enough, Mr F was able to continue bringing up these two children himself. He had not remarried. He went back to work with the same company he had been employed with before the accident but in a reduced capacity since the job involved considerable responsibility and long hours, and Mr F was experiencing continuing problems with his back which meant that he had to rest for a substantial part of the day. When asked, Mr F explained that he was coming for help now partly because of being prompted by hearing the friend talking about the Unit, and partly because of his awareness that he was now constantly bitter and cynical. He was often inappropriately angry and trusted nobody. These things he linked to the experience of the accident. Subsequently it seemed too that he came because of a deep but less conscious anxiety about his increasing vulnerability; his back pain was getting worse and made it harder for him to get about easily. As well, of course, he was getting older.

The questionnaire revealed some details of his background. He was the eldest of three children; the others were six and eight years younger than he. His father was still alive, but mother had died several years ago. Mother was described by the patient as being unaffectionate, not maternal, and this was linked by him to mother's having lost her own mother through illness when she was still a toddler.

Mr F came to the first interview smartly dressed, carrying a sheaf of papers. He appeared at first friendly and in control, stepping forward to shake the therapist's hand when he emerged from the lift. Once in the room he quickly began speaking, in a rush and heatedly, not about the accident but about the way he had been treated by his employers afterwards. He felt that they had not supported him sufficiently, and that he need not have been 'demoted' within the firm to the extent that he had been. His bitter complaint about this filled much of the first half of this first meeting, and created a particular kind of atmosphere in which it was difficult for the therapist to formulate anything which might be helpful to the patient since she felt so bombarded by this outpouring of complaint. Mr F described feeling aggrieved and resentful, and this was very obviously so. He said that he wanted to see justice being done. The interviewer made some comments about Mr F filling the session with his feeling of complaint, perhaps rather than speak about the accident itself. She suggested that he was anxious that if he did talk about the accident it would be like reliving it, and he would feel plunged back into all the pain, helplessness and horror he had felt at the time. Although she did not suggest this to Mr F, the grievance could also serve as some protection against aspects of his guilt about what had happened to his family. This guilt, as we shall go on to describe, related not so much to his actions during the accident itself, but to a pre-existing ambivalence towards his family. In the session, Mr F agreed with the therapist's comment, and did then begin to say something of the accident itself, showing considerable distress whilst relating the detail of what had taken place. In fact it did indeed feel to the therapist as if the event was as alive in Mr F's mind as though it had just happened, which was probably a truer representation of his psychic state than that the accident had happened seventeen years ago, largely because it was so unmourned. However, talking about the accident itself was interrupted by his repeated comment that he had said enough about how upset he was many years ago, when he had been seen by counsellors shortly after the tragedy took place. For much of the meeting he seemed in a bitter and aggrieved state of mind, and this appeared to push away something more vulnerable and distressed, as well as keeping at a distance the therapist's attempts to offer Mr F something helpful through her own intellectual and emotional resources. It seemed essential to this patient to maintain a defensive omnipotence, in which he was convinced of the veracity of his grievance – that he had been demoted unjustly, that he had been badly treated and let down by those on whom he depended and therefore could only trust himself and his own views.

The therapist's attempts to make contact with him represented a serious danger, threatening to undermine this omnipotent stance by offering helpful understanding and emotional containment. In fact, as the therapist went on to address with the patient his fear of collapse and helplessness, he began to speak of needing a further operation on his back, and his fear of the enforced dependency that this would lead to, at least temporarily whilst he recovered. He said that he was going to stay with one of his children while he recuperated, but spoke about this bitterly, it seemed resenting that his child had established herself successfully in life, with a job, marriage and family, when he had lost so much that he had had in his own life.

Gradually it also emerged that the holiday during which Mr F's wife and child had been killed was the first he had taken for many years. He had always been an extremely hard worker, maintaining that he could then build up enough savings to retire early and that the family could then enjoy the money. However, this had meant, it seemed, that the family had been neglected by him during these years as he spent long hours employed at his office desk. He related this hard-working nature to a lifelong feeling, sharply apparent in the interview, that you had to look after yourself, that you could not rely on anyone. He explained to the therapist that this attitude came from experiences he had had from well before the accident. His parents, for example, had not allowed him to take advantage of the scholarship he had won to go to grammar school. They had insisted he stay at the local school with the rest of the family, and he had always felt let down and resentful about this.

In describing these events during the consultation Mr F was allowing us to see that the current situation was not the only or original source of his aggrieved feelings. He felt that his life had been afflicted by unfair treatment from his childhood years and in his description of this, he appeared to be mounting the evidence to prove his position. It seemed it was very important for him to show the therapist that this was a true representation of his life. Thus, the traumatic accident and subsequent treatment by his employers were unconsciously experienced as 'welcome' events, adding further and indisputable cause for his claim to have been unjustly treated by life. Although it was not possible to explore this at any length within the time Mr F allowed for the consultation, it seems possible that his grievance was a response to earlier experiences. He had described in the questionnaire, for instance, his 'non-maternal' mother, by whom he felt let down and betrayed through her lack of maternal care.

What became evident during the consultation was the way in which

87

subsequent events were taken up by him in this very particular way, as if substantiating his grievance that in life he was always the one who came off worst, the one who was dealt with unfairly. Furthermore, this sustained sense of grievance justified his omnipotence, his not depending on anybody. It could therefore function to defend him against whatever was painful in his early relationships. But as well as protecting him from this acute sense of loss and the consequent pain, importantly he was also protected from feelings of guilt, related to having become like the non-maternal parent himself in his neglect of his own family. This was evident in relation to the accident, about having given so little of himself to his family before they died, and of having chosen to attend to the two children who survived the train crash first, before then turning to his wife and other child. His grievance and feeling of blame towards others was fending off this unconscious *self*-accusation, an unconscious feeling of fear that he was the one to blame, related also to earlier feelings of rivalry with siblings, and ambivalence and destructive feelings towards parents and others. As Steiner (op. cit.) describes, the child's encounter with the realities of the parental couple introduce him or her to a situation experienced as shocking, and which 'can lead to a deep sense of hurt, injustice and betrayal'.

For such an individual the trauma, tragic as it is, can be embraced by the part of the personality that can put it to use – to defend against feelings of jealousy, loss and guilt by justifying continuing feelings of grievance, of life as unfair and of other people as traitors. The reality of not having mother exclusively to oneself is felt as too painful and humiliating to acknowledge, and the destructiveness of the revenge that would be sought were such acknowledgement to be made is felt to be unmanageable. Feldman (op. cit.) describes that the wish for possession of an idealised maternal object can indeed be replaced by holding on to the grievance like a precious object that cannot be given up and which gives a sense of power and control, and of specialness. It becomes essential in this situation for the grievance to be maintained. In such circumstance, the trauma becomes a 'peg' on which to hang the grievance, and so maintain it. In coming for help, the individual may be coming less out of a wish for psychic change than to sustain and reinforce their existing internal structures. Some people are, in other words, ready to find further cause for feeling 'hard done by'.

Perhaps predictably, for Mr F the consultation became a further source of grievance, rather than a source of understanding and help. He did not attend more than one meeting. He telephoned, and spoke to one of the Department secretaries, and told her that he found the meeting too harrowing, partly because the therapist was unfriendly and unsupportive, in not offering a handshake at the start, in not offering a cup of tea or coffee. He described thinking that she had been disapproving and judgmental when he had spoken of his wish for such things, and that she did not show him respect or consideration. The therapist wrote a letter in response, acknowledging Mr F's distress and disappointment, giving some sources of therapeutic help nearer to where he lived, and also offering a further meeting, perhaps with another therapist from the Trauma Unit rather than herself if he so wished. Nothing further was heard. Feldman (op. cit.) points out that the therapist can be hated because of their representing the quest for psychic truth, including facing painful oedipal realities and taking personal responsibility for destructiveness and damage done in fantasy and reality. He writes that if the therapist threatens the defensive grievance structure through his interpretive work, the patient is likely to react with a feeling of threat and betrayal rather than insight.

We suggest that for some patients, like Mr F, the *unconscious* function of coming for treatment around the trauma is in order to give new life to a focus of grievance. Mr F had suffered a very real and terrible injury seventeen years ago, when his wife and child had died in a train crash. Consciously he was coming for help because of his inability to get over that injury, to mourn his wife and child. This was a very real problem for Mr F. Unconsciously, however, he was coming to add fuel to the sense of oedipal grievance he had held from his early life, and this impeded his attempt to get help to move on from the trauma of seventeen years ago. Such a patient hashes over with the therapist the grievance that exists and then incorporates the therapist and/or their institution as a fresh focus for an aggrieved state of mind. It is important clinically to understand that these patients have a double purpose in coming for help, and, if possible, to distinguish and attempt to address both – the conscious, and unconscious aims.

### Ms G: grievance and the possibility of reparation

A second patient, Ms G, also displayed an aggrieved state of mind, in which she felt herself to be a victim. However, it seemed she was more able to make some use of the consultation, the internal grievance structure seeming both less entrenched but also less threatened.

Ms G, a 34 year old woman, was referred to the Unit following an assault whilst at her work as a bus conductor. A passenger got into an argument with Ms G over the fare, and began to push and shove her, eventually toppling her to the ground. The bus was almost empty, and as Ms G lay on the ground the woman attempted to push her off the bus, potentially into the path of oncoming traffic. The driver was alerted by one of the few passengers on the bus, and the assailant, noticing this, instead jumped off the bus herself as it slowed in traffic, and ran off through the streets. Ms G escaped with some painful bruising but was not seriously injured. The assailant was caught and tried, with the outcome of a heavy fine and a suspended sentence. Ms G was very shaken by the event, and felt that she had been lucky to have just escaped more serious injury. She remained unable to sleep, with flashbacks and nightmares about the incident, and had been unable to go back to her work at the time she was first seen for a consultation, some four months after the assault.

The questionnaire revealed some facts about her background. She was one of two children, with a sister 9 years younger. Both her parents were still alive. She described her parents as loving, caring and supportive, but that they were hard-up financially, and that during most of her childhood the family lived in a small one bedroom flat in Glasgow. She mentioned that her parents argued a great deal, but that they always stopped when she appeared. She thought that their arguments were provoked by their less than adequate living accommodation. However, her mother tried to 'care for their needs in every way she could', and father worked very hard, as a manual labourer. Ms G herself had never married, but did have a partner, 8 years older, with whom she had lived for 2 years. Before her current employment as a bus conductor, she had worked with a large catering suppliers, but had been made redundant and was unable to find similar work with another company. After a period of unemployment of over a year she had found her current position. She was dissatisfied with the job and would have liked something else, but had had no success with any applications.

When seen for the consultation, Ms G presented as a softly spoken, rather diffident woman. However, from the outset, much of the meetings were filled with her quietly bitter descriptions of the unfair treatment she felt that she had received in the last few years. She had been made redundant, had then to apply for and accept the job as bus conductor which she did not want, after which she was assaulted. She explained during the consultation that even before the redundancy she had been an active campaigner against the abuse of wealth and power, latterly through trade union involvement, but some time ago through her work with a socialist organisation. It seemed clear that she was preoccupied with fighting 'unfair' treatment, and also felt that such treatment had dogged her life. As the consultation progressed, it was possible to link this more clearly than had been possible during Mr F's one meeting with aspects of Ms G's early life. During the second meeting, Ms G told the therapist that when her sister had been born she felt that she had lost her 'special' place as the only child in the family. She described that her sister still often asked for money from her parents, and she deeply resented her for doing this, explaining that she thought that she should know better than to take money from their parents, who could not really afford it. In this way, she presented herself as the one more able to understand and be generous towards their parents than the sister. It was suggested to Ms G by the therapist during the consultation that this 'generosity' protected her against a less conscious feeling of grievance towards her parents rather than towards her sister, a feeling that it was unfair that her parents should offer only the sister money. This 'generous' state of mind also allowed her to remain in a position where she felt herself to be 'in the right', rather than rivalrous with the sister for their parents' affections. Ms G responded to the therapist's comments about this by a description of her feeling that their parents were unjustly generous towards her sister, and she wished she could change their attitude towards the sister, but felt helpless to do anything.

Ms G went on to relate how much of her life she felt was filled with unfairness. She described the redundancy and how upsetting it had been. Friends were losing their jobs, which was awful in itself, and then she lost hers too. She described being unhappy at secondary school, because those who were more able were picked out by the teachers for special attention. This was unfair, she thought, because they were picking out children who were already doing well in order that they should do better. The therapist related this to her feelings about her sister, whom she thought had always had more attention from their parents than she. She agreed and then described an early memory of hitting her sister when she would not stop screaming, and her own guilt now in remembering how powerful she had felt in relation to this little baby, wanting to stop her demanding screaming. The therapist suggested her own infant feelings of demand could not tolerate *any* rival. Ms G agreed and added that she felt that she could have killed her at that moment when she was screaming, wanting food, attention, something, she did not know what, but just because the baby was there, alive and wanting something. Her current partner wanted a baby, but Ms G told the therapist that she was not sure of this herself, and agreed with the therapist's interpretation that this was maybe because of her fear that she would feel rivalrous and murderous towards this new baby too.

It also became apparent during the consultation that Ms G could avoid feeling guilty about her own demandingness, her own murderous rivalry, by maintaining her sense of being justified in her complaints because she was not being treated well. An example of this had been evident at the beginning of the consultation. Ms G came straight up to the therapist's room, five minutes before time and before the therapist was ready. When this incident was raised with her, Ms G explained that she had seen the reception desk, but felt that the receptionist had been busy; Ms G did not want to bother her when she was already busy, so decided she would find her own way. She then found it difficult to find the therapist (she had no idea where the therapist was located in the building), and eventually, near to tears and feeling lost, had had to ask a secretary on a different floor who had pointed her in the right direction. She complained that these buildings were so complicated, too big, too busy, and there should be more signs, and more people on the reception desk. She would leave a complaint in the 'suggestions box' in the foyer, she said. In this she felt herself to be a victim of the workings of this powerful Clinic, which pushed away any sense that she herself could have any guilty feeling at having claimed the kind of immediate access to the therapist which she later agreed she wanted; to avoid having to negotiate the reality boundaries of time and receptionists. It was possible later in the consultation to begin to link this with her wish to have her mother to herself, not to have to face the reality of mother's having her own partner, made so apparent through the birth of the sister, and thus that she did not have mother all to herself.

Towards the end of the third consultation Ms G spoke of her awareness of feelings of rivalry and rage, and at moments of a guilt about this. She came to the last of the four sessions she was initially offered, reporting that she had gone back to work, to a desk job, which suited her better. At follow up three months later, however, she complained that while she still did like the job, she thought the others in the office did not work very hard and left it all to her. She was considering making a complaint to her immediate superiors. At this meeting Ms G was offered further therapy in the Department, but decided against it; she said she did not think she needed further treatment. Although she had been able to begin to explore her feelings of deprivation and grievance, it seemed that it was not possible to sustain this exploration, which might have led to a shift in her current identifications and perhaps indeed, could not be sustained *because* it may have led to more radical internal change: the facing of her own responsibilities and consequent guilt. Steiner (op. cit.) suggests that the individual has to enact his wish for revenge in fantasy and also in mitigated forms in relationships, including in the transference relationship with the therapist. It is only when the destructiveness and damage done has been faced that reparation and forgiveness is possible. Feelings of resentment may not be able to be acknowledged because it is too great a blow to pride; destructiveness may not be able to be faced because it is felt to be too damaging, or there is a fear of retaliation. In such circumstances, the grievance has to be preserved.

## Discussion

For both Mr F and Ms G, it seemed that the sustained feeling of grievance was necessary as a way of managing the acute pain of the experience of deprivation, of not being loved as wished, and the resentment and subsequent guilt that this stirred. For both, it seemed that the primitive experiences of deprivation had not been resolved to any satisfactory degree; reparation had not been made. When this is the case, it may be due primarily to the particular nature of early external reality, or may be due primarily to constitutional factors, but always it involves some intermingling of both.

Dennis Carpy (1987) suggests that the impulse to blame is almost invariably present in debates over the relative contribution of internal and external reality to mental health problems. He argues that the blame is either of the child if phantasy is deemed to be primary, and of the adult/parent if it is the environment which is given most emphasis. His argument is that this particular kind of 'moralistic' blaming arises from primitive psychotic areas of mental functioning, and exist in everyone to a greater or lesser extent:

> I think, however, that this attitude is universal and is associated with a deep sense of grievance that each of us feels towards the parents whom we feel have mistreated us. In this moralistic attitude we want to blame these parents, and be able to demonstrate with certainty that they are in the wrong, that they have perpetrated injustice upon us as victims, that we are entirely justified in our accusations, and that we have a right to have this generally recognised.

He puts forward the idea that this kind of grievance can be at the root of and maintain narcissistic personality disorders, where any experience of dependency is avoided *because*, the individual maintains,

93

it always leads to profound disappointment. The grievance serves to protect the individual from the immense psychic pain which would result from an awareness of actual dependency, and the ways this has been on a less than *ideal* object, and perhaps involving substantial physical or emotional deprivation or violation. Carpy writes: 'It is therefore essential that the sense of grievance be maintained in an active state'.

For such patients a traumatic external event in the present may be greeted unconsciously as a fresh source of nourishment for an older grievance, and it may be then particularly difficult to move on from the event.

Although all three patients described in this chapter seemed to be making some use of grievance as a defence against psychic pain, against feelings of vulnerability and helplessness, and against feelings of guilt for destructiveness done in phantasy or reality towards others, there were also distinct differences. For the first patient, aggrieved feelings seemed to have been more able to be worked through and made use of in a reparative effort to establish reality and truth. For both Mr F and Ms G, there was more sense of an entrenched grievance structure. This can both lead to greater feelings of internal devastation, greater guilt, and greater need for defences and so for a shoring-up of the grievance structure, creating a psychic vicious circle. For Mr F the search for help did seem unconsciously motivated by a need to shore up rather than address and potentially change the internal grievance structure. For him, the consultation then became the focus of further grievance, rather than a source of help.

Of course in any consultation where a patient feels themselves to have been badly treated, it is important to attempt to understand the nature of this, and how much we as therapists may indeed have contributed. What is notable with Mr F is that he would not allow any possibility for such exploration with the therapist, as if determined for it to remain a bad experience with a bad object which he could feel aggrieved about.

The differences between Mr F and Ms G's presentations may elucidate the different ways they made use of the consultation: either as a source of some help or as something which itself became a focus of grievance. The differences are connected both with the extent to which the defensive grievance structure feels necessary, and the extent to which it feels threatened.

It is possible that for Mr F, the original focus of grievance was no longer sufficient to sustain the aggrieved personality structure, without

94

fresh sources of complaint. The grievance then had even more to be strengthened, rather than understood. He was now older and retired, and so his job no longer provided ongoing occasion for aggrieved feeling. As well, ageing and retirement, meaning less activity, could expose him to the risk of painful guilt and acute depressive anxiety. A depressive breakdown could be avoided through righteous rage. Indeed, because of increasing age and reduced life opportunities, Mr F also perhaps felt that there were fewer possibilities open to him for reparation; both Ms A and Ms G could still have children and had other possibilities in life. If there is not a sense of potentially being able to repair the damage done in reality and phantasy then facing the damage is not possible. For the first patient, Ms A, litigation seemed a possible route towards reparation; Ms G also seemed more able to use the consultation as a means of addressing her psychic reality and so also as a means of internal reparation. It was perhaps also the case that Mr F felt a greater need for this particular psychic defence as some of his family members had actually died, and he was threatened by devastating feelings of guilt. He could not bring them back to life, he could not have more children of his own, and as his own life was nearing its end, he was also in phantasy facing the ultimate triumph of their retaliation: he would now die too.

## Conclusion

Aggrieved feelings are often difficult to address. Both therapist and patient have a tough task, since for the patient the suffering of being a victim of an identifiable external event may be preferable to the kind of psychic suffering outlined above. In trying to help traumatised adults who appear to present this picture, it will be necessary both to explore the traumatic event in the present, and to explore carefully and sensitively the nature of the grievance, including as it arises with the therapist *in vivo* in the consultation. It can be all too easy for the therapist to be felt to be adopting a blaming stance, and to seem to be discounting the very real trauma experienced by the patient. However, it is only by such exploration that it may be possible to locate and work through the original anguish that was defended against by adopting the identity of aggrieved victim, in order to free the personality for a more creative life.

# 6

# Mental Work in a Trauma Patient

*Graham Ingham*

## Introduction

In the novel *The Adventures of Augie March* (1953), Saul Bellow has Augie, his hero, sit in a café and reflect upon himself.

> ... all the while you thought you were going around idle, terribly hard work was taking place. Hard, hard work, excavation and digging, mining, moling through tunnels, heaving, pushing, moving rock, working, working, working, working, working, panting, hauling, hoisting. And none of this work is seen from the outside. It's internally done. It happens because you are powerless and unable to get anywhere, to obtain justice or have requital, and therefore in yourself, you labour, you wage in combat, settle scores, remember insults, fight, reply, deny, blab, denounce, triumph, outwit, overcome, vindicate, cry, persist, absolve, die, and rise again. All by yourself! Where is everybody? Inside your breast and skin, the entire cast.

In his depiction of Augie's mind at work Saul Bellow is showing something particular taking place: Augie is involved in creative work and labour. But how particular is this work? It is the stuff of mental activity, of mentally processing the elements of moment to moment, day to day, existence. The absence or insufficiency of this labour suggests that the mind is not working properly. It is also, Saul Bellow asserts, work often undertaken out of view, from within or without.

I begin with this passage because although the patient I will present is 'a trauma patient', inasmuch as at the point of referral he was devastated by the accidental death of his girlfriend and the preceding illness and death of his mother, he now, however, describes himself as having a problem with 'mental work' (his phrase, not mine). In a way this is not a new insight for him. Indeed on entering therapy he would sometimes describe himself as having 'a philosophical problem', of being a cynic, nihilistic, ignorant of and uninterested in the workings of

96

the mind. Someone, as he put it, who goes to the garage with his car and says 'The engine's not working'. His favourite joke, which he told me early on, was 'How do you make God laugh? Tell him your plans!'. He is someone who could make what he called 'a synaptic leap' – 'I can press a mental button and produce an infusion of soothing substances'.

Now, you could think a person who speaks in this manner is showing evidence of mental work, of purposeful self-reflection, of a capacity for metaphor and symbolisation. He is certainly an intelligent and sensitive man, cultivated, politically aware and in many respects thoughtful. Such statements have, however, stuck in the memory because they were unusual in their directness and communicativeness; they were also said with some pride, as if asserting the superiority of the patient's viewpoint and of his strategies for maintaining a psychic equilibrium. The context of such comments was of someone's maintaining that they never dreamed, nor had daydreams, could not describe a fantasy, had scarcely any memories from childhood and apparently found the notion of an internal world utterly perplexing. Someone who when, as a child, found himself isolated and in a state of massive anxiety turned to a medical textbook, taught himself about adrenaline and thereafter 'understood' – 'explained' mental experience as neither more nor less than the consequence of physiological phenomena. The graft and struggle of Saul Bellow's hero, an inner landscape of motive and pain, populated by figures in conflict and resolution was alien, and anathema to him.

I will return to the patient shortly, but first I wish to say something about the concept of mental work and its relationship with trauma. (I say 'something' advisedly because, of course, mental work is a vast subject.)

When Freud is writing about trauma in 'Beyond the Pleasure Principle' (Freud, 1920) he conceives of it as 'a consequence of an extensive breach being made in the protective shield against stimuli' (1920, p. 31). Like other organisms, the mind develops 'a special envelope or membrane resistant to stimuli' (1920, p. 27). This external surround or shield is typically inorganic or dead, like the skin. 'By its death', writes Freud, 'the outer layer has saved all the deeper ones from a similar fate' (1920, p. 27). For some individuals the dead outer layer reaches further inside than for others. It can be the case (and perhaps this is especially true of some schizoid patients) that the dead outer layer renders the living self almost unreachable. For all of us, however, this layer, which has come, via Bick and others, to be known as 'the psychic skin' or 'the skin ego' is an essential for mental survival (Bick, 1968). Freud repeatedly emphasised its necessity: 'protection against stimuli is an almost more important function for the living organism than reception of stimuli' (1920, p. 27).

I think it is correct to say that psychoanalysis would now view 'protection against stimuli' and 'reception of stimuli' as deeply interrelated. It would suggest that a functioning receptor, capable of processing stimuli, is necessary if physical sensation and raw perception are to be made into manageable and thinkable-about experience and the mind therefore protected from excessive, overwhelming and paralysing stimuli. What I am describing brings us into the area of Winnicott's 'good enough mothering' (Winnicott, 1965) and Bion's 'container-contained' (Bion, 1962).

What Bion formulates is that the mother's mind functions as a container for the infant's chaotic, unintegrated, raw sensations and through what he termed the mother's 'reverie' – a capacity to receive, fantasise about and metabolise these sensations – the mother transforms these into what Bianchedi calls 'personal imaginative experiences' (1995, p. 128). This capacity for making the undigested stuff of experience into the material of mental life – dreams, daydreams, thoughts, memories – Bion refers to as 'alpha function' (Bion, 1962). It is a capacity, a function, that the infant internalises, takes in and makes his own from the mother. Segal emphasises that it is crucial to development, 'an identification with a good container capable of performing the alpha function is the basis of a healthy mental apparatus' (1991, p. 51).

To recapitulate: in a trauma the mind has been subjected to excessive stimuli and the protective shield has been breached. Not only that but the mind's capacity to deal with, manage, process stimuli has been overloaded. In Bion's terms, alpha function has broken down and instead of the mind's containing 'alpha elements', the building blocks of experience, the dreamable-about, thinkable-about, storable elements of human experience and understanding, it is instead filled with chaotic, fragmented, unrecognisable sensations – Bion's 'beta elements'. These have then to be expelled and evacuated into any available location. In passing I might mention that in the course of his therapy my patient has recounted how as a child he lay awake in the middle of the night, in a state that he could not give words to but he knew to be awful, and to which Bion's term 'nameless dread' might be applied (1962, p. 116). The patient's awareness focused on the ticking of a clock in his room, the clock and its ticking being, I think, the closest approximation he could find to a container for something unnameable taking place in his mind.

So we could say that a traumatic event demands that enormous amounts of mental work be undertaken, mental work along the lines of the alpha functioning I have briefly described. Trauma, by definition, occurs when this work, this alpha functioning, is overwhelmed and unable to contain and digest the quality and quantity of stimuli involved and therefore breaks down. Perhaps the relationship between trauma and mental work is even closer and more interdependent than this suggests. After all, it is a traumatic anxiety relating to separation and absence that psychoanalysis views as a foundation of mental work. It is in the recognition and the acknowledgement of separateness and the working through of the experience of the absence of the providing mother, that thought and mental work are constituted. The link goes further, in as much as this process of recognising, acknowledging and working through absence is essentially a mourning process. It is self-evident that for the trauma of a bereavement to be successfully worked through, mourning is required. Losses of any sort – a job for example – are seen to involve mourning. Indeed change itself, we now know, initiates mourning. Melanie Klein writes that 'any pain caused by unhappy experiences, whatever their nature, has something in common with mourning'. She continues, 'the encountering and overcoming of adversity of any kind entails mental work similar to that of mourning' (1940, p. 360). She views any enrichment of the self as dependent on this mental work. I suspect it is what Saul Bellow is also referring to in the passage I quoted, when Augie's internal work occurs because he is 'powerless and unable to get anywhere, to obtain justice or have requital'. In the absence of this struggle with adversity and loss, and the mourning processes it involves, internal and external reality are impoverished. Klein writes of the stifled and severely restricted emotional life that results (1940, p. 368), and I think Saul Bellow is pointing to something similar when he writes, 'Everybody knows there is no fineness or accuracy of suppression; if you hold down one thing you hold down the adjoining' (1953, p. 3).

Trauma then not only demands and can damage mental work, mental work itself is founded on, constituted by a capacity to face, manage, contain and negotiate traumatic anxiety. The pain and shock of recognising need, helplessness and dependence, of acknowledging that one is not omnipotent, these function as an engine of development. Trauma and thought, trauma and knowledge are indivisible.

I will attempt to illustrate these themes by describing something of the treatment of a patient referred for consultation to the Tavistock

99

Trauma Unit and subsequently taken into once and later twice-weekly individual psychotherapy.

## Case Illustration: the consultation

My patient, Mr D, is a 31 year old man, the third child of an Irish father and a Scandinavian mother. His older sister and brother were born within three years of the patient. He was referred shortly after his girlfriend, Alison, with whom his relationship had been on/off and at times stormy, died in a hang-gliding accident. His mother had died a year earlier and at referral he complained of a combination of panic and despair. He was seen at the Trauma Unit for a four-session consultation which he found helpful. He remained, however, at best able to get through his days and nights in a cut-off automaton-like manner and, at worst, totally incapacitated by a state that managed to be both unfeeling and panicked.

The particular features of his assessment which have stayed in my mind were a series of deaths – not many years before the consultation a close friend had died in a road traffic accident, and he, like Alison, had lived 'on the edge'. Mr D's work, which involved him in front line rescue services, was close to matters of life and death. There was also a sense in his early account of he and those around him having considerable ability and at the same time lacking the internal resources to deal with life. His father, an eminent professor, was presented as a decent and concerned but emotionally restricted and in some way damaged man. His mother had faced her painful illness and death with great stoicism but this also seemed indicative of something 'shut off' about her. Alison had been beautiful, intelligent and creative but unknowable and never quite of this world.

In the initial interviews with the Trauma Unit the consultant had noticed a concern with the capacity of the other 'to take in and survive distress', a fear of 'encountering an exhausted incapacity in his object'. Most if not all patients are initially centrally preoccupied with the capacities of their therapist and consciously or unconsciously, explicitly or implicitly, they set about establishing the therapist's strengths and weaknesses, limitations and capabilities. Perhaps this is especially the case with the trauma patient, where the therapist's or indeed any listener's task of being open to and partially identified with an experience that the patient finds unthinkable, *and* at the same time thinking about it, is testing, and sometimes so in the extreme. In Mr D's case, as I have touched on, significant figures in the picture were presented by him as lacking a capacity to contain. When the patient was in his early teens his father had taken him to a psychologist friend, ostensibly because of exam-related anxiety, but the patient could not recall his father ever speaking with him about his anxieties. Nor indeed could he recall arguing with father, although he had furious and interminable rows with his siblings.

## The Treatment

Early on he was at pains to establish what I would do if he became so depressed or suicidal that he couldn't function. Would I medicate or hospitalise him or arrange for someone else to do so? Could therapy help, if so how, and how long would it take? In what way would talking about Alison help? I found myself worried and anxious about the patient. All this took place alongside a recounting of Alison's death, her memorial service and so on, that was quite desperate in its urgency and pressure. Such accounts would alternate with an assertion of the validity, if not superiority, of the patient's own long established means of manipulating his state of mind, in particular his ability to switch off, his 'synaptic leaps'.

Nonetheless there is no doubt that Mr D had in some way recognised his need for a container and that this had been partially met in his consultation and the initial stages of his therapy. Anzieu, writing of trauma, suggests that 'the pain caused is less if someone can be found as quickly as possible to function, both by the words they speak and the attention they give, as an auxiliary or substitute skin ego (or envelope) for the injured person' (1993, p. 140). This truism of responses to trauma is developed by Anzieu who conceives of something he terms 'a psychical envelope' (1993, p. 140). To put it crudely, it is in this envelope, this container, that Anzieu formulates daydreams and more especially dreams as taking place. A major function of these is to repair the tears and rents that everyday experience causes to the envelope. The external container is turned to when the trauma has overwhelmed the containing capacities of the psychical envelope.

As I mentioned at the outset, however, my patient claimed to have no dreams, to be unaware of personal fantasies or daydreams and thus to have no internal container. It is not that he lacked for thoughts as such, for in many ways he was and is a thoughtful man, professionally gifted and more than able to hold his own in argument. In fact, something I heard of when the immediate pressures of loss and grief had relented was his propensity for heated debate with friends. Or rather debates in which his adversaries would become heated whilst he remained cool and detached and took hidden pleasure in dismantling their arguments, especially and typically when the other was upholding a system of belief – religious, political or philosophical. He would be perplexed (as well as secretly triumphant) when his adversaries became angry or upset. Naturally enough I was invited into such arguments, especially in relation to the efficacy of psychotherapy. Sometimes these invitations would be issued with apparent playfulness, sometimes with an urgent and frantic tone. In either case my belief and conviction in my work with the patient was very much under scrutiny. As I said, this is in a sense grist to the mill of any therapy but I think in Mr D's case there was a more destructive element in which hope, meaningfulness and the connection between ideas and people could be remorselessly stripped of value. A vicious circle was set up, in which it was at times possible to observe the patient taking the life out of my interpretation and then panicking having, I think, realised that he had damaged precisely what he needed. The container was scarcely given a chance to do its job before it was rendered inoperable.

This process, observed externally, was also one that unsurprisingly took place internally. It became clear over time that Mr D subjected his own mental contents, at least those concerned with feelings, wishes, longings and their representation in fantasy and dream to the same treatment. In his attacks on these contents, he aspired to avoid pain and suffering but actually stripped himself of the equipment for processing and ultimately analysing his experience.

I will try and illustrate these themes with some clinical material. About eighteen months into his therapy, at which point Mr D was attending twice weekly, he had begun to describe to himself and to me, in some detail and with growing concern, how he could rarely put words to feelings. Internal events would occur, which would be expressed as somatic sensations (for example the excess of adrenaline referred to earlier). They would not be linked by him to a perceived emotional state, for example anxiety or need and even less so to a cause such as the absence of a person.

In a subsequent session he told me of his interest in serial murderers. He went on to give an account of a popular science programme on television which had featured a particular form of psychopathology where the patient pursues gratuitous amputations. One particular patient had successfully persuaded surgeons to amputate a leg, at which point the amputee's mental state was much improved. The patient was struck by this man's 'affability', a word I had used to describe the patient's apparent attitude towards me. He went on that such cases were, according to the programme, hopeless. It was possible to see this in terms of the patient's own assaults on his and my effectiveness and how an affable presentation concealed his frequent violent severances of his capacities and means of connection with others. The consequence was that he was left feeling hopeless. There was a good deal of contact in the session as we looked at these themes, such that, most unusually, the patient brought a dream to the next session. Its relevance had been so transparent that for once he had found no difficulty recalling the dream. He reported how, in the dream, his hand had been severed and he had managed to persuade someone, it wasn't clear who, to sew it back on.

Despite my best efforts, my interpretations and the session as a whole fell flat. Towards the end of this particularly dead session the patient was silent, then seemed to smile to himself. I asked him what he was thinking. He told me that he had realised that he did in fact have one daydream. It had escaped his notice though he had turned to it more than once as a means of getting himself to sleep. In brief the daydream involved his taking the role of the assassin in a scene from the film 'The Day of the Jackal'. In this scene he, the patient, is rehearsing the assassination at the window from which he plans to shoot. He then skilfully dismantles the rifle, placing the parts in its special case, and effortlessly leaves the building via a meticulously planned and re-searched route.

I think it is possible to see that this daydream which had been kept out of view, mine and I believe the patient's, actually reflects his underlying knowledge of himself as someone who dismantles connec-tions and kills life. Yet he takes pride in his skill and his consummate ability to act without breaking cover or leaving trace. Once the day-dream had been reported he had broken cover and thereafter, albeit intermittently, these processes were more detectable and attacks on life and meaning, as they occur in the session, comprised a major focus of the work. How, though, are these processes linked to the trauma that brought Mr D into treatment and what do they reflect of his internal situation?

To return to the first year of therapy. When the immediate sequelae of Alison's death, the feelings of panic and despair had begun to ease, a process of some months, I became aware of intermittently but increas-ingly feeling that I was not doing my job. There was an 'easy' quality to the sessions in which I felt vaguely well-disposed towards the patient and I had reason to think he towards me, but no real work appeared to be taking place. From time to time Mr D would wonder aloud if he was 'cured' and ask me if I thought he should continue with his treatment. I was also aware of feeling rather cheated of an experience, more particularly of being deprived of the satisfaction that comes from the experience of a reasonably substantial exchange with someone. I tried to take this up in various ways, to what effect wasn't clear, but what Mr D did do was gradually give me a picture of his mother. I say 'give me' but in a sense this was a picture that was also new to the patient in as much as initially he maintained he had little feeling for or memory of his mother and only a very shadowy image of her, at least prior to her terminal illness when he had been impressed by her uncomplaining dignity and courage and had played a full part in her care. It increasingly troubled him that 'great chunks of memory' in relation to his mother, as well as more generally, were missing.

Over time the picture of his mother and of his relations with her, became increasingly complex and substantial. It seems that his birth was traumatic, with a question at one point as to whether mother and baby would survive. His older brother and sister were still toddlers, the family were poor, father preoccupied with his work and mother in an unfamiliar and alien environment. One of the first things he said of her was that she never touched him; he later mentioned that she never answered his questions and always looked at him at an angle. When she spoke to him it was 'to give middle-class injunctions to do well at school, and eat properly'. It then emerged that he and she had engaged in pronounced and persistent anorexic battles, apparently from the age of ten or eleven onwards. He would store food in his cheeks and try and disguise that he had not swallowed. They eventually hit on a compromise. He could choose packaged meals which he knew tasted like sawdust but had not been cooked by his mother and therefore allowed him some control.

The insubstantial, bland, facsimiles of exchange that were evident in the transference clearly had precursors, as did the patient's absence of appetite for his therapy and my feeling of not being allowed to gain any satisfaction from my role. What I am not conveying (and neither, for some time, did my patient) is the bitter, hostile, life and death qualities of these struggles with his mother. You will remember the affable amputee, the violent assault on his capacities and connectedness with those who care for him, all done in pursuit of freedom from conflict. The patient had once described his mother as someone whom he experienced as unyielding, not so much cold as impermeable, unpenetrable, a beautiful woman, mysterious, opaque and unknown. Someone he has no recollection of being held by, verbally or physically engaging in play with, or having strong feelings about. The ambivalence at the time as well as being displaced into furious rows with his siblings was perhaps more fundamentally shown in his failure to thrive. Despite his ability he had failed to realise his potential at school and until fairly recently also in his work. In the treatment any progress has been shadowed by a need swiftly to dismantle it and show me, often with a cruel element, how what might seem like a development – for example a fairly secure relationship with a girlfriend – was in fact an illusion or utterly precarious. Similarly a significant achievement, a promotion at work, could be thrown away in favour of 'dropping out' and seen as 'a middle-class injunction', which he had been foolish enough temporarily to subscribe to.

Some progress has been secured I believe. There has been considerable retrieval of memory, he has an appetite for finding out about his mother, researching in fact and fantasy her childhood, and he has an understanding of how depressed she may have been in his early years. He has also movingly described her illness and his profound sense of loss. In short some mourning has taken place. With mock belligerence he reviewed his treatment, telling me that he could no longer effortlessly cut off, he worried about his relationships and was depressed about his losses. We both took this as a statement of progress.

I realise in writing this section of the paper that I have been struggling with the wish to tell a story, to select and render coherent and meaningful a host of disparate facts, memories and experiences related to the patient. Clearly there are dangers in such a construction of narrative and meaning, not only that it may not correspond to reality but also that the therapist can become the sole provider of meaning for too long, leaving the patient in an empty state, akin to the anorexic's projection of appetite. Locating the patient's material in the transference is crucial. For example, when Mr D recounts a favoured senior having told him that in the patient's line of work it is essential to keep an aspect of the self 'inviolate', this only takes on meaning or resonance if it can be linked with, in this instance, the patient's perceived need to protect and retain control over a raw, vulnerable and hidden aspect of himself in the therapy. In this sense clinical facts are not reported, they are experienced in a relationship between patient and therapist where they can be observed, articulated and confirmed or discounted. Notwithstanding the dangers of overly speculative interpretation, I think this giving of meaning to experience is at the essence of our work and never more so than with the trauma patient. The trauma has often devastated the meaningfulness of experience. Fonagy writes of the analysis of borderline children: 'only the gradual elaboration of mental representations of thoughts and feelings will free them from the crushing grip that the concrete experience of reality imposes upon the human mind' (1995, p. 43). This is, I believe, an accurate formulation of the task in working with trauma. My patient indicated that he was taken aback and perplexed by my use of analogy and metaphor, stunned by his girlfriend's ability to intuitively recognise his feelings and give a name and meaning to them; for example 'You're angry with me'. For whatever reason – his mother's apparent incapacity for reverie, his incapacity to make use of it, or a combination of both, Mr D failed fully to develop, or partially retreated from, the world of imaginative experience and sought refuge in the world of things and physical facts. Fonagy tells us 'this adaptation, the disavowal of reflective thought, deprives the child of the possibility of metabolisation and resolution of psychic trauma' (1995, p. 43). I believe that this has been an adaptation pursued by my patient. For whatever reason he lacks a good enough maternal object, a container, a psychic envelope that could help him dream, fantasise, imagine and store in memory his experience. In its place there is an impermeable object from which his experiences and impulses bounce back in a raw, undigested, aggravated and deeply alarming condition. In a way we could say Mr D is perpetually traumatised, constantly attempting to suppress with an infusion of soothing substances (concocted of denial, dissociation, disavowal, splitting and so on) the impact of his impulses. In the absence of the mental work I have tried to outline, the repeated, moment to moment working-through of what Anzieu terms the 'microtraumas' (1993, p. 140) of the frustration of need and its consequences, the alternative can be a suppression of mental life, an impoverishment of the mind, and in consequence an unreadiness or ill-preparedness for external traumas such as accidental loss. Khan in his notion of cumulative trauma is describing something similar when he writes that these microtraumas 'operate and build up silently throughout childhood right up to adolescence'. They may be 'muted into obeyance'; the individual can 'arrive at a fairly healthy and effective normal functioning, nevertheless [he] can in later life break down as a result of acute stress and crisis (Khan, 1963, p. 56).

Mr D's susceptibility to trauma may be seen then to lie in the constraints placed upon his mental life which I have outlined. Then there is also the nature of the traumatic event to be taken into account. It perhaps goes without saying that he has a marked *ambivalence* towards the population of his internal world, particularly focused around his maternal object. As I have said he has been able to movingly express his love and concern for his mother and describe his tender, reparative nursing of her as she approached death. There is, though, also the hatred and hostility she provoked, especially by his perception of her emotional unavailability.

It is possible to see how, given this internal situation, a succession of deaths culminating in Alison's sudden and violent, if accidental, death would cause massive turmoil and intolerable guilt and conflict. In the absence of an effective identification with an involved father, capable in the patient's mind of intervening and protecting the mother from the patient's ambivalence and an internal world sufficiently alive and resonant to enable a working through of guilt and mourning, Mr D's hopelessness and despair on referral is understandable. I have suggested that the components of this vital working through are, at least in part, such activities as fantasy, imagination and dreaming. Segal notes that daydreams 'undoubtedly have a bad press in psychoanalysis'. She continues that they 'are often repetitive and shallow and always egocentric'. At the same time she maintains that 'it is only the most defended, restricted and rigid individual who is bereft of daydreams' and goes on to argue that imagination, which involves more contact with pain and struggle, is a development of the capacity to daydream. She adds that in patients lacking the capacity for daydreaming or imagination 'one may well suspect that the unconscious phantasy is too horrifying to be allowed any access to the waking life and the daydream' (Segal, 1991, p. 103). Mr D is not only up against the violent and fearful nature of the unconscious phantasy but also the disadvantage that it is directed at the very object that he needs to contain, face and work it through. Perhaps, as Oscar Wilde suggests when he writes 'Every man kills the thing he loves', this is to some degree always the case but the elegance of Wilde's formulation belies the anguish and struggle involved in encountering this fact and mourning its consequences. Naturally, we dedicate a good deal of our resources to avoiding this painful work. What I have tried to show is that when, as in the case of my patient, the mental musculature for grappling with traumatic anxiety has gone undeveloped, when imaginative mental work has, for whatever reason, been stunted, then psychic survival becomes equated with a dependence on soothing substances of one sort or another and further damage is done to the capacities needed to address the underlying situation.

# 7

# Issues in Treatment

## A Case of Rape

### *Caroline Garland*

### Introduction

In this chapter I hope to draw attention to two features of therapeutic work with survivors which, although relevant in clinical work as a whole, are particular issues for those who present after a traumatic event. First, there is the way in which a current trauma can link up powerfully with events of the past, through long-established existing internal object relationships. It is not simply that traumatic events in the present unearth events from the past, as of course they often do. It is more that in the survivor's mind the current event takes on some of the emotional resonance of past fears and phantasies, and may eventually be perceived as having some structural resemblance as well. To the extent that this link becomes entrenched, the trauma is felt to confirm existing unconscious phantasies about certain deeply troubling kinds of object relations, and this in turn contributes forcefully to the difficulty of 'getting over' the event in the present.

Second, I hope to show how the failure of containment by the maternal object, represented by the fact of the traumatic event's having happened at all, leads inevitably to difficulties in the area of symbolisation. A traumatic event is a breakdown in containment, and vice versa. The earthquake, the train-crash, the fire, the rape, the kidnapping, the mountaineering accident, all represent a massive failure of the maternal container. The outcome is a disintegration of the thinking, behaviour and defensive organisation of the individual caught up in the event – a breakdown. Both the external and the internal containers are lost: the world itself has become unpredictable and dangerous, and the dangers are such that one's good internal objects are powerless to prevent the worst from happening. The capacity to symbolise, to use aspects of the

108

actual world to represent internal objects and object relationships for purposes of thinking and understanding, depends upon the proper functioning of an internal container. In a trauma that container is lost; in treatment an attempt is made to restore its function.

I shall describe an individual, a seventeen year old girl, and the impact on her of a highly traumatic rape. I first saw about 6 months after the rape, and took her into twice-weekly psychotherapy for 18 months, before she gained a place at University and started her degree. After a gap in treatment during her first term, she travelled to London once a week for a further three years. Her attendance was patchy at times, sometimes for justifiable reasons, but sometimes also because of resistance to treatment and to change – resistance which exists in the treatment of trauma patients no less than in any other.

Ms O was hard to engage in treatment, in part because of her age, and in part because emotional contact exposed her to feelings she had spent her life defending against – need, vulnerability and dependence. Her tight and often ruthless control over these feelings had broken down following the rape, and from time to time would also break down in treatment, when she would be flooded once more with helplessness and extreme anxiety. At these times she required containment which had to be literal and total. By this I mean that she would sleep on the floor of a friend's room at University rather than spend the night alone and terrified. She was also a patient for whom certain words that occurred inevitably in the treatment (*rape*, or *knife*) were no longer symbols that stood for an event or a thing, but instead had become equated with the event itself. To hear them was to suffer that kind of breakdown in ordinary functioning that often gets called a *flashback*.

## Containment

When all goes well, containment is a fundamental of what goes on between a mother and a baby. It means that the mother can grasp the importance of, and take into herself, something of the baby's earliest and most primitive anxieties – about being dropped, about being forgotten or abandoned, left to starve, about states of disintegration, or fears of annihilation. She can think about such things in her own way without being caught up in them, overwhelmed by them herself. Babies with mothers who can take the panic out of their anxieties, eventually take into themselves some version of a mother who can manage – who can get hold of something important emotionally without being knocked off balance by it. Eventually the baby takes into itself, along

109

with its mother's milk so to speak, the mother's capacity to tolerate and manage anxiety – her own and her baby's. And this internalised version of the mother forms the basis of the child's eventual ability to manage, and eventually to think about its own anxieties ... *about* them, rather than just going on being caught up in them. This job is done intuitively by most mothers, with help from a supporting environment. In therapy it is more easily described than done, particularly with events of the violence and horror that many of our patients have encountered.

Bion (1967) described this process as transformation. He linked what the mother can do for the baby with what the therapist can do for the patient: help transform the unbearable into something that can eventually be thought about, held in the mind and considered, rather than responded to as an overwhelming experience that causes a further breakdown of the ability to think. This might be particularly true for therapists when working with a traumatised patient. Often the traumatic event has exposed the patient to the fear of imminent death, perhaps the most fundamental of all anxieties – and no less so for the baby, for whom states of 'nameless dread' link quite directly with the fear of annihilation.

The process of containment links in particular with one very recognisable feature of the thinking of survivors, the *flashback*: the sudden gripping sensation that you are not just thinking about what happened in the past, you are actually reliving it in the present. I suggest that the flashback is the experience of the loss of the container: the internalised place, or vessel, or space, intimately connected with good early care, in which *thinking-about-something* can occur. To be able to think about something, implies an 'I' who is a bit separate from the event or experience that is being considered. Most of us can most of the time recollect the events of the day without that experience being so vivid that it is equivalent to reliving those events. Reliving – or having a flashback – seems to indicate that the distinction between the *I* and the *event* has been lost, that the container has been lost or overwhelmed and the individual flooded with extreme anxiety – and as a result *recollection or remembering* has been replaced by *re-experiencing*. So that apparently simple process, thinking 'about' something, is hard when it comes to a gravely traumatic event. For the survivor, achieving the 'about' may even be impossible, and an unconscious decision is made to try to *not* think about things, instead to try to wall up the experience in some not-to-be-visited place in the mind, that may eventually only become visible in nightmares.

110

## 7. Issues in Treatment

### Symbolisation

Good-enough containment is also a necessary basis for a capacity to symbolise. Hanna Segal (1957) was the first to make this link by describing how this internalisation of the mother's own capacity to think *about* something, which technically we would call the internalisation of a containing object, is central to the development of real symbolic thinking. In symbolic thinking, the symbol is recognised to *stand for* the thing symbolised, but to differ from it, to possess its own unique properties which distinguish it from the thing it represents. Once the ability to symbolise is achieved, events can be thought about and dreamed about and worked on and eventually transformed in a variety of ways. However, after a serious trauma, the ability to symbolise, which has been developing from infancy onwards (thumbs, the special blanket, toys, all have symbolic as well as actual value), may be damaged, or lost. Its place may be taken by what Segal called a 'symbolic equation', an earlier version, developmentally speaking, of true symbolic thinking. For example, after a major fire in which a number of people choked to death in thick smoke, one of the survivors could not go outside the house when it was foggy. In fact, she could not even bear to draw her curtains back and see the fog outside. She knew with the rational part of her mind that this was fog, but at a different and more urgent level of functioning she felt about it and responded to it as though it were smoke.

In a symbolic equation, the symbol – in this case fog – does not in any substantial or convincing way stand for the thing symbolised – in this case smoke; it is felt about and responded to as though there were no difference between them. When it is foggy, this survivor shuts herself in her room and stuffs towels along the crack at the bottom of the door. So, to repeat, after a serious trauma, that ability to symbolise may be gravely impaired, and, particularly in the area of the traumatic event, be replaced by the symbolic equation. In some cases, the symbols that lose their symbolic value may be words themselves. In this situation, it is not hard to imagine that psychotherapeutic treatment of the survivor, based upon verbal communication, may be affected by the way in which the words we might hope to use about the traumatic event carry the impact of the event itself. To utter the word is at some level to recreate the traumatic event, which, as it has before, overwhelms the containing object with catastrophic anxiety and reproduces, via the flashback, a brief glimpse of the earlier breakdown.

Once the container has been lost, the particular nature of the anxiety

111

experienced in any situation that is even minutely reminiscent of the original traumatic event may itself make a further contribution to the failure of symbolisation. As I have described in Chapter 1, the traumatised ego can no longer afford to make a distinction between signal anxiety, which warns of impending danger, and automatic anxiety, which occurs in a situation of actual danger. The ego has become hyper-vigilant, a state often seen in survivors; it now responds immediately to all warning signs (symbols) as indicating an actual, not a potential danger. From the point of view of survival, it cannot afford to do otherwise. The sights, sounds, smells, certain configurations of relationship, certain words can all produce the flashback, the event-in-the-present, rather than the memory, the-event-in-the-past. The loss of the internal container results, through the loss of symbolisation, in the flashback, and the flashback in turn leads to automatic rather than signal anxiety – which adds in its turn to the failure of the internal container. A self-perpetuating cycle is produced, which leads to increasingly stuck and repetitive behaviours. The striking literal-mindedness of the survivor, the apparent concreteness of his or her thinking faced with certain evocative stimuli, are evidence of the existence of the helpless and disabled area of functioning that is the longer-term legacy of the original breakdown. This phenomenon does not improve with time alone: the survivor simply becomes more adept at finding ways of avoiding such stimuli.

## The Traumatised Response

After a traumatic event, there are two (often merging) stages of development in the survivor, as described in Chapter 1. There is the initial breakdown, the catastrophic disruption of normal mental functioning which follows the breaching of the protective shield, that is to say the mind's normal capacity to filter out excessive or painful stimuli (Freud, 1920). The survivor is shocked and confused, perhaps unable to take in what has happened. He may become silent and withdrawn, or compulsively talkative and active, but in either case his normal functioning is in a state of disintegration and he is unable to think or behave in a coherent manner.

The second stage is slower to make itself visible. To the outside world, the survivor may appear to have 'got over it'. He may even be back at work, or socialising again. However, internally the picture is different. This longer-term internal situation is the outcome of two powerful drives. First, there is the way in which we have from infancy onwards attached all our experience to some notion of an agent, an object felt to be responsible for this or that perception, sensation or other internal state of affairs. Not surprisingly, the kind of relationship associated with such a catastrophic event is felt to be intensely persecutory, linking with the earliest and most paranoid of phantasies about the nature of one's objects. It is therefore not surprising that survivors can feel overwhelmed with confusion, demoralisation and a sense of persecution.

Second, there is our powerful inbuilt drive to make sense of our own experience, perhaps especially the apparently arbitrary. In the struggle to give meaning or sense to the catastrophic event we link it with what is already familiar, or with whatever resembles it in some important respect. This process, which is linked to what Freud (1920) called 'binding', is partly responsible for the entrenched quality that can so often be part of a traumatised response. A trauma in the present will link up with troubled relationships and disturbing events from the past and give fresh life to old or buried issues which may have been more or less manageable up to that point. The certain outcome is that whatever the physical damage, the long-term problem will be the repair of the survivor's relations with his social world – both the actual people around him and the representations of those figures, or aspects of figures, he carries inside him for good or ill: his internal objects.

The outcome is that the current external event will cease to feel like a new experience, since it is the external confirmation of old fears about the unpredictability or untrustworthiness of one's internal objects, of the world itself. These are the serious and difficult issues that have to be addressed in treatment.

## The Patient

Miss O was 17 years old when she came to the Clinic. She was nagged into it by a school-friend, the only person to know Ms O had been in touch with the Samaritans. The friend (whose own mother had once been a Tavistock Clinic patient) was terrified by Ms O's suicidal state, because she knew that Ms O had resolutely refused to tell her parents, her school, or her GP about the traumatic event, and was trying, and failing, to manage it more or less on her own. Ms O had tried to manage it by cutting herself off from it, banishing it from her mind, through developing a phobic avoidance of situations or places that could provoke a recollection of the traumatic event. It was when this defence began to break down – for instance when the clocks went back and Ms

O could no longer avoid being out alone after dark – that she began to become uncontrollably panicky.

She was a slim, pale-complexioned girl, with long tangly brown hair and striking blue eyes – an unusual, intelligent face which was not conventionally pretty, but which became animated and attractive when she smiled. She wore jeans, T-shirts and baggy cardigans. She was watchful, quick-witted and highly defended. She was in the first year of her 6th form studying for A-levels, which included Latin-American Studies, and contemplating a career in third world development projects. The summer before her exams she had travelled to South America with an organised tour, to learn more of the language and culture. At six o'clock one evening, before supper, she had left the hotel and her group, and gone for a walk by the town's river, when a man emerged suddenly from the bushes behind her, and held a knife to her throat, asking her in his own language, 'Do you want to live?'

She was terrified, but summoning up her GCSE Spanish, replied yes she did want to live; and as he was tearing at her clothes and she realised what was going to happen, told him desperately that she was only a school-girl, and a foreigner, and that she had AIDS, all of which were ignored. The man forced her at knife point to lie down and then tried to penetrate her, but Ms O had never had sexual intercourse (or indeed any kind of sexual contact before) and the man found it impossible in spite of repeated and increasingly violent attempts. Ms O described with a small, rather forlorn laugh how while this was going on, and her eyes were tight shut, she was quoting *Hamlet*, one of her A-level texts, to herself: the passage where the bewildered girl Ophelia, rejecting Hamlet's menacing advances, chides him by saying, 'You are keen my Lord, you are keen ...' and then she quoted Hamlet's savagely punning response, in which he twists Ophelia's reference to his sexual desire into a reference to the keenness of a knife blade, 'It would cost you a groaning to take off my edge'.

This was a courageous defence, a deliberate attempt at dissociation in a struggle to keep her head, to keep her wits about her. In terms of her psychic survival, it relates to the fear caused by the loss of omnipotence, the terror of the utter and prolonged helplessness that is in and of itself traumatic. For Ms O, having access to her wit and intelligence was closely linked to feeling all right, since it was an important part of an identification with a particular aspect of one of her parents, and therefore part of the functioning of a rather brittle and two-dimensional internal object. When he failed to penetrate her, the man turned her over – and at this point Ms O believed that in his rage and frustration he would kill her, stab her to death. She became terrified, in a state of extreme fear and disintegration. He told her to stop making a noise. He then had anal intercourse with her, and committed further acts of perverse sexuality. Afterwards he robbed her of what small possessions she had about her, and ran off, leaving her to crawl back to the hotel, the tour leader, the police, the police surgeon, the British Consul and so on.

The drive to make sense of catastrophe, through the unconscious linking of external events with familiar internal object relationships, meant that the assault and rape came to achieve a sort of congruence with existing conditions in Ms O's internal world. In a way that was problematical for her future, they provided a kind of confirmation of some deeply troubled phantasies, both conscious and unconscious, about the nature of these relationships. Ms O was the only child of parents, then in their late 40s, who divorced when she was 3. Her mother never married again, and apart from one unsatisfactory affair some 8 years earlier, had remained single, unemployed and depressed. Her father, an obsessional, controlling and apparently schizoid business man, had had a long string of short-term relationships with women, all of which ended in disappointment for the woman and in mutual recrimination. Ms O divided her time between her two parental homes. Each parent complained that she spent more time with the other; neither had any contact with the other. Ms O felt she was a chameleon: when with her mother she 'fitted in' to that view of the world, reversing the mother-child relationship so that it was she who acted as the caretaker for her depressed parent. This was part, though only part, of her reason for not telling her parents of the incident – she could continue to project the turmoil, upset, and fear into her internal representations of her parents and then look after it in its projected condition. When with her father, she would adopt his stance: a mocking and sardonic view of the human comedy, exasperation with the current girl-friend, and a fine line in invective for what she called 'wishy-washy women's talk, *feelings* and stuff'. Father and daughter tended to communicate through their shared enthusiasm for the latest developments in software for the word-processor.

The rape therefore achieved an easy congruence with her pre-existing psychopathology, given her hatred of a vulnerable, despised, contaminated female aspect of herself which she kept controlled by a slightly cocky, omnipotent, intellectual self. It was when the denied, split-off, vulnerable aspects of herself came flooding back, and she was overwhelmed with feelings of fear, vulnerability and disgust, that she was at her most suicidal – wishing to kill off the despised female altogether.

Internally, there seemed to be two distinct and separate identifications: a depressed, vulnerable and hopeless version of her, which she identified as female; and a clever, ruthless and rather perverse version, which she identified with some version of a male based upon her perception of her father. The central organising feature of her internal world was the belief that these two identifications could not be brought together in a tender or loving or constructive manner. The only sort of intercourse of any kind possible between any two people was one that was conceptualised as, at worst, bullying, sadistic, hurtful; at best, incapable of hearing her in a sympathetic or helpful way that was not simultaneously weak and despised.

This is perhaps illustrated by a dream she brought in the sixth session. In the dream she was on her own, walking past a very large building, a huge department store (perhaps the Tavistock), trying to find her way to a tube station without knowing quite where it was. She had to go through a sort of amusement arcade on the way; it was full of rabid dogs which she was terrified would bite her. Then she was with her parents who were feeding her, but she felt afraid they were poisoning her, and when she turned to her friends for help they seemed vague and distant, offering her false sympathy before turning away to their own preoccupations. She had woken terrified from this very bleak dream, and I took up with her the way she was describing a world with no-one in it who could be expected or trusted to help or support her, or to whom she could turn with any expectation of being understood. And this of course included me, and her need to be safe and understood by me, which was felt to be profoundly at war with the feelings of vulnerability this stirred up, leaving her with the fear of an object who was helping in a falsely sympathetic way, leaving her worse off than before.

This view of intercourse (not just sexual intercourse, but all ways in which objects might engage) was given weight several weeks later, as I learned that within the last year, Ms O had approached in person three of the London teaching hospitals in the hope of getting someone to perform a total hysterectomy on her. She had also been to a birth control clinic, invented a name, address and boyfriend to obtain supplies of the contraceptive pill which she took continuously to avoid all bleeding. Why not, she said, watching me carefully: she never intended to marry or have children, and she detested her periods, they disgusted her.

116

I said I took what she was telling me very seriously. I thought she was describing her own murderous assault on herself, a ruthless attack by a bullying, contemptuous self on a vulnerable, depressed aspect of her own functioning, which she located in her female reproductive apparatus. She could then maintain an aloof, superior, if lonely stance. She seemed startled: she began to argue, but I also felt she was somewhere at some level relieved to have had her destructiveness recognised and spoken about. It was the first moment in the treatment when I felt her take something in, as opposed to a mere hearing-me-out. In the transference I had to tread a very fine line between coming too close, which was labelled as 'all that pathetic women's talk', and being a fraction too far away, when I would get a sudden glimpse of the lost small girl, who had constructed for herself, and lived in, a lonely omnipotence – a fantasy of being self-sufficient, of needing no-one, of being superior to people who suffered from messy uncontrollable things like feelings and needs. And consequently of someone who had never internalised a steady reliable caretaking function, which could take a realistic view of the risks involved in going for a walk alone in a strange city, as opposed to an omnipotent and cocky view – that she could take care of herself, she was invulnerable.

Thus this treatment was not primarily about the rape itself, but about the state of her internal world, in which brutal, unsympathetic, rapey kinds of encounters – attacks by knives, rabid dogs, unhearing people, people who fed you poison, who fobbed you off with false sympathy – were the norm. Nor was I blind to the kind of poison I was felt to be feeding her: to do with being in touch with her own neediness, vulnerability, her own longing for an intimate contact that would not also be a violation of her privacy or individuality. (There was also of course some real investment in sustaining a narcissistic belief in her own self-sufficiency, allowing her to avoid knowledge of any good coupling anywhere, and thus in turn to avoid – or delay – being exposed to more ordinary oedipal pains and conflicts.)

However, a second dream six months into treatment suggested that as she gradually became more able to tolerate becoming part of a couple, the therapeutic couple, some sort of shift had begun to occur in this girl's internal world. She'd had, she said, a few nights ago, a really absurd dream, quite meaningless. She'd been leading a camel along the Edgware Road in London, she couldn't think why. It had been a very sweet camel with big round eyes and long fringy lashes and a rather wide soft-lipped mouth; she had enjoyed being with it. This, she said, was not one of the older, hardened sorts of camel that could survive on its own in the desert without food or water yet, it was only a baby camel. It only had one hump ...

There are many ways in which one could have approached this dream. Camels' humps are of course very tempting to psychoanalysts, but I chose to ignore this bait, and said instead that I thought she was telling me about a rather kinder relationship that was beginning to be possible between the two aspects of herself, the controlling, leading, in-charge, competent part, and the appealing, vulnerable, not-knowing-the-way infant part, in that helpfulness, even tenderness could be included. She went on to tell me in the same session, that two days after the dream she had had her eighteenth birthday. She had passed her driving test a few weeks earlier, and had decided to celebrate the beginning of her officially 'adult' life by driving out into the countryside about 40 miles beyond London. As evening came, she had suddenly felt exhausted and lonely, and daunted by the prospect of driving back in the dark while trying to map-read. She had phoned her mother and asked for help, and her mother had borrowed a car – in fact her father's car – and had driven out to find her daughter, and then led her back into London and home. The link with the dream was quite direct: it was in some ways was a restatement, a description, of this experience. A shift towards something a bit softer in the internal object-configurations had been followed by a change in behaviour, a change for the better in external relations. At about this time, she also managed to tell her parents (shortly before she took her A-level examinations) about what had happened to her nearly a year earlier; and she weathered the storm of upset that followed this painful revelation – doubly painful, because it involved not only the traumatic incident itself, but also the fact that she had kept it from them. She brought them together in order to break the news to them, a significant step for her; and no doubt for them.

As the treatment continued, the difference in the child, who had undoubtedly contributed to the parents' inability to come together on behalf of their daughter, seemed in turn to have affected the parents themselves. When their daughter got As in her examinations and gained a place at university, for the first time in ten years the father entered the mother's house, and in front of his daughter embraced his ex-wife, saying, 'We produced a clever child, didn't we?'. Ms O told me this with some real emotion. Subsequently after ten years on her own, Mother met someone and fell in love, and although the relationship was not able to be sustained for longer than six months, during that time she offered her daughter the potential for a rather altered model of sexual relations: a woman who could feel pleasure and happiness rather than fear or pain from being with a man. Simultaneously with this development, the daughter began to have a social life, something she was virtually incapable of before, in part through a narcissistic pre-occupation with an idea of herself as needing no-one, and in part through an intense shyness and self-consciousness with people her own age. She was more sociable, and that meant, she would complain to me in a self-mocking way, more boringly ordinary.

And what about the rape, the traumatic incident, in all this? Although she spoke briefly about it at first, for a long time it went underground and was not mentioned specifically, although a lot of the work that went on about her feelings about her body and her *own* murderous assault on its specifically female attributes of course related to the terrifying and obscene violations she had experienced. Later she began to talk about the rape again, and many details that had been repressed at first began to emerge, just beginning to be somewhat freed from the intense affect that characterised the early weeks. The violent rage and destructiveness that, turned on herself, emerged as intense suicidal wishes, became more able to be known about and directed outwards. In part it was channelled into a quite remarkable campaign, conducted entirely on her own initiative, but making good use of the help and cooperation of the British Embassy and the local police, which eventually resulted in the identification and reimprisonment in a maximum security hospital of the rapist, already known and convicted for two other identical offences, in fact upon boys. This campaign and its success also had a powerfully restoring effect upon her sense of control of her own life. In my view it replaced her earlier omnipotence, her narcissistic conviction of self-sufficiency, with an almost equally powerful but by no means unrealistic belief in her capacity to get people to help her.

By the time treatment ended, Ms O had succeeded in establishing some long-standing and close friendships with both men and women contemporaries. She had also sustained for over two years a good sexual relationship with a man who took on considerable importance for her. There were times when the rape again became a horrifying and dominating feature in her mental life, but interestingly, we came to recognise this symptom as a sign that something still more frightening was oppressing her, something so frightening she could not contemplate it openly. The memories of the rape served as a kind of screen behind which the greater fears were lurking. (She is not the only patient to make use of a trauma as a screen memory in this way.) Not surprisingly, these greater fears concerned her own enormous vulnerability to separation and to loss, and hence to the recognition of her own dependency and need. Although she still has some important issues to be faced – both in this area, and over the question of whether she will contemplate having children, and thus irrevocably facing and accepting her own female body – she is moving again, taking part in life.

### Discussion and Conclusions

I hope that I have illustrated through the clinical material the way in which the traumatic event in the present links with and gives fresh life to existing persecutory phantasies concerning primary object relationships. The longer-term treatment of the survivor of any traumatic event will involve early object relationships, revealed in the transference, that are central to effective treatment of the trauma in the present as well as the past. As well, as I have suggested earlier, the damage to the capacity to symbolise is a characteristic and problematic feature of the thinking of the traumatised, and one which can circumscribe some aspects of treatment. When individuals are caught up in a catastrophically overwhelming event, inducing total helplessness, their sudden enforced regression takes them back to a stage before the use of words and symbolic thinking have emerged in their own developmental history. In the early hours of a disaster, the use of words at all can be misleading – they may be emptied of their habitual symbolic freight, and carry the significance primarily of cries and groans, utterances of despair, ways of remaining in touch with anything or anyone that may be perceived as capable of listening. At a later stage, symbolic functioning may be more or less restored in all but the area of experience directly connected with the disaster itself. Here, there can be a chronic impairment. Certain words said out loud may retain for a long time, perhaps for ever, the psychic impact of the event itself: the word does not denote the event, it *is* the event, is a symbolic equation and not a symbol. Events where the bodily envelope is penetrated, or seen to be penetrated in others, and life ebbs out of the perforations, are perhaps especially likely to produce this breakdown in the capacity to think symbolically about the event itself. This return to a stuck and concrete mode of functioning in the area of the trauma is also responsible for the flashback, which is itself a concretised way of 'remembering', and for much of the disabled repetitious symptomatology of trauma, including the impulse to repeat the traumatic events in both active and passive forms.

For Ms O, damage to her ability to symbolise concerned not things, like fog, but words: the words 'knife' and 'rape' were particularly affected. When, about a year later, sitting in a pub with some friends

120

one night, one of the boys said teasingly that they couldn't let the girls walk home on their own for fear of rape, Ms O became filled with feelings of terror she could not articulate, and she resorted to acting in a way that forced those feelings out of her and into her companions, through a process of projective identification. She left the pub and climbed swiftly some sixty feet up a scaffolding on a nearby warehouse, walking precariously along the planks at the top, terrifying her friends and making them beg her to come down. When she'd frightened them enough, and felt sufficiently relieved of her own feelings of agitation (gazing down upon these feelings from a lofty position), she came down, not really able to understand why she'd felt driven to do what she'd done. It seemed that each time we were able to understand one of these incidents there was a small shift in the valency of those two significant words, but there remained a constant drift back *towards* the state of equatedness and *away* from the symbolic. The behaviour that she had used to induce a state of alarm and fear in her companions was still concretely enacted on a large scale, although it began to modify over time.

This breakdown in the capacity to think symbolically about the traumatic event is perhaps partly responsible for the way in which the event so often remains encapsulated as a foreign body in the mind, a 'no go' area. The foreignness of this body is sustained by the real differences in the nature of the cultures (language and behaviours) on each side of the border: the concreteness of the symbolic equation, and its associated behaviour, on the one side, and the flexibility and creativeness of true symbolisation on the other. To some extent those borders have a defensive value, to prevent the concretised culture of the sealed-off territory from encroaching on the areas where symbolic functioning has remained possible; and this affects the whole mind, personality and functioning. 'Working through' – the analytical process that is necessary if traumatic events are going to be understood, thought about, and integrated into conscious functioning, rather than unconsciously sought out and helplessly repeated – is particularly difficult when the words one might use about the event are felt to recreate the event itself.

However, the treatment of a patient who presents following a traumatic event offers the chance of a transition from the stage where the survivor is stuck with the trauma as the dominating feature of mental life, to a subsequent stage in which it has become a *part* of the whole, still present, still painful, but able to be contemplated without upsetting the apple cart, losing the container, all over again. In other words, the possibility of a future is there once more. I hope I have been able to show something of the way in which when that treatment is of the person and his object-world, not the event, it allows for integration of the event into an overall view the individual has of his or her own self and life. It therefore allows for the possibility of letting go of and mourning the loss of the pre-disaster existence, which has sometimes involved a kind of blissful ignorance, and an accompanying sense of omnipotence, even of immortality. The outcome in Ms O's case was a sadder but saner individual, one more in touch with the reality of her entirely human vulnerabilities and needs, and beginning to be more accepting of them. This is the aim of treatment: for the traumatic event to become part of the survivor's overall thinking and functioning, instead of remaining a split-off, encapsulated and avoided area, a 'foreign body' in the mind, ready to break open once more at the next unforeseen and frightening incident.

# 8

# Dreaming After a Traumatic Bereavement

## Mourning or Its Avoidance?

*Elizabeth Gibb*

### Introduction

In this Chapter I will describe some aspects of the therapy with a woman who had suffered a traumatic bereavement, the suicide of her adolescent daughter, her eldest child. I will outline aspects of the management of this case, but will be concentrating on the state of the patient's internal world. This patient from the beginning regularly brought vivid dreams to her treatment. They were an important part of her communication with me. Her dreams were always significant to the patient; she remembered and thought about them. However, there was a sense in which they, and her relationship to them, were an escape from reality, a reality of fractured, rivalrous and disturbed relationships. They illustrated an aspect of the patient which turned away from knowledge of herself and her objects, internal and external. I will suggest points at which I thought this was most marked in the transference relationship and where this had seemed less so. The question I wish to raise is whether or not we can think of these dreams as illustrating a shift in the patient's internal world as she tried to accommodate this devastating event. This has implications for considering the function of the therapy and some aspects of management.

Dreams were first given recognition as important products of our mental life by Freud in 1900. His oft-quoted phrase 'the royal road to the unconscious' indicated the supremacy of the dream at that time in trying to understand the patient. He emphasised the dream as a vehicle of psychic work, and as such, evidence of a capacity in the ego to do such work. Subsequent Kleinian thinking about unconscious phantasy,

123

that set of underlying beliefs that dominate and determine how an individual interprets their experience, has tended to place the dream *alongside* other communications in the therapeutic relationship, particularly the detail of the transference and countertransference. Greenson (1970) argues strongly against this position. Segal (1981) emphasised the form and function of the dream, that use to which it is put in the mind, and in the analytic relationship, as illuminative of disturbances in ego function. Here the dream operates to rid the mind of unwanted parts of the self and its objects, rather than to work them through; and in the therapeutic relationship it is used as a way of avoiding painful emotional truths.

In everyday life empathically we can all recognise the terrible problem in mourning posed for parents when their child commits suicide. The loss is unmitigated by realities, perhaps of the natural order of life, accident or fate, considerations which can relieve persecution and guilt in bereavement, and hence facilitate mourning. In her paper 'Mourning and its Relation to Manic Depressive States' (1940) Klein writes movingly of the internal dilemma provoked by bereavement. I wish to outline some aspects of what she has said that I have found helpful in thinking about this patient. She says, and I quote, 'The poignancy of the actual loss of a loved person is ... greatly increased by the mourner's unconscious phantasies of having lost his *internal* "good" objects as well. He then feels his internal bad objects predominate and his inner world is in danger of disruption' There is a need not only to reinstate the lost loved object into the ego, as Freud (1915b) tells us, but also the previously internalised good objects, ultimately the loved parents, in order to restore security. In order to accomplish this re-creation the actuality of the loss has to be acknowledged – the first step in the work of mourning. It is necessary to renounce in order to recreate. Mrs Klein describes how the loss of a loved figure realises universal infantile phantasies, death wishes and the need to inflict punishment against parents and siblings. The more the lost person carries representations of these internal figures, then, as well as sorrow and grief, triumph over hated rivals will be activated, and hence more guilt. Also in suicide, perhaps especially that of one's child, the fear that the dead object is inflicting punishment for one's wrongs or deficiencies by their absence is reinforced. She describes how this fearful internal situation impedes mourning, and it is only the realisation of the loss and consequent pining that will diminish persecution and allow relief. Where the bereaved person feels incapable of re-instating their lost loved objects they must turn away from them more than previously, denying their

124

love for them by an increase in manic mechanisms of control and omnipotence, and by reinforced projection into the external world. This provides an escape from the deeper anxieties of the depressive position, but stifles emotions and inhibits working through. The depressive position (Klein 1935) is the developmental point at which the infant is aware of the mother as a whole person, one whom he both loves and hates. This leads to anxieties about the damage done to the internal object, guilt, sorrow and a wish to make reparation. This developmental step is not reached once and for all but moved to and from in the person's experience of the world.

## The Suicide

I first saw the patient, Mrs D, about a month after her daughter's death. She was referred to the Trauma Unit by an out-of-London Adolescent Unit where she and her husband had been seen shortly following the suicide of Anna, who had shot herself. Anna had been seen briefly in this local unit some years previously and at the time of her death was waiting for a new appointment. On the day of her concert performance rehearsal, when her parents were away together, she had gone into the cellar at home where she had killed herself. She was found by her father on their return surrounded by a circle of lit candles and flowers. The sense that has always been conveyed to me is of an elaborate ceremony with herself as the sacrificial victim. The patient rushed to the cellar on hearing her husband's screaming. She has said that in those few seconds she was able to prepare herself for something awful, a warning that had been denied her husband.

Anna was the eldest of this couple's four children, the others being some years younger. She had been in evident difficulty for the previous three years, engaged in delinquent behaviour, a source of profound anxiety to her parents and unable to take the normal developmental step of leaving home. Particularly in the last year her disturbance had dominated the household. The parents had managed this in a way that reflects the prevailing dynamics in the family. Mother and daughter were overtly rivalrous for father's attention, a situation in which he played his full part. In this household Anna and mother each had their own rooms, the other children shared a room and father slept in his workshop. Father and daughter would talk together for hours, a relationship which the patient envied and from which she felt excluded. She and her daughter would argue terribly, the patient often provoked and enraged by her. She was clearly persecuted by the continual accusation of being a bad mother, reflected in the girl's disturbance and rage and her husband's criticism. About a year previously she had reacted to Anna's taking an overdose with anger and denial and at the time no outside help had been sought. Some months later Mrs D had spoken to a relative of her concerns about her daughter who then suggested various possible avenues for professional help. However, on hearing about this her husband had accused her of betrayal of the family and nothing came of this possible intervention.

A few days before her death when Anna had again threatened to kill herself her mother had snapped at her to go ahead then. On the day of her suicide, as well as the parents going off for the day to visit friends, her father had told Anna she could no longer continue to speak to her mother like that. 'Like that' seemed to be with a mixture of contempt and anger. I have felt, and hope it is conveyed, that this was a cut-throat oedipal disaster, a drama inexorably enacted to its inevitable end, the death of one of the participants.

One can also get a glimpse of the almost impossible nature of the mourning which faced the patient and the limited strength and capacity of the available internal resources with which to accomplish this.


## The History

Mrs D, an American, was 55 years old at the time of the treatment, although looked much younger – rather adolescent in fact. She is the eldest of six sibs and had an intensely rivalrous relationship with her only sister. Both her parents were living, and she had a poor relationship with them, although worse with her mother. She said that mother – daughter relations had been bad in her family for generations and she thought of this as the transmission of a destructive mutant gene. The patient was said to have been the quarrelsome member of the family, difficult and rebellious. At the age of six she had been sent to live with an aunt for some months. She had always taken this as evidence of her parents' incapacity to deal with her difficult behaviour and this had fed her derision of them. Subsequently, in this therapy, she realised it was when her fourth sib was born. When she was eight the family fortunes declined and they moved into cramped accommodation. The patient was angry and unhappy at this loss of her previously unrestricted life, but it was from then that she began to eat properly, having never previously done so. To this day she found her mother's food suffocating – her word – and didn't eat much she prepared. Father too was described as extremely thin, referring to the food prepared by his wife as poison. At twelve she had a reconciliation with her sibs, realising with guilt and distress that she had cut them out of her life. It seems likely this was at the time of mother's pregnancy with the last child. She was hurt that her parents refused to allow her to participate in the care of the new baby, trusting her sister more.

She said that during her teens her father went into therapy because he was troubled by the degree of violence and overinvolvement he felt towards her. From then her parents' marriage deteriorated. They rowed constantly. Her father stopped hitting her, and she turned towards him and away from mother. They would talk together, for hours. She subsequently went into therapy for three years, a secret between her and father, kept from mother in an atmosphere of intrigue and mental incest.

Mrs D married her husband on the rebound from a failed affair. Financial strain had been a source of constant trouble between them: her disappointment that he could not support the family easily, and his that she had never contributed. When the children were young she went back into once weekly treatment with her previous therapist. This was in part because of the constant difficulties she had with Anna, whom she always experienced as demanding, and as alienating her by coming between herself and her husband. This repeated the family patterns of her childhood. She left this treatment on bad terms with her therapist. He had suggested she come more often than once a week and, feeling he wanted her to work analytically, she stopped her treatment. It seems likely she would not have been able to tolerate coming more often than once a week.

Anna was supposed to be a very promising musician and, from the photos I saw, was extraordinarily attractive, more striking than her sibs. A 'special child' perhaps. Her mother had taken great joy from this, as well as feeling narcissistically gratified. No doubt it had also however fuelled the jealousy and envy that was such a part of their relationship. It is perhaps worthy of note then that Anna removed this loved and admired body, representing both the realisation of her own femininity and as such a physical demonstration of her identification with her mother, and also that which had alleviated some of her mother's own emptiness and self-hatred. She left her mother only with what was in her mind. Mrs D was terrified of forgetting her daughter's physicality and kept a garment which she had worn and which retained her smell, packaged in clingfilm. This seemed linked to the fear of having nothing good remain inside herself of her relationship with her daughter, projected as it was out of her mind and into her physical body.

Following Anna's death, her father moved into her undisturbed room, and it was eighteen months before he allowed it to be changed or was willing to move out. The parents were little able to comfort each other. Mutual accusations of blame and inadequacy flew between them. They could only join in agreement that the patient's mother, because of her failure to have mothered her properly, was to be held responsible for murder.

## The Treatment

I saw Mrs D every other week initially, all I could offer at the time. After eight months I was able to offer her a weekly vacancy. I am going to describe these months and then, briefly, some subsequent material.

At the time of referral the patient was disturbed and agitated at home, a source of terrible anxiety to her family, as her daughter had been to her. The family were very afraid she would kill herself. She was preoccupied with what she experienced as the ununderstandable difference between herself and her daughter: at the age at which she had gone into psychotherapy Anna had killed herself. She attributed this to Anna's erroneous belief that she could always rely on her father, whilst she from an early age had known she had to stand on her own feet. She gave herself something she called 'interpretations' which she either recalled from her previous therapy or had subsequently read in books. These were usually persecuting, for example about suicide being the killing of the introjected bad mother. Given in this way, these are not interpretations but instead a kind of mantra, a magical formula which it is hoped will take away pain without having to experience the reality of the loss. My overriding impression as she spoke about her daughter was of the long-standing inability to recognise how ill this girl had been, in a state of angry desperation and possibly in the last few days of her life actually psychotic. This negation seemed to be due to the unbearable nature of the helplessness and humiliation the parents would have felt if her disturbance was fully recognised and *outside* help sought. Mrs D felt terrible about how angry she herself had often been with her daughter. There were of course many 'if onlys' but I wish to draw attention to one in particular, the patient's belief that had she not got Anna out of bed that day to go to the rehearsal she would not have killed herself. Mrs D spent large parts of the eighteen months following her daughter's death in bed.

For the first few months of her therapy I, and the other professionals involved with this family, were concerned Mrs D could kill herself. This

128

was probably a realistic concern. However, I was also preoccupied with the fear that I could say something that would drive her to it and so would be held responsible. My knowledge of countertransference and projective identification were reduced to theoretical concepts and as such were not enough to help me hold this experience in my mind and enable me to think. Instead the experience of actual murder, and the internal accusation of being the murderer, were brought into the session in all concreteness. The therapeutic position was hard to hold, as I too became drawn into the need to gather evidence, locate blame and assign the deserved retribution, the death penalty. There was little space in the therapeutic relationship – my experience was of finding myself either colluding with a view of the patient and her daughter as victims of her mother or alternatively finding myself being heard as accusing her of murder and becoming instantly an object of suspicion and fear.

In the first session she told me that since the suicide she would at times feel all right, but at others be filled with panic with associated unbearable chest pain. When not in bed she would be screaming and crying. She described a dream from the previous night, of a photograph of Anna as a baby. She had woken with chest pain, panicking and unable to breathe.

She came to the next session and told me talking no longer worked as a way of making her feel better, believing Anna to be not dead. She had begun to have flashback dreams of her: in the cellar, in hospital lying shrouded on a trolley, in her coffin.

There is more than one way these dreams can be understood, but I took it that the dream of the photo of the baby represented an image of hope and possibility, new life, and also a memory of when Anna was a baby, alive. It is at the same time a lifeless image, a photograph. I thought therefore it was highly condensed, containing both what she knew and what she could not bear to know, in hidden form the knowledge of this death. It also indicated her state of mind in coming to the therapy, the extreme dependency typical of the traumatised patient looking for an object to relieve them of suffering and mental pain, to make everything as though it had not happened. It links to the prolonged helplessness and dependency of infancy when an actual mother is needed, since there does not yet exist any internal mental container to process and integrate sensation and experience.

This broke down quickly as she brought the flashback dreams, again typical following a traumatic event. There was an accusation around at this time that I had not fulfilled my function since talking no longer worked to obliterate pain. She told me she was wearing shoes that Anna

129

would often borrow, this intrusive borrowing a source of much irritation to her. I was filled with anxiety at this point about her identification with her daughter and its possible consequences, and have never forgotten this moment – or rather that at which I sent her out of the room at the end of her session.

The flashbacks, although night dreams, indicate the stuckness and inflexibility of thinking about the event, a frozen unmodifiable image in the mind, not able to be thought about or subject to symbolisation. It is an unelaborated throwback to the event, rather than being a dream as a potentially symbolic representation of an internal state. It is as though the mind is overwhelmed once more by unmanageable experience so thinking breaks down. Even her bed, believed to be the place of safety for her daughter, was no longer available as a retreat. At this point I would suggest she was briefly recognising the reality of what had happened, that her daughter had killed herself and she, the dreamer, was alive. She then filled me with anxiety about her safety, that which she had not been able to provide her daughter. As I could not help her deny this tragedy I then had to bear what she bore in all its concreteness. In this session too she told me a dream of herself and her daughter, both crying and holding their arms out but unable to reach each other.

Shortly before Christmas, that is three months after her daughter's suicide, she became hysterical again at home, running about, enraged, shouting and throwing things. The family contacted the GP, who contacted me. This was one of a number of conversations her GP and I had in these few months.

Mrs D came to her session, the last before this first Christmas, enraged with the Clinic. Her main theme was of our negligence and unavailability. Did we not know that patients could kill themselves? How could we shut for Christmas? She brought a dream of Anna as a vampire, spoke about being sent away when she was six, and her preoccupying fear at the time of being abducted by an eagle. She spoke of when she was 14 and had become anxious about going out of the house and in particular about using the Underground after an incident when a man had fired into a crowd there. She said she had been as she was now, demanding and fallen apart, at other times when she felt exposed to tremendous danger. She was aware of her wish for revenge, to ruin Christmas for everyone, including me, as Anna had ruined it for her. She was afraid of being admitted to hospital, stating that the family would fall apart if she was.

I think at this time she was fully identified with her daughter. The vampire, both dead and undead, was inhabiting her, sucking out the life blood of herself and her family. Under the pressure of its being Christmas, and the break, the threat of the pain of this intolerable loss had come closer. The patient interpreted her dream as indicating herself as Anna's victim. Of course, in so doing she could deny what she had become herself and was asking those around her to carry. Perhaps then the previous dream of her daughter and herself with their arms held out to each other was indicative of the pull to death, a warning that her defences were failing.

Mrs D saw another therapist over this break, a man whom she decided she preferred to me, finding him more sympathetic. Shortly after her therapy with me had resumed, and without telling me beforehand, she contacted the therapist whom she had seen as a young woman. However, she was unable to keep the appointment, paralysed by anxiety about betrayal and dishonesty with me. After I took this up as her anxiety about my retaliation and rivalry with her relationship with the man in the break, the preferable therapist, she was able to speak to her previous therapist and tell him about her daughter's suicide. She was relieved by his nonretaliatory response and genuine sympathy, and also that he did not recall the end of her therapy as being due to her refusal to work. This was a relief as in part her wish to contact him and tell him of the suicide was to punish him for not having done his job properly, to make her into a better mother, linking him with her own mother. At this time she agreed also to see a psychiatrist in whom she found a benevolent figure.

At this point she read her daughter's diaries again. This time, she saw Anna's struggle to live, whereas when she had last read them she had seen only her preoccupation with suicide for the previous two years. This had of course added to her sense of persecution about how unavailable she had been to her daughter. One can however also see the degree of lack of differentiation between herself and her daughter – the patient now too was struggling to live. However, she had agreed to allow in another parental figure (the psychiatrist), which was both an admission of her own need and disturbance, and an offer of containment for me. It is interesting to consider how far the patient sensed this latter. It links to the child who *is* too much for mother to manage on her own – a father's help is needed.

Following the conversation with her first therapist Mrs D brought some photos of her children to the session. There was one of herself and Anna. The dead girl's attractiveness was striking, as was the clear happiness of mother and daughter. It seems to me to be significant that this remains one of the few recognitions in my mind that there was a wanted and treasured daughter to be grieved for. As I commented on this photo, the patient was able to tell me of her pride in her daughter's beauty, her resentment and wound at being left with the children who were less so, and her shame about these forbidden feelings, not allowed to good mothers. It seemed likely she had brought the photos in order to open up this conversation. She then told me she had been in the cellar, wondering how Anna had done what she did, what the gun had felt like in her hand, looking at what was still scattered on the floor. She went on to tell me a dream. She was looking at Anna in her coffin, seeing her breathing through the window in the coffin. She opened it and the two spoke together, about the girl's life, her feelings. In the dream she told her mother why she had killed herself. At the end of the dream Anna stayed alive. Mrs D did not remember the reason the dreamed Anna had given for killing herself. However, it was quite clear that had she done so, she would have taken this as the real cause, not that *she* had *dreamed* this.

As she told me this dream, to which she had no associations, other than the wish to have remembered what the dreamed child had said, I was very aware of the painfulness of the dream, the awfulness of the situation, identified with a mother whose daughter would be dead by suicide. This was of course partly because of the communication of the essential human pain. But it was also a reaction to the previous material: I had been very concerned as she spoke of wandering in the cellar as to just what her state of mind was. I also did not think I could rely on her to tell me if she were to feel in danger of killing herself. Or indeed, if she did not feel like it, that it would be possible to tell me this in a straightforward way. I spoke to her of her need to have me know how unbearable her feelings were for her, her loss and her desperate wish for facts, to *know*, in order not to feel helpless, exposed, vulnerable to disaster and unpredictability. I felt I recognised this state of mind very well. I had found myself in sessions listening to her material and her dreams as reassurance about her survival until the next time I saw her. This was a fruitless occupation, replacing any attentive listening and effort to understand the patient. In fact in this session she had spoken of mother not hearing her when she complained of being excluded from a family holiday everyone else had enjoyed. She told me, not for the first time, that I did not see her often enough and this was why she had so much to say when she came.

I took this up as her belief that I was impervious to her, that she felt abandoned during the week and moreover that I was critical and angry with her for asking for attention and for complaining . She ended that session very distressed and angry about her daughter's suicide – what kind of a statement had her daughter felt she had to make? – and about the painful reality that they were both deprived of the chance of having a better relationship.

Mrs D then returned to the next session with a similar dream about opening the coffin and speaking to her daughter. However, at the end of the conversation Anna became incorporated into a greetings card in 3-D relief. For the first time the patient had associations to this dream. She mentioned a recent newspaper item where a woman who had been certified as dead had been found to be alive in the mortuary. ( In fact I had been aware in the previous session of this news item but she had not mentioned it). She also spoke about a rather surreal film she had seen where a girl had gone into her mother's head and brought out a previously dead and unmourned child. The three had spoken together before the child had returned into the mother's head. The mother then began to grieve. The patient went on to tell me about her own adolescence when it seems as though she had caused as much anxiety to her parents, and been as delinquent as Anna had been.

This was the first time she was able to have an association to her own dream. She had gone on to speak about her troubled teens, owning also for the first time some of her own disturbance rather than just seeing herself as the victim of misunderstanding, neglect or violence. In addition, by having both dream and association the patient implicitly asked for my input. This was in contrast to the more usual situation where she brought a dream and then 'interpreted' it to substantiate already existent beliefs about herself and her relationships with others, often very condemning of herself or them. Perhaps the dream, where Anna returned to a three dimensional image on a two dimensional background stood for an aspect of the patient moving towards the border of a potentially symbolic relationship to the contents of her mind – to a 3 dimensional world. This would open up the possibility of building some internal sustenance which would allow her to grieve and make real reparation. To do this, she needed to acknowledge her ambivalence about this death, the relief that she no longer had the alive Anna with whom she had to struggle.

Following this session Mrs D got drunk at a family gathering and blurted out that she had had a termination of pregnancy when her youngest son was five. There was great consternation – the boy felt he could also have been an abortion, and her pregnant cousin became agitated. However, there was also concern and discussion about her husband's having left the decision about continuing the pregnancy to her and about his having refused to come with her for the abortion. That night the patient had had a dream of herself cleaning up an 18-month-old toddler. It seemed to me, on hearing this, that there had been a disguised confession of murder with the possibility of the emergence of something other than retribution. Subsequent to this she arranged to see the senior doctor in the Adolescent Unit and took her to task about the failure of the services provided for her daughter. Whilst this did contain split-off aspects of her rage with me for how little I was providing, I think her object had become a less fearsome figure, less suffused with murderous projections and consequently more approachable so that an arguably necessary meeting could be had. Following this meeting she came to her next session in a very agitated state, speaking of her hatred of her daughter when she was alive and her consequent fear that she had caused her death. She described her daughter saying she would kill her and then herself. Mrs D had severe chest pain – heartache perhaps. She was more aware of the reality of her daughter's death and of the unbearable thought that it might have been preventable. Her ambivalence was more available, and this lessened the identification, consequently increasing pain and anguish. Again, however, the quality of resentment at being exposed to these memories and feelings was present, as well as the possibility of anguish.

I think this sequence of events illustrated the nature of the dilemma for this patient. When she could genuinely feel some help, it opened up the possibility of hope for herself, of maternal objects being available *to her*. This opening is immediately filled with guilt about what she could not provide for her loved daughter and the awareness of the impossibility of being able to now repair this in reality. It possibly also reactivated triumph – she is not dead, the other is (the hated rival, the embodiment of the parental relationship from which she is excluded), with an immediate increase in persecutory guilt and fear of retaliation. It was hard for the patient to hold this without immediately having to project the responsibility to another object, who was to be pursued for wrongdoing and negligence.

This patient also had many dreams of oedipal conflicts, rivalries, competitiveness with her sisters, her attractive mother going out with father, that is dreams where the content would seem to indicate the possibility of working through her anxieties and defences. However, the most marked feature was the quality of the way in which she reported them. This linked to the real difficulty presented by her dreams and in trying to understand their role in her treatment. This patient knew dreams were important to therapists and she, I think genuinely, invested them with significance. I had a sense however of being presented with an irrefutable fact: there was nothing to be explored, discovered, thought about, there was no depth or latent content and few associations, and so there was no role for me other than to function as the passive recipient of – royal material. Of course this can resonate with the difficulty of bearing my own sense of not knowing what to say when a patient in such need brought material I did not understand, be it dreams or anything else. And of course this therapy, like much work with traumatised patients, was dominated by an irrefutable fact – of terrible and irreparable external damage, that is not just in phantasy.

I want to come back to my experience in the sessions of listening to the dreams in the way I sometimes did, that is, as a kind of secret evidence for her state of mind, looking for material that would alleviate my own anxieties . It is of course likely this was related to the difficulty of helping this patient to bear what had to be borne. I think though it was also related to another quality that pervaded the sessions. There was a sense of rarely being in receipt of a direct communication from her, but rather of being operated on in some way to feel guilt and anxiety with a vaguely indefinable feeling that this was my responsibility. I had done something wrong or missed something with potentially dire consequences, but was not in a position to know what. I think it linked to an aspect of the patient about which she slowly became more open. This was a tendency to take things belonging to others, be it goods or private information. She had various justifications and supports for all of these. So, as well as a controlling and rather torturing quality in the communication, there was no sense of a readily available object to give to and take from. A feeding relationship had to be established on the sly. The kind of awareness that would acknowledge indebtedness and the need for boundaries was then evaded.

Mrs D was able to speak at times of her anguish and puzzlement. How could love become as embroiled as it did? She realised that she had so much thought of her daughter as a part of her she had not realised she had to have a relationship with her. And to do this, they had to be separate beings, not fused.

After about eight months I was able to offer Mrs D a weekly session. She felt grateful for this but resentful. I would want her to work as her first therapist had done and this was cruel, and evidence of my being uncaring. Despite this protest she came to the next session with the first dream for some time which carried an overt acknowledgement that her daughter was dead. In this she was telling another woman she had had four children but one daughter was now dead. This was a rare event.

135

There had been a lack in this patient of dreams typical of mourning; for example where a loss is directly acknowledged, a death or a funeral, perhaps displaced onto another figure but still present in the dream. (It was not until some eighteen months after the bereavement that the patient could more consistently have dreams where, for example, her daughter walked away from her.)

At this time in treatment she went on to dream that Anna was alive and she felt joyful. I have wondered if this was related to her mother being diagnosed with a potentially terminal condition immediately after this, so not long before the anniversary of Anna's death. The patient had almost seen this as a deliberate ploy on mother's part to gain attention for herself, a kind of competing demand for her feelings. Any attempt on my part to interpret this as a defence against pain was heard as my demand she pay attention to mother. Her mother did recover. Although she overtly maintained an attitude of unconcern, it was then that mother began to enter her dreams. The patient's attitude to this was one of astonishment that she could allow her mother mental space. There was an overt wish to deny her mother a meaningful existence. At the same time it became possible to understand with her that the internal, and at times actual, poisonous arguments with mother over which of them was causing the conflict and bad feeling between them was also an argument over who caused the death of her daughter. With this came a little recognition of mother's actual frailty and a wish for better feeling between them, a rare desire for her to have.

Mrs D then began to have dreams she has had repetitively for many years and which she had not had in the months that followed her bereavement. These were of herself either walking in fields of faeces, or of going to the lavatory or to shower, only to find a bathroom covered in faeces and nowhere clean to use. She eventually told me she used to smear as a child, and spoke of her parents' fastidious attitude to cleanliness. There were indications that she remained preoccupied with her bowels in various ways. The content of the dreams do seem to indicate the lack of an object available to clean up, to sort out and make good. I am not sure why these dreams stopped and started when they did.

To end this account I will give a dream which the patient had very near the termination of her therapy. In this she is supposed to be on a stage playing a part. The audience are waiting. She realises she has not brought the shoes to play the part and so someone else has to play it. She felt very upset in the dream, as yet again she had done something self destructive. When we talked about this dream she told me Anna

136

used particularly to borrow her shoes. She spoke of her irritation at her own ever present tendency to please or make an impact on others. I had immediately recalled the session shortly after the suicide when she had come to her session in the shoes her daughter regularly borrowed. She told me she remembered it. I think this dream illustrated her conflict at the end of therapy – would she be able to allow her daughter to play her part and she, the patient, play hers, or would she leave me as her daughter left her? Her pull is to play the other's part, but in the dream she has to leave the stage, play her own. It could be considered as a gift to me.

## Conclusion

The pressures on the therapist in this treatment were twofold. One was the need to hear and hence to help the patient bear the enormity of what had happened to her, its effect on her concept of herself and her future life, as well as the unavoidable anguish and guilt. This is an expected therapeutic task, essential in mourning. The other was however more indicative of the patient's own disturbance and more problematic in the countertransference. This was the quality I have tried to describe in my experience of her dreams and her relationship with me. Insofar as the experience in the room was overwhelming for the therapist, often leading to my listening for reassurance about her survival, then my capacity to *think*, to know this was countertransference, was impaired. When I listened in this way, for reassurance, I repeated the inattentiveness to the patient's real state of mind. This is the complaint against her maternal object – one of not being properly attended to, thus little basis being established to begin to bear separateness. Thus ordinary 'neglect', parents going out together, the end of a session, turn into concrete and absolute murder of the self.

There was an aspect of the patient, indicated by this means of communication, that was not aligned with the therapist in the provision of help and the continuance of life and hope. This is terribly important to assess and take proper account of. It is important not to underestimate the malignity of the forces against life. Unlike some patients, with Mrs D it is not that deliberate plans for suicide would have been concealed. It is more that the secret pull to death, the fusion with the daughter, could overtake her limited capacity to bear the pains and losses of everyday life. It was the provision of real external figures, who could be available to the patient in different ways, providing concrete support, sometimes medication, sometimes advice, the knowledge of a

137

potential actual 'place of safety', that allowed the therapist to work analytically. In addition the communication between professionals allowed us all to function in our different roles, and hence to think about anxiety and assess risk properly. I would suggest this can only work well when each party values the others' function – a good, not a rivalrous or envious, parental couple is achieved. Father is needed to support mother in her task of caring for the baby.

There was a dangerous secret: that the therapy existed to keep her daughter alive. With the end of the therapy would come a crisis. One can see the hints of this – her anger when I exposed her to reality or to pain, a need for me to not take another view which would serve as a reminder of my separate existence, the seductiveness of the 'inside' knowledge. This indicates a further management problem. With patients like this the pressure, unspoken, on the therapist can be such that the end of therapy cannot be contemplated and both shy away from thinking about it. Or alternatively, in order to end, the therapist can turn away from his or her knowledge of the extent of the patient's own disturbance, a view promoted by these patients. Despite what seems like an acknowledgement of their own vulnerabilities, examination of their beliefs indicates how far others are held responsible for the position in which they find themselves. This is perhaps indicated by the infliction on themselves of terribly persecuting interpretations and accusations from others, not in fact real insight although sometimes appearing to be so.

In these situations the therapist may again need the presence of a third figure, either in a supervisory capacity, or an actual resource to which the patient can, if needed, turn. This may include consideration of future treatment, psychotherapeutic or other, or the provision of consultation or follow up. With patients where there is a seeming idealisation of analysis or therapy this can resonate with the therapist's own omnipotence, making it difficult to keep in mind not only the stresses of, but also the help provided by, the external world. The recognition within the patient of an ongoing vulnerability to the vicissitudes of life involves an internalisation of a non-omnipotent figure. This can help avoid the need for blame to be projected into others, or the need for a further crisis, even tragedy, so that others are required to act. Bit by bit it then becomes more possible for failings to be faced, shame to be overcome, and a need for help acknowledged.

# 9

# Identificatory Processes in Trauma

*Shankarnarayan Srinath*

Jorge Semprun was a young inmate in the concentration camp at Buchenwald when the first allied soldiers arrived at the camp to liberate it. Here he sees his fear and panic mirrored in the soldiers' horrified faces, a horror which belonged to both of them. The soldiers are, at that moment, identified with the man: *'They stand amazed before me, and suddenly, in that horror-stricken gaze, I see myself ... they stare at me, wild-eyed with panic ... And if their eyes are a mirror, then mine are those of a mad man'*, (Semprun, 1997).

Identification is not only an important developmental process, contributing significantly to the formation of identity and character, but it is also a mechanism of defence, one of the ways we have of maintaining psychic equilibrium. It plays an important role in the overwhelming experiences of survivors of trauma. It influences how survivors react to their sense of inner fragmentation and dislocation, and attempt to reintegrate their experiences. In this paper I shall discuss the psychotherapy of an adult patient who was severely traumatized as a child, concentrating on the identificatory processes as they presented themselves in the sessions. I shall highlight how these processes maintained the patient's predicament and how their eventual recognition helped in allowing them to be relinquished. The gradual development of new identifications has contributed towards some resolution of the patient's most severe pathology.

## Identification as a Developmental Process

Primary identification is defined as a state that exists before a firm boundary between self and object representations has been established. In secondary identification, the more commonly implied meaning of the term identification, 'the representational boundaries between the self and the object is not lost, but the subject embodies in the self-

139

representation attributes of the object, real or phantasied' (Sandler and Perlow, 1987).

Our sense of identity is derived from identifications with different aspects of our objects. We discover ourselves through the images that we perceive in the eyes and looks of others, seeing ourselves in others and finding ourselves in the process. We learn to relate to others through a complex process of identifications and dis-identifications, developing a capacity to move between one's own point of view and those of others.

Schafer (1968) states: 'In its fullest sense, the process of identifying with an object is unconscious, though it may also have prominent and significant preconscious and conscious components; in this process the subject modifies his motives and behaviour patterns, and the self representations of that object; through identification, the subject both represents as his own one or more regulatory influences or characteristics of the object that have become important to him and continues his tie to the object'.

Identification, according to Freud (1921), is the earliest emotional tie. Character is based upon the memory traces of our earliest identifications. Although he used the word loosely and did not write directly of mother-infant relationships, he spoke of 'the oceanic feeling' which was a reflection of the earlier blissful union with the mother (Freud, 1930). He seemed to refer in this context to the primary identification with the mother when there was no differentiation between the self and the outside world represented by the mother.

Winnicott (1952) felt that we could speak only of baby and mother as one, and that there was 'no such thing as a baby'. The baby gains his early sense of security through the exploration of his first social relationship. He sees himself reflected in his mother's eyes and expressions. He actively searches her face to meet her eyes. She responds with her smile and voice. He reacts with pleasure to her, which evokes further responses. 'What does the baby see when he or she looks at the mother's face? I am suggesting that ordinarily, what the baby sees is himself or herself. In other words, the mother is looking at the baby, and what she looks like is related to what she sees there.' (Winnicott, 1967) Searles (1963) makes a similar point that the child recognises his own feelings through the mother's emotional responses to him. Bowlby (1969) speaks of the importance of the baby's recognition of the mother's face and the mother's smile in the development of the baby's attachment to her.

Melanie Klein, in 'Notes on Some Schizoid Mechanisms' (1946),

140

took the understanding of the complexity of identification further with her description of the process she called *projective identification*. In projective identification, a part of the self that is felt to be unacceptable or the feelings of pain and fear (or other forms of psychic pain) that are evoked by certain intolerable experiences are split off and projected into the outside world. It is, in an infant, also a way of communicating unconsciously with the mother, and therefore important for both biological and psychic survival. Thus projective identification, as well as being an intrapsychic process like projection, occurs in a relationship with an external object and affects both the subject and the object (Sodre, 1995).

Bion (1962) extended this concept to introduce the notion of the mother as the container of the infant's intolerable feelings, communicated to her through projective identification. The distressed and helpless infant evokes a corresponding experience in the mother by his verbal and non-verbal behaviour. A receptive mother, by a strong introjective identification, allows the evocation of these feelings in her. The mother, through her reverie (derived from the French word, 'to dream'), gives significance to the infant's somatic and sensory experiences (beta elements) and transforms them through thinking into something more manageable to the infant (alpha elements). The infant stores the experience in his mind and eventually can sustain himself in the event of his mother's absence. The absent object thus becomes an impetus for the development of thought and a mental space (O'Shaughnessy, 1964; Segal, 1983). Winnicott (1966) writes of the mother: 'She was a baby once, and she has in her memories of having been a baby; she also has memories of having been cared for, and these memories either help or hinder her in her own experience as a mother'.

The child thus begins to develop his own identity through progressive identifications, by links and changes in self and internal representations of objects. His development is of course influenced by the dynamic organization of the family, by how his parents assume their roles and relate to each other (Ackerman, 1958), and by their reactions to his developing identifications. This process would inevitably be affected by traumatic experiences such as loss of parents or siblings, exposure to situations of violence, seduction, illness and deprivation, physical and mental illness in the family and major changes affecting the whole family. How a child is marked by these events will surely depend on how his parents react to them, on the availability of significant objects other than the parents and on the child's stage of development (Schafer, 1968).

### Identification as a Defensive Strategy After Trauma

A massive traumatic experience profoundly affects a person's perception of the world. Survivors struggle with a confusion of feelings such as sadness, despair, guilt, shame, anger and aggression. These provoke intense pain. Identification, in its various guises, may be used defensively for one's psychic survival. It may be guided by various motives, for example to deny distressing feelings of loss and abandonment, to gain independence from the object or traumatic event, to master fear or to get rid of intolerable feelings of guilt and shame.

For example, following a profound loss or separation, there can be a narcissistic identification of the ego with the lost object. Freud (1915b) describes it with his famous statement: 'The shadow of the object fell upon the ego and the latter could henceforth be judged by a special agency, as though it were an object, the forsaken object. In this way, an object loss was transformed into an ego loss, and the conflict between the ego and the loved person into a cleavage between the critical agency of the ego and the ego as altered by identification'.

A shadow implies the presence of darkness and Freud (1905) links the fear of darkness to the loss of a loved one. The ego, overwhelmed by the loss and in its attempt to deny it, becomes the lost object. Freud (1921) cites an example of a child who was unhappy over the loss of a kitten. The boy declared that he himself was the kitten, crawled on all fours and would not eat at the table. Thus during mourning identification with the lost object is a defence against the trauma of loss.

Anna Freud in 1936 described the defence of identification with the aggressor. This identification need not necessarily be with the aggressor himself, but may be with his aggressive act, or indeed simply with the aggression itself. The roles are reversed in this defence; the victim attempts to render the object he dreads harmless by identifying with it and thereby turning into the aggressor. We have the common saying, 'If you can't beat them, join them'.

Anna Freud illustrates her point with several examples. A little girl was afraid of seeing ghosts in the dark, and would run across the dark hall making magical gestures. 'There is no need to be afraid in the hall,' she said triumphantly to her little brother, 'You just have to pretend that you are the ghost who might meet you'.

Identification with the aggressor can thus be seen as a person's attempt at control and mastery over a traumatic or threatening situation by turning the passive role into an active role (Freud, 1920). Freud believed that the chronic repetitive post-traumatic nightmares of soldiers following battle were an unconscious attempt by the ego to master the overwhelming experience. He thought that children's play in the wake of a trauma might have a similar creative function to help them gain control of the situation. 'As the child passes over from the passivity of the experience to the activity of the game, he hands on the disagreeable experience to one of his playmates and in this way revenges himself on a substitute.'

This defence, like all defences, can become pathological. For example, the sexually abused child becomes an adult paedophile; a bullied child becomes a bully himself; children mistreated by their parents in turn treat their own children badly, thus perpetuating pathological family patterns.

Bettelheim (1960) gives examples of identification with the aggressor in concentration camps. Some long-standing prisoners tended to assume the attitudes of the Gestapo towards new prisoners who were seen as weak, unable to withstand the hardship of the camp and unlikely to live beyond the first few weeks. They were also considered more likely to turn traitors. They were therefore thought to be a liability and the old prisoners, in order to hasten their end, assigned them the dangerous tasks and did not assist them when they needed help. Old prisoners adopted the aggressive behaviour of the SS, both verbal and physical. It was sometimes motivated by the wish to appease the guards, but it was also believed to be the right way of treating prisoners in the camp. They also tried to copy the appearance of the SS by sewing old pieces of SS uniform to their prison clothes even though they were punished for doing so.

## Rescue Phantasies as a Defence

Survivors of trauma may sometimes be preoccupied with rescue phantasies or be driven by a compulsive desire to rescue others. Although this behaviour may have something genuinely reparative in it, it can also be an attempt to deal with the survivor's own intolerable feelings of helplessness, impotence, guilt and humiliation, via a projective identification into others of those feelings. This defensive strategy can also become grandiose and omnipotent. The rescuer, in his attempt to protect someone he perceives as the victim, can become an aggressor himself, through re-enacting in the process the traumatic situation he has himself endured in the past, thus playing the roles of both victim and victimiser. For example, a depressed young man, who had suffered horrific abuse from his father in a violent family setting, sought help

143

because of his fear that he would harm his own little son. On one occasion he had seen a small boy being chided by his father in the street, and he had felt impelled to protect the child. He separated the father and son and seriously assaulted the father, and the police had to be called in to drag him away from the scene.

This represents one of the ways in which projective identification can be used defensively in traumatic situations. In other situations using the same defence, the hatred of the terror or despair originally felt by the survivor may be directed towards the object who is perceived as containing those disowned parts of the self (Klein, 1946). Alternatively, the survivor may take into himself, appropriating as his own, good or bad characteristics of the object. I shall give an example of this kind of introjective identification in my clinical illustration.

There is an interplay of projective and introjective mechanisms in projective identification (Sodre, 1995). It affects, at least in the subject's phantasy, the identity of both himself and his recipient, often resulting in confusion of identities (Rosenfeld, 1949). The loss of aspects of the self may result in loss of contact with himself and thus make the task of recovery, whether in or out of therapy, more difficult. In the long term, a determined forestalling of the return of the projected parts of the self may lead to emotional depletion and a rigidity of character.

Survivors may resort to other defensive manoeuvres to protect themselves from, or provide opposition to, feelings and experiences when they become intolerable. Pathological organizations of the personality (Rosenfeld, 1971; Steiner, 1987), intended to protect the individual from pain, also hinder or prevent any resolution. Feelings may also be evaded by denial of the traumatic experience and by attempts to obliterate the event or minimize its impact. But 'every denial requires further denials to be able to maintain the original one, and every repression, to be continued, demands further repression' (Bettelheim, 1952). The survivor may assume a total identity related to the trauma, for example, as a victim, a refugee or as sexually abused. He may become emotionally detached. Or he may develop a pathological hatred of himself. The experience for some may be so overwhelming, as with victims of the holocaust (op. cit.), that they may feel that reintegration is impossible. Often survivors seek repeated reassurances from others that they are not guilty and deserved to be saved, but feel crushed if these reassurances are not easily available.

## 9. Identificatory Processes in Trauma

### The Need for Mourning

Successful working through of a traumatic experience depends on the survivor's capacity to mourn. He needs to separate from the lost object and from the event by painfully relinquishing what belongs to them and refinding in the process what belongs to himself. This separation demands repeated dis-identification (Sandler and Joffe, 1967) and the creation of firm boundaries between himself and the object. It is only then that true reparation is possible.

The capacity to mourn the traumatic event and its consequences is determined by both external and internal factors (Garland, 1991). The traumatic event, when too horrific, may buckle even the most stable and resolute psychic structure, making mourning difficult or impossible. The event may also revive feelings related to earlier traumata, both conscious and unconscious. What these might be will of course be influenced by constitutional factors, the earliest experiences with the mother, the stage of psychic development at the time of the trauma and the accompanying phantasies.

### Clinical Illustration

I shall now illustrate these processes as they occurred in the case of Mr A, a young African whom I saw in once-weekly psychotherapy for a number of years. He had visited his family doctor for some time, complaining of long-standing anxiety. When on one of these visits he revealed that he had witnessed, as a seven year-old, his mother being killed by his father, his GP recognised the important connection between this event and his present state, and referred him to the Trauma Unit.

Mr A had always been an anxious person, but had experienced increasing panic, terror and rage for no conscious reason in recent years. He was afraid that he would fall apart and go mad. He was often immobilized by these feelings and stayed indoors. He had been frozen with panic on his way to work one day, unable to go forward but yet frightened that he would not be able to leave again if he returned home. He was also phobic, afraid of spiders, of travelling on lifts and the underground. He had waited outside his house for several hours once, terrified of a spider inside, until a friend had arrived to remove it. He had nightmares of his mother's formless presence in the house transforming itself into a spider and chasing him out.

He was an only child who had grown up in an unhappy household

145

dominated by the violence between his parents. His mother was secretive as Mr A had himself become. She beat him and told him not to mix with other children in the neighbourhood as she saw other families as beneath them. He had also been also told not to speak to others about the family. He had nonetheless tried to tell people what was happening between his parents, but none had intervened.

Mr A had been the only witness to his mother's murder. His father had returned home on that fateful day with a present for him, and the mother had felt excluded and ignored. An argument had erupted between the parents, which had escalated into violence. The little boy sat outside the kitchen and listened to the shouting inside, wanting to go in but also frightened of it. Curiosity had however got the better of him. He had pushed the door open and had seen, at that moment, his father plunging a knife into his mother. He had become, unable to speak the unspeakable, mute for a long time after the murder and this had protected him from the demand to testify against his father. He had been placed in a residential school and had regained his speech gradually with the help of a kindly teacher. He had refused to see his father in prison. His father had hanged himself in prison several years later.

Mr A had shown remarkable resilience during his life-time by educating himself and having a stable job. However he had led an isolated hermetic life. He had been married in the past to a woman who had been unable to have children, and they had led separate lives, choosing not to socialise together. His wife did not know of his past. He was most comfortable in the company of his dog.

He used humour and irony with a deceptive charm, often making a joke of painful things. He would say, for example, of his suicidal feelings that he could not jump off a building because he was afraid of heights, or throw himself in front of a bus because the buses in his area never arrived. He would try to fix me with an intense wide-eyed gaze as if testing me to see if I had believed or understood what he had said. He was extremely sensitive to changes in the setting, and reacted with alarm and agitation to unavoidable changes in time or to shifts of furniture in the room.

For a long time in the course of therapy, I needed to be more like the mute witness that he himself had been, an unobtrusive listener to his story. He seemed to see me in no particular way, but there was a certain fragility in his manner which betrayed a precarious sense of personal balance and the threat that it could easily be disturbed.

Mr A's way of talking about his tragic experience and the measures he took to deny the event were complicated. Persecutory feelings of

146

shame and guilt compelled him to split off and deny his previous identity. He spoke of it not as his experience, but as that of a clingy seven year-old boy with whom he had nothing to do. The event was nevertheless alive in him. He felt pursued by his monstrous past and was frightened of exploring and acknowledging the full implications of what had happened to him. He had, after his father had killed himself, left his home country, changed his name and destroyed all evidence of his past. He had mutilated or thrown away all photographs and severed contact with relatives and people he knew or who had any knowledge of the incident.

He had created a whole new world for himself. He had constructed various accounts of his life from his childhood and had identified strongly with these constructions. He had conjured up idealized parents for himself, modelling them on the parents of other children at school whom he had admired. The idealised family was warm and protective. There were no threatening conflicts in it. He got into relationships with people who impressed him with stories of their own family life. He desperately wanted to be included by them, but became threatened when they wanted to know about him. He would then become indifferent towards them and withdraw, and they reciprocated similarly. He would then want to spite them for keeping him at a distance and would want to avenge his hurt. He also judged these families with the ideal family in his mind and inevitably found them disappointing. There was a complex mixture of envy, idealization and contempt in his interactions.

These strong split identifications – on the one hand with the tragedy from which he was trying desperately to escape and on the other with the stories he had compiled to defend against it – presented a dilemma. There was often a confusion of internal and external reality for both of us in the sessions and it was difficult to know what was real and what was not in his stories. His sense of identity was confused and confusing as a consequence.

Mr A felt stigmatized by the identity that the killing had imposed on him. He felt ashamed of himself and his parents. He felt guilty and responsible for what happened because the argument between his parents had begun with the gift that his father had brought for him. The feelings of shame and guilt influenced his behaviour inside and outside the sessions. He was secretive with me, taking care not to reveal the identities of the people or places in his narrative. He warned me against what he saw as my intrusiveness and was afraid that I would take him over. He was frightened that psychotherapy would destroy the firm

147

identity that the event had given him and he would not know who he was. He was scared of inviting people to his house. He thought there was little for them to see and yet was concerned about what they might find, implying that there was little inside him apart from his shameful secret. When he was offered a lift home by colleagues, he was careful to get out at a fair distance from home lest his house was identified.

He was frightened that a catastrophe would befall him again and he tried to protect himself against it with obsessional defences and by attempts at an omnipotent control. For a long time, he seemed to be always dressed against bad weather. He was alarmed by any change of routine. He checked things over again and again before he left the house, the hobs, the oven, the switches and the locks. He pulled out all the plugs in case of fire. When we met for the first time he was agitated, afraid that his house might have burnt down while he was away. He had gone home from work before he had come to see me, to ensure that the house had not been damaged.

He was often afraid to speak. He felt that his thoughts would become real when he put them into words. They would then have a life of their own and he was concerned that he would have no control over them.

While Mr A was hesitant to speak about things, he conveyed his experiences through projective identification and enactments. For example, he desired closer contact with others but was also terrified of it because for him intimacy carried the risk of violence and murder. His feelings of dependence were split off and located in his wife, and his contempt for those needs were then directed at his wife. He was mocking of her attempts to care for him, and of her close relationship with her own family. He also projected his curiosity, his wish to be noticed and his awareness of things into others and was then assailed by thoughts of what others might be thinking of him. He talked pejoratively of his colleagues as nosy and gossiping. He tantalized me with snippets about what he did, but was careful not to give me details. He took care never to reveal the names of the people or places in his narrative, so that my own experience was often like reading the headlines in a newspaper with no small print. He came excitedly to a session once carrying a large shopping bag but rapidly became agitated that I might want to look into his bag.

There was in his mind no object with curiosity that was also not persecutory. Interpreting gradually that his own fear of the curiosity of others about him was also partly his own curiosity about himself and the threat that it carried for him, helped to alleviate the feelings of persecution.

148

He had heard, about a year into treatment, that a colleague had been killed in an accident while on holiday. For many sessions he struggled with whether or not he believed this story. The event brought into the open his feelings about his mother. He felt her to have been provocative, wilful and aggressive, and like the colleague, had invited her own death. He thought he too was like his mother, but was more successful than she had been; he felt strongly that he would have avoided the killing. His identification was therefore with his mother, but he dealt omnipotently with the feelings he had introjected and identified with.

Mr A told me just before a break with a mixture of urgency and excitement, while being dismissive of the break, that he stole things, sometimes things that he wanted but more often simply what was available. He felt he was a ghost of a person and nobody saw him. It was when he felt irrelevant and unreal that he stole. It made him a man of substance, a man with a history and a past; but each episode was soon followed by guilt and depression. In fact, he had been stealing from the age of eight. He had hated it when other children in the residential school went home to their families during the holidays while he had to stay in the school. He would steal when he was invited to his friends' houses, sometimes what he felt should have been his by right, sometimes what he rationalised was not important to them and would not therefore be missed.

The confession of stealing at this time was an unconscious communication of his various feelings evoked by the impending break, at the same time as he was consciously denying its impact on him. He aroused my concern by informing me that he got into dangerous situations when he felt abandoned. He conveyed his sense of desolation and deprivation, his feeling that others had families that he felt deprived of, and I was stealing his sessions. Also while he consciously obliterated his past, he also seemed to entertain an unconscious wish to be caught, which would have made it inevitable that his history was revealed. Perhaps this way he could have felt real and ceased to be a ghost. There was also a compelling excitement in it. The stealing, with its manic excitement, helped him to override the awareness of the aggression in his stealing and the accompanying feelings of guilt. Interpretation of these processes brought some conscious recognition of his various motives into the sessions, and helped him to tolerate the sense of abandonment and to avoid stealing during the break.

While Mr A struggled to keep control over what happened to him, particular external events two years after the start of therapy forced him to enact his internal situation. He and his wife had taken a lodger to supplement their income. The lodger was apprehended by the police for drunken driving and was brought home in the early hours of the morning. Mr A had panicked, shouted at the police and refused to let them in. He felt implicated and accused, and was at pains to tell me that he had done nothing wrong. He was agitated that the news, with his address, would appear in the local newspaper. He was afraid of being found out and wanted to run away.

The incident became a living nightmare for him. It brought out forcibly the previous incident, the killing of his mother, the publicity surrounding it, his feeling of shame and guilt, and the upheaval and exposure he had re-experienced when his father had committed suicide. He shifted back and forth from one incident to the other in the sessions and it was often difficult to recognize which of them he was referring to. Time had reversed its course and in his mind the past and the present had become inseparable.

Another theme that has been prominent is an identification with his parents' marriage manifested in his jealousy and aggression. He was incensed when he discovered that his wife was having an affair with another man. He stabbed her in the arm with a knife during the argument that ensued. He was alarmed by what he had done and took her to the casualty department of the local hospital. He wanted to confess to the staff what he had done, but was dissuaded by his wife from doing so. He had felt that the kitchen had been contaminated. He had scrubbed it repeatedly and, dissatisfied with it, had changed it at much expense. Mr A had replayed the family drama, identifying with the father as the aggressor and identifying his wife with his mother. His jealousy, like his mother's, had been explosive and had resulted in violence.

I often wondered why Mr A had sought help now when he had split his life successfully to survive for so long. One possible factor was the death of one of his two dogs five years ago. He had found the dogs as mongrel pups abandoned behind a railway yard. He had taken them home and doted on them. The dog that had died had been run over by a car and he had felt devastated. Things had not been the same again and something inside him had collapsed. He had felt punished for awful things that he had done. His panic attacks had begun not long after this death. He could no longer wholly identify with the dogs and take care effectively of his own dependent parts projected into them. Recognising the breakdown in his functioning (the breakdown of the projective identification) enabled him to seek help from the external world in the form of therapy.

Mr A has made significant changes in himself. His claustro-agoraphobic anxieties have diminished. There is a more flexible use of space and of his objects. His world has enlarged. He can now travel on the underground. He is able to tolerate changes in the setting. There are more people in his social life. He is now able to invite friends to his house. The dreams in the early phase of treatment were set in dark and dingy houses and boxes, full of dangerous spiders and cobwebs. The houses have gradually developed extensions and gardens, and are inhabited by people.

The burden of his secret has lightened in the telling. Although still frightened of others knowing about him, he no longer feels on his own. He is surprised by his own thoughts and awareness, and more able to tolerate curiosity in both self and others. There is often a request that I enlarge on my train of thought to show how I have arrived at an interpretation.

### Conclusion

I have tried to show the enormous and formative impact of massive childhood trauma on my patient's sense of identity. His identification with the event and its characters, and his counter-identifications to deal with the mental pain of this situation conspired to blur the distinction between phantasy and reality. These identificatory processes are complex, never easy to understand fully, and are particularly powerful and compelling following a trauma. In Mr A, changes gradually became possible through an exploration of these identifications in his enactments. Eventually he was able to begin the reconstruction of an internal – and hence external – world through gradual dis-identifications and the concurrent growth of new and more lively internal objects.

# Part Four

# Psychoanalysis

# 10

# Developmental Injury

## Its Effect on the Inner World

### Nicholas Temple

### Introduction

The concept of psychic trauma or injury has been associated with psychoanalysis from its beginnings. In adopting the concept of trauma from medicine and surgery, psychoanalysis carries the three ideas implicit in it to the psychic level: these are the ideas of violent shock, a wound and disruptive consequences affecting the whole organisation.

Freud (1916b) described the notion of trauma as an event which overwhelms mental processes by being too sudden or extreme for them to accommodate and process. As he puts it, it is 'an experience which within a short period of time presents the mind with an increase of stimulus too powerful to be dealt with or worked off in the normal way and this must result in permanent disturbances of the manner in which energy operates'.

Freud (1895) said in 'Studies in Hysteria' that the cause of neurosis was related to past traumatic experience. Effective cure was sought by means of abreaction and a psychical working out of the traumatic experiences. Abreaction derived from this early theory and has remained as a treatment in psychiatry and in those therapies that believe in catharsis as a therapeutic method.

This view changed. The part played by the external event came to be seen as less important, since external events were felt to derive their traumatic power from the fantasies they activated and from the excitation they provoked. This view has been the subject of some recent controversy. Freud has been accused of denying the importance of sexual abuse of children as a real trauma, by attributing children's memories to oedipal fantasies.

Trauma as a consequence of separation and loss rather than sexual

155

seduction was taken up first in 'Mourning and Melancholia' (1915b) and then in 'Inhibitions, Symptoms and Anxiety' (1926). Freud discusses the pathology of those who cannot come to terms with loss through the process of mourning and who develop instead the pathological state of melancholia – this is equivalent to the diagnosis of endogenous or psychotic depression in modern psychiatry.

In melancholia blame and reproach against someone who has been lost is turned on to the self in a masochistic fashion, so that there is an inability to accept the loss or failure of the person to recognise valuable aspects of the relationship. A repetitive process of recrimination is set in train. A depressed patient is preoccupied with a sense of loss and bitter grievance against a parent who has failed to measure up to their expectations. Not surprisingly, this is likely to be repeated in the transference relationship. When it occurs in a psychiatric setting it can cause the psychiatrist to feel overwhelmed by the patient's despair. The psychiatrist's wish to retaliate is aroused; hence the resort on occasion to punitive forms of treatment for depression.

Freud's work on melancholia gave rise to different developments in psychoanalysis. Melanie Klein (1935 and 1952) described the details of the struggle to come to terms with separation and loss in normal development. She described how the inability to mourn early losses and to retain a connection with good experiences results in an obstruction to development with a defensive return to a more paranoid way of functioning.

'Mourning and Melancholia' was also the inspiration for the study of traumatic loss in children. This theme was developed by Winnicott (1958) in his discussion of the anti-social tendency which he saw as a form of protest to force the environment to help to repair a trauma. Bowlby's work (1944) investigated the *traumatic effects* of separation of young children from their mothers. A letter written by Bowlby, Miller and Winnicott to the *British Medical Journal* (1939) warned against the long term traumatic consequences of separating young children from their mothers by evacuating them from cities. They warned that the risk of psychic damage caused by separation might be as great a danger as the risk of physical harm through remaining in the city during bombing.

Many analysts have followed Winnicott in being interested in the effect of pre-verbal trauma on the individual's development. Pearl King (1978) has demonstrated how this may be first detected in the analyst's affective response to the patient. These lines of development in psychoanalysis have come into conflict. One side emphasises the environment

156

and gives insufficient attention to the person's inner psychic world. Blame is put on past environmental failures for present problems in an unhelpful way. The Kleinian view, in contrast, is criticised for ignoring the traumatic effects of the environment and having no sympathy with the individual's suffering and disturbance resulting from it. This controversy is important not just theoretically. It is also significant in therapeutic technique. It is important therapeutically to keep both aspects in mind to achieve a balance, understanding the importance of the events of the past, while not colluding with the patient's wish to hold the past responsible for the present difficulties and to justify revenge. In traditional religious terms this could be seen as a conflict between the idea of original sin and the idea of sin as a reaction to injury or damage. The latter is Winnicott's view in 'The Anti-Social Tendency' (1958) and an important issue in treatment and in morality.

The justification of murder and war often goes back to a grievance or injury from the past. Shakespeare makes Richard III, in the opening soliloquy, justify his evil behaviour through the trauma of being a hunchback who was sent before his time into this world, as if he has the right to revenge himself on those who are happy because of this injury and misfortune. Thus a debate about the origin of sin is part of the conflict as to the effects of nature versus nurture, or ill nature versus the ill effects of failed nurture. Some psychoanalysts still do not accept Freud's concept of the death instinct (1920) as a primary source of destructiveness and attribute destructiveness to the effects of past trauma. This view is difficult to sustain in the face of the evidence of primary destructiveness and the use of grievance to justify harming others. Although the term 'death instinct' is somewhat unsatisfactory, implying a fixed unconscious drive, the compulsion to repeat past trauma and to use it to justify the gratification of cruelty and sadism is very strong.

The compulsion to repeat the trauma is a striking clinical feature of traumatised patients. Originally Freud, in his paper 'Remembering, Repeating and Working Through' (1914b), saw this as a resistance to remembering. This compulsion to repeat the trauma poses complex and interesting questions which I would like to explore in the discussion of my patient.

Psychic injury can occur during childhood development when serious disruption occurs in the primary relationship between mother and child. This form of trauma may be obvious and external when a mother dies or becomes seriously ill. It may be less obvious when it occurs as a result of disturbance in the mother/child relationship – for example, where a mother fails to bond with her baby.

A rather different situation exists where a phase of development proves to be difficult because the relationship between mother and child cannot adapt to changed circumstances. For example, this may occur where a mother who is happy with a compliant, rewarding baby may find it difficult when that baby becomes an active and rebellious toddler. The birth of a sibling can radically change the nature of the mother/child relationship so that it is experienced from the first-born baby's point of view as having been damaged. This will be emphasised if the mother has become depressed after the birth of the second child.

This form of trauma can be represented in adult life by a tendency to repeat the traumatic episode. A relationship that begins well may be disrupted by a tendency for the individual to bring about circumstances which resemble the point at which things originally went wrong between mother and child. This form of repetition may be an attempt to achieve reparation of the past by entering into a similar situation with a hope that something can be repaired and changed. The hope is that a different outcome can be achieved, but the repetition can result instead in reinforcement, compounding the inability to recover from the painful sense of loss derived from the disruption of the primary relationship. There is a bitter preoccupation with the failure and a tendency to anger and resentment in the repetition of it in later relationships. This will emerge in the transference with such patients, where the analyst is perceived as failing in the same way that the primary relationship with the mother had failed. This failure is felt to be unforgivable and there is a desire to punish by some form of retribution. There may be an unconscious phantasy that if the original object is punished sufficiently the wrong will be put right or made good. This is similar to the assumption behind the Spanish Inquisition where the subject was tortured to save his soul by renouncing the heresy, thus giving the torturers full justification for their deadly, cruel gratification. This preoccupation with punishment can lead to a depressive illness or chronic depressive symptoms when it is turned inward against the self and the self is tortured. It is likely that such a set of forces is normally at the root of depression.

The stage of psychosexual development at which the trauma has occurred may be represented in an individual's character by symptoms which have their roots in fixations around that particular developmental stage. These symptoms can be neurotic or psychosomatic in nature. For example, a man whose mother had a puerperal mental illness after the birth of his sister when he was 18 months old had bowel symptoms of psychosomatic origin and obsessive-compulsive traits which had their origin in this traumatic period. Thus the trauma may have a profound long-standing effect on an individual's personality. The traumatic period will remain as an active part of the individual's internal world, because it cannot easily be worked through. Unconsciously it remains the focus of resentment, pain and guilt. This preoccupation may overshadow and distort other good experiences in the individual's relationships which are pushed aside and only emerge in analytical treatment when the traumatic experience is able to be worked through sufficiently for the preoccupation with it to fade and for it to exert a less dominating effect.

While Bowlby's (1944) and Winnicott's (1958) studies have emphasised obvious traumas such as separation from mother, the traumas can be caused by subtle and complicated interactions in the mother/child relationship which are often largely unconscious to the patient, as are the subsequent patterns of their repetition. Only close observation and understanding can reveal evidence of the nature of the trauma and the way it is repeated in an individual's adult life. These are powerful influences which are hidden in the internal world. The extent of the influence of an obscure period of trauma on development is often underestimated and its enduring effect may not be realised.

## Case Discussion

I shall describe the case of a woman where a traumatic phase during her early development led to a serious disturbance of her personality, which overshadowed her positive capacity for relationships and her considerable creative abilities. She continually came back to the point at which things had gone so badly wrong between her and her mother.

The patient was referred to me after having two years of once a week therapy, because of her concern that she was making little progress in her life. She had sought help at the age of 30 because she felt she was stuck. Although she had a highly paid job in advertising, she was always short of money and lived in neglected and dirty accommodation. She drank and smoked heavily and frequently used marijuana as a way of dealing with bouts of extreme anxiety.

Her preoccupation with the past had meant that she had made little progress in adult life, and in her mid-thirties she had no relationships with men, no proper home and constant uncertainty in her career.

Her relations with others, both friends and employers, were often

159

troubled by crises in which she would feel let down and would retaliate with vicious language which usually caused her serious trouble, but she was left with a sense of satisfaction that she had had her revenge, however much damage it caused her. She was frequently in trouble with minor officials such as guards on trains or taxi drivers whom she would provoke and abuse, usually ending up successfully humiliating them, but often with serious and risky consequences to herself. At these times she was intensely excited and gratified by her sadism and later by masochism when she suffered the consequences of her outburst.

The patient believed that her difficulties were caused by the fact that when she was aged four her parents had started a business which preoccupied them for the rest of her childhood. She described spending a great deal of time on her own, in miserable loneliness. She was angry that she had been blamed for being unhappy and was criticised as a troublemaker in the family. She was dirty and untidy and suffered from encopresis and soiling until mid-adolescence. At times she deliberately soiled herself to annoy and embarrass her mother who was obsessionally clean and tidy. Thus throughout her childhood she had been characterised as rebellious, foul-mouthed and dirty. These epithets would still apply to her and are associated with a strong tendency towards sado-masochistic relationships with others. Sometimes she felt guilty about how she had treated her mother, particularly as her mother became seriously ill with breast cancer when she was 15 and had died when she was aged 20.

Work in the analysis demonstrated the likelihood that the original trauma had occurred much earlier than the age of four, as the patient had always believed. There is evidence to suggest that something had gone seriously wrong between the patient and her mother at the age of one. It is hard to know precisely what had happened but the patient found a photograph of herself at the age of 18 months, an overweight, miserable looking child; her mother was probably depressed. She did not learn to walk until the age of three. There are indications to suggest that the first year of life was one in which she was close to her mother. Her warmth and capacity to form relationships seems to be based on this earlier experience.

In her version of the trauma her mother was close to her and devoted to her and when she was four turned her back on her. The serious encopresis and the patient's interest and involvement in dirtiness and mess indicated that the second year of life may have been quite traumatic. There is much to suggest that her mother was obsessional and rigid and found the patient's assertiveness, anal preoccupation and greater independence in the second year of life difficult to cope with; hence the patient's belief that her mother turned her back and withdrew from her.

She accused me of being like her parents, self-satisfied and preoccupied with money and conventional success. This occurred at holiday breaks, after weekends and whenever she felt that I had failed to understand her. This was most often due to her conviction that I had a rigid, unbending view of her, including a fixed analytic dogma which condemned her bad behaviour over being dirty, taking drugs, missing sessions or being in a financial mess. It was necessary that I should be able to bear the chaos and mess without condemning and judging, despite her accusations, but that I should also take the mess sufficiently seriously without being overwhelmed by it. It was not always easy because of the power of the patient's capacity to project: at times, I would feel provoked into feeling critical and angry and found it hard to control a desire to shout at her. At such times she conveyed an overwhelming sense of panic.

The patient described herself as constantly accusing her parents as a child. She had exciting sadistic exchanges with her father with perverse oedipal overtones. She was at times extremely provocative in the analysis and attempted to draw me into rows about the rules of the setting or the stupidity of my comments.

For this patient there was a sense that her life remained dominated by the trauma of her childhood. She described experiences in the present which she reacted to as if she were reliving the past. If a rejection or disappointment occurred she would react in a furious, abusive way. Equally, if an opportunity arose for progress in her work or in her social life, she found herself compelled to destroy it in order to remain in a familiar equilibrium with the past. An overpowering and primitive form of guilt seemed to exist which meant that any opportunity for change had to be sacrificed. She was unable to free herself from the traumatic past and was compelled to live close to it. This had been true of her childhood, when she had turned away from help and support at school. There appeared to be two forces which maintained this state of affairs. First of all she was preoccupied with an overwhelming sense of grievance and injury and, secondly, and perhaps as a consequence of this, she had an intense sense of guilt which demanded that she should sacrifice good things in her life. These forces maintained an equilibrium which resulted in the unchanging chaos of her life.

161

She had experienced the analysis as a hopeful opportunity for change which she had consequently undermined and attacked. This first occurred in a major way when, during the first summer holiday, she embarked on a homosexual affair which had the effect of blocking the analytic work for over a year. It was also understood as the acting out of an unconscious wish to return to a fused relationship with her mother. The affair ended in trouble and bitterness when she rejected the partner.

When the analysis had seemed to her to have let her down, either by a break or by her belief that I did not understand her, she launched bitter attacks on my competence. She was full of suspicion and doubt towards me and constantly searched to discover my failings. She believed that I was not good enough for her. She especially expressed this belief when she was anxious that I was irritated with her and disapproving and had turned my back on her as she felt her mother had done, such as after a holiday or a weekend break.

The analysis was characterised by periods of progress when the patient became aware of the distorted and pathological nature of her preoccupation with the trauma and began to allow it to become less centrally important in her mind. At these times she showed the capacity to be sad about what went wrong and also to take some responsibility for the fact that she had caused a great deal of damage by her preoccupation with it. At these times she could make some progress in her life without destroying it. She made quite important changes including buying a house and having a partially successful relationship with a man. She ceased to act out so much in her career but still could not allow it to develop commensurate with her ability.

Periods of progress in the analysis seemed to be linked to the patient's sense that I could bear her destructiveness without retaliating against her. This required a capacity for me to acknowledge my shortcomings as well as to be able to tolerate her attacks without blaming her or retaliating against her. At the same time, it was important that I had a capacity to be firm with her as she tested my toleration. If I was too tolerant she became more destructive and became excited in a sadistic and triumphant way which she justified by reference to how badly she had been damaged. She easily saw tolerance as weakness which invited her to become more destructive and then guilty at the damage done.

These periods of improvement and change were not stable and easily collapsed into periods of destructiveness when the preoccupation with the past trauma was intense and the patient tended to destroy progress that had already been made, as if she would not let go of a sense of being traumatised and deprived. In these destructive phases her guilt became powerful in relation to the damage she was doing and tended to cause her to intensify the destructive spoiling of her opportunities as a form of masochistic self-punishment.

This slow work involved a constant examination of the interplay of these processes and an attempt to create a working atmosphere in which both the patient and I could examine what was going on. She always responded to what I said by feeling attacked or blamed at first, but then could gradually accept a discussion which did not blame her, but supported her capacity for responsible guilt. When this worked well it increased her insight into the seriousness of her disturbance and the way that it had wasted much of her life.

This awareness was intolerably painful to her and made her feel guilty and overwhelmed by what she had done, leading her to want to escape from it to refuge in the excitement of further destructiveness or of drugs or alcohol which could blot out painful feelings. It was thus very difficult to maintain her capacity to remain in touch with the pain and for this reason five times a week work was crucial for her. She did have the warmth and capacity to form a relationship and indeed did this intensely, but it was then disrupted and damaged by the repetition.

## Discussion

For this patient the trauma in the primary relationship had done serious damage to her capacity to reach a depressive position in which it would be possible to let go of her resentment at her mother's failure and to cope with a mother who was both good and bad at the same time. The trauma had led to a destructive and bitter preoccupation with the loss, as if she had lived all her life since that point wanting to punish the person who failed her and believing that the trauma could and should be cancelled out by revenge. Equally, her punishment and persecution led to a belief that retaliation would occur, leading to primitive guilt, based on retribution, which meant that she could not enjoy anything good and sustaining without having to destroy it. She then used the gratification of drugs, alcohol or sadistic fantasy to enable her to escape temporarily from the guilt and despair.

The effects of the trauma that has severely damaged the capacity to mourn loss have been made worse by the experience of losing an object that was strong enough to remain with her and to contain her destructive feelings. Instead, the object was experienced as retaliatory, punishing and abandoning her.

It is possible that in the eyes of her mother, the patient changed from being a good, compliant, rewarding baby to being a bad, dirty, angry, difficult infant who was extremely disturbing and whom she could not bear.

In view of the mother's probable obsessional disorder, it is possible that the patient became part of the mother's bad internal world which she then had to control with obsessional defences. Hence, I believe that the patient began to represent something in the mother's own early development and inner world which was intolerable to her. The patient had the experience of being a bad object in the eyes of the mother and of having something intolerable attributed to and projected into her. This crisis in their relationship was never healed and mutual resentment prevented later opportunities for the repair of the damage before Mother's illness and death from cancer when the patient was aged 20.

In the analysis the transference was such that frequently the analyst was characterised as being the bad object who had failed and should be punished, but also the analyst was seen sometimes to be the good object who was damaged and could not be repaired and who would turn away because of having been damaged. The patient felt that as much as she would like to give up this preoccupation with damage, she could not do so and she remained trapped by it. She feared giving it up, as if the consequences would be a psychic calamity. The sense of a grievance and the bitterness about it operated as a defence against the real acceptance of the loss and the guilt about the damage she herself had caused.

There is evidence to suggest that the trauma was treated as a kind of *cause célèbre* which justified an attack on the objects that had failed her. This attack had a strong element of sadism in it. The attack had become the focus of an organised perverse fantasy which took on a life of its own, one in which the excitement and gratification of sadism were justified, but which also served as an escape from the real sense of emptiness and loss which had accompanied the original experience of the mother's turning away. It therefore prevented any possibility of her coming to terms with that original loss. Its effect was to damage hopeful situations which made her more sharply aware of guilt. The perversion appeared in the analysis when the patient mounted extreme attacks on the analyst after small failings, or when she attacked hopeful or realistic interpretations. The perversion was also represented in forms of masochistic fantasy and acting out in which the patient was gratified by being punished or made to suffer. She had a repeated fantasy of a masochistic

164

kind in which she was violated by a revolting old man. This served both to punish her and to relieve guilt, but also to excite her.

There was some evidence to suggest that the patient's family members, particularly her father, were also excited by sadism and the patient may have met with little opposition to the development of this perverse organisation. In fact, she may have been unconsciously encouraged by the family to use this form of defence. Certainly many of her interactions with her father had a strong sado-masochistic flavour, both in the present and in her account of their past relationship.

This emphasises the point that a person's response to a trauma is complicated and may involve the secondary development of a psychic organisation such as a perversion which has predominantly sadistic or masochistic features. Some individuals may have much more help from their close relatives in coping with loss than others and some may be able to make better use of that help than others. This patient believed that she had very little support of any kind in trying to come to terms with her experience of the loss of her mother; but a number of people who did try to help her in her childhood and adolescence had to work very hard against her resistance to accepting help. Eventually her teachers did manage to help her to study and go to university. The analysis appeared similar in that all too often she fought against it as a source of help, but eventually accepted that it could help her.

What is it that the analyst can do to shift this kind of internal world? The analyst's capacity to bear the rage and the suffering is important, while also remaining separate enough to describe the patient's use of perverse and destructive omnipotence. The patient's tendency was to create such chaos in her life that she felt she had nothing left but her exalted sense of grievance and the triumph of revenge. Frequently she felt her life was a mess of damaged situations and people, making her feel that she had nothing to live for to make it worth turning away from further spoiling. At these times it seemed important to take a firm stand against the spoiling and the omnipotent excitement, without at the same time condemning her. This could be difficult when she had wrecked good and hopeful developments and was attacking the analytic work. She did manage, despite the chaos, to continue working at her job, although it was sometimes hard to understand how she managed this.

At times interpretation of the nature of her perverse excitement gave some relief and she calmed down. This was followed by missed sessions. She then reported a sense of desperation that she was losing this form of relief and would be left with the desolation of her damaged life without the escape into excitement. The growing awareness of the fact that she had brought about much of the desolation and damage in her life was the cause of intense shame and guilt which was hard for her to bear.

This patient demonstrated the continuing importance of a trauma as a preoccupation in the inner world. She could not easily be understood without reference to it. Her character and symptomatology were structured by the experience and the stage of development at which it occurred. She was similar to one of the children studied by Bowlby (1944) traumatised and hurt by the experience of sudden and inappropriate separation. As a consequence, she turned away from the earlier good experience of her mother, making it impossible for her to achieve an integrated picture in which both good and bad could exist.

Her awareness and overwhelming bitterness about the loss led to a failure to form stable relationships, except for those which involved perverse elements. She used the sense of grievance at an unconscious level to justify retaliation and sadism. This gave rise to omnipotent excitement invested in destructive narcissism which was used as an antidote against depression and against an overwhelming sense of guilt about the damage she had done. The tasks of the treatment were first to deal with the perverse excitement and sadism and then the primitive guilt which prevented the patient forming links with helpful objects. As far as the effects of the trauma were concerned, it was necessary to acknowledge the real wound she had suffered with her mother, while engaging her in the task of grieving so that, ultimately, she could move away from her grievance. This also meant standing firm against the regressive wish to use the grievance to hold the past responsible for all her difficulties and to justify the destructiveness of revenge.

# 11

# External Injury and the Internal World

*David Bell*

## Introduction

This paper is concerned with the relationship between external adverse, or traumatic, events and the internal world. Psychoanalysis is particularly well placed to study this relationship, as each patient brings the events of everyday life and shows how they are internally experienced. Each patient brings his own central anxiety situations, and lives them out in the treatment, thereby demonstrating his attempts to master or evade certain types of anxiety or psychic pain. In this process he shows what sort of object relations dominate his internal world and also how they are perpetuated and realised in his lived life.

The word 'trauma' is used in many ways – to indicate a single event, or an accumulation of events, or the subjective experience of this event (the reaction to it), or the sequelae of the event. The more we know of a patient, the more complex becomes our understanding of any particular trauma, as we come to understand the context and the state of the patient's inner world at the time of the trauma. For the purposes of this paper, I prefer to use the term 'traumatic situations', by which I mean the breaking through (often described as a breakdown) of unmanageable anxiety or mental pain; a breakthrough which is brought about by a combination of internal and external factors.

Some external events, apparently almost trivial, will overwhelm a particular individual because of their particular meaning. Other events – loss, major life changes including successes (a potent source of trauma in some people) – are generally accepted as traumatic, though their particular effect on any individual will depend on the prevailing anxieties and defences at the time. There are some patients for whom almost any event which involves emotional contact with another human being evokes the most primitive catastrophic terrors.

The events that we as analysts are able to understand with most clarity and certainty are those events that happen within the treatment setting – for example, reactions to starting, the way the patient deals with interpretations, reactions to breaks in the treatment.

Here is a brief example:

Mr A arrives late for his first session. He is clearly anxious and talks in a hurried way offering dreams, bits of history and so on. The atmosphere of the session is such that the analyst feels that the patient is not offering this material for the mutual work of understanding, but in a more desperate way – the patient hints at some claustrophobic terror and worries whether he will be able to stay for the whole session.

In one of the dreams there is a huge dog in his kitchen. It is so big that he can hardly move round it. In order to keep the dog away he throws it bits of food to keep it occupied. One can immediately see how this patient's experience of starting his analysis is represented internally. It gives expression to a primitive infantile anxiety situation that is realised in the external world. A huge persecutory figure has moved into the kitchen of his mind, threatening him – the figure is placated by giving it something to do: dealing with bits of history, or dreams. He revealed in the analysis over and over again a powerfully intrusive internal figure that had constantly to be placated in order that he may be allowed to keep the odd morsel for himself.

## Theoretical Considerations

I will turn now to the understanding of this relation 'internal-external'. These categories are often placed in opposition to each other. However from a psychoanalytical point of view we are more interested in the relation between them: how, in the interplay of projection and introjection, external experiences are represented, internalised and dealt with.

In *The Interpretation of Dreams*, Freud (1900) showed how the mind makes use of everyday perceptions in order to give representation to certain internal situations that are pressing forward into awareness. The unconscious mind is constantly scanning the external world in a very active way, seeking out events and situations which can be used to represent these internal situations. The dream is like a window into this continuous process. The unconscious is therefore making use of perceptions of the external world *for its own purposes*. These representations manage to both express and hide these inner situations – or become objects of projection. The analyst examines the material the patient brings to analysis from this perspective: it is less a question of whether an event has had an effect but more of what it has come to be used for. The capacity to make use of the external perceptions to represent inner concerns provides one mechanism for 'binding' anxiety.

The ego is constantly striving to preserve its integrity, so that it is not 'overwhelmed' by stimulation from either external or internal sources. Events which are sudden, for which there can be no preparedness, may lead to disorganisation of the ego. This is felt as annihilation, falling to bits. The mind defends itself from such events by what Freud described as a 'stimulus barrier' or 'shield'. Traumatic events, which are those that break through this barrier, derive their pathogenic effect for a multitude of reasons – varying from their suddenness and violence (like accidents), to the type 'which owes its importance merely to its intervention at a point in the psychical organisation already characterised by its own specific points of weakness' (Laplanche and Pontalis,1973). Freud stressed the internal factor in these events. Even in those episodes of trauma in childhood, the traumatic effect is maintained in adulthood through the memories, and the fantasies that they activate in the mind of the individual.

The eventual outcome of a traumatic breach in the shield is the construction of a defence. I shall later describe two very different types of such a defence. Some patients for whom the threat of overwhelming anxiety is ever-present, for whom there have been fundamental problems in the building up of an adequate protective system, are forced to live a life in which they endeavour to do the impossible: to be prepared for anything and thus able to do practically nothing. The analytic situation is particularly terrifying for these patients, because it threatens the known with the unknown.

Freud was hampered in his early thinking about trauma by his lack of an adequate conceptualisation of a living internal world. This did not acquire a proper theoretical underpinning until he wrote *Mourning and Melancholia)* (1915b) which gives a model of how external figures are internalised. Later, in the *Ego and the Id* (1923), he stated that the 'ego is the graveyard of abandoned object cathexes' . In other words we see how external objects, combined with fantasies projected onto them are installed within the ego. Freud (1930) had recognised that the archaic, cruel character of the superego could not be accounted for purely by the reality of the parental figures but must acquire its character from the destructiveness projected onto it.

The main contribution to our understanding of the internal world, however, comes from Melanie Klein. She maintained that from the

169

beginning of life there is a rudimentary ego that alternates between states of relative cohesion and states of unintegration and disintegration. She emphasised the constant interplay of projection and introjection in the building up of an internal world of objects to which the ego relates and which are also experienced as relating to each other (e.g. an internal parental couple).

She described two fundamentally different states of the internal world, which entail two different orientations to internal and external reality. In the *paranoid schizoid position*, experiences are widely split: the destructive impulses are directed towards an object felt to be bad whilst the loving impulses are directed toward the good object which is protected, through idealisation, from this destructiveness. The infant, in projecting his violent and destructive impulses, feels threatened by violent and persecuting objects. In this paranoid world, the ego has to disown aspects of itself – or of certain internal situations – and locate them in objects separate from the ego. Certain aspects of psychic reality are thus disowned. The developmental task is the building up of a secure enough internal 'good' object for integration to occur. Integration leads to the capacity to see the damage done to the loved objects and, if the guilt can be borne, the wish to make good the damage done through reparation. These are some of the elements of the depressive position. The move towards the depressive position entails a fundamental change in the orientation to reality, both internal and external. These are distinguished as the projections are withdrawn – the objects cease to be identified purely with aspects of the self, and so their own attributes can be perceived.

This gives us a model of the function of the external world. The infant, who has in his mind, destroyed his mother out of frustration and hatred of frustration, will be internally strengthened by the appearance of an undamaged mother externally. In other words, one function of external reality is to disprove the horrors of the internal world through supporting the internalisation of undamaged and unpersecuting figures.

Adverse experiences diminish trust and confirm anxieties about inner annihilation and persecution. Severe mental illness in one parent, particularly in the mother, is likely to deprive the child of having an external reality which can disconfirm his worst terrors – for example, the annihilation of the world including himself. In situations where external reality confirms inner terrors the result is a grave difficulty in distinguishing between them.

Klein suggests that the extent to which external reality is able to disprove anxieties could be taken as one criterion of normality. The final point I want to make here is to emphasise the difficulty, even the horror, of facing guilt and ordinary human sadness, and yet how the inability to manage this leads to an inhibited and joyless life: the inability to suffer pain means the inability to 'suffer' joy.

Some patients live out their life just on the edge of experiencing depressive pain. They have been unable to face the reality of damaged objects and are always on the run from a terror of being trapped in situations in which they feel faced with the recriminations of these objects. This situation is particularly common in survivors, where they have had the mental equipment to make something of their lives and yet feel constantly threatened by guilt of a particularly unbearable and persecuting kind. Such patients often greet success in their lives as a very mixed blessing and progress in their analysis is constantly impeded. It is as if the patient is saying 'If I get well I have done it at the expense of my loved objects who are in a terrible state. I fear they can never be repaired and I can't stand the pain of their suffering. I can protect myself by being ill'. By being ill the patient also avoids guilt, through identification with his damaged objects.

### Clinical Illustrations

This first illustration is a brief piece of clinical material from a patient whose treatment I followed.

Ms B is a woman in her thirties. Her mother was chronically mentally ill and her father died when she was in her adolescence. The family were described as being very impoverished. The patient went to school the day the father died, a matter about which she felt intensely guilty. Her sister committed suicide when the patient was in her early twenties, leaving a note which the patient read, though then hid, protecting her mother from its contents. The patient ensured that she got her schooling and complained to her teacher that she could not study because of the noise at home, enlisting the teacher's support for a temporary move so that she could get through her exams. She went on to become a teacher, teaching very impoverished and deprived children. She has however been unable to have much real pleasure and satisfaction from her achievements, which include a very supportive relationship with her husband. Her life has a driven quality.

There is much to support the idea that this patient's determination to get away from the impoverished and deprived family was an expression of her wish to live and not be dragged down, but also such a situation would be likely to support a very omnipotent view of herself in which the helpless and impoverished parents are unconsciously triumphed over.

The patient arrived for a session after she had taken a week's holiday. She looked terrible. She had a terrible time. She kept having the figure of a child in her mind, a child whom she teaches. The child was saying to her, 'You didn't listen to me reading'. She felt intensely persecuted and kept frantically busy to blot out this image. Every time she stopped it reappeared. She commented that she didn't have her record with her so that she could check whether she did or did not listen to the child. She also said that she knew 'that it was something in my mind'. This brief bit of material gives, I think, quite a vivid picture of the state of mind from which this patient has been on the run for much of her life.

In her job she struggles in a desperate way to repair all her damaged objects – the deprived and impoverished children. She does recognise the damaged objects in her internal world, but they have to be omnipotently repaired, as she cannot allow herself to face the reality of any irreparably damaged objects. Such objects would face her with situations which support her inner state of persecution, threatening her with retribution – 'look what you have done to me'. Klein (1940) stated that 'the death of a sibling, however shattering for other reasons, is to some extent a victory and gives rise to triumph and therefore all the more to guilt'. Death by suicide is particularly devastating as it gives reality to fantasies of the object's giving in to the death wishes directed against it and enacting them. A further point here is the mother's vulnerability. One gets a picture of an internal mother who would not be able to support her child in facing the guilt of the sister's suicide. She (the mother) is protected from any accusations (the letter), and although this may have been an accurate perception by the patient it again supports her omnipotence. The rather banal external event, the possibility of a minor failure in her work, has because of this patient's particular circumstances, lodged itself in her mind as a persecuting object whose recriminations she cannot escape though she attempts this by her driven activity. I think this situation also represents a type of 'intrapsychic claustrophobia': she feels trapped with damaged objects who persecute and blame.

There remains the question of why this situation came to light now. One possibility is that the holiday was not experienced as a separation from a therapist whom she needed. Her history makes it likely that she would experience herself as turning away from a vulnerable internal mother projected into the therapist, who is then experienced as needing her, fuelling her sense of superiority and triumph over the object who

172

complains that she never listened to her. What I am emphasising here is how the patient repeats in the transference her central anxiety situation – she triumphs over a vulnerable object – which then lodges itself in her mind persecuting her with recriminations.

However, this patient is able to say that she knows that 'it is in her mind' and she is also expressing her acknowledgement of her need for the therapist (the book that she did not have with her that could help her distinguish reality from fantasy).

This patient has then already managed some quite fundamental achievements. She shows an ability to distinguish internal and external, to acknowledge a helpful mother therapist who can help her think about her experience. There are patients, however, who have not acquired this level of development, and are dealing with unmanageable anxieties of a psychotic nature.

Freud's model of anxiety bound by representation through symbolic function – in dreams, sublimations and neurotic symptoms – assumes the presence of a mental apparatus which can perform this function. Klein (1952) demonstrated that the early psychotic anxieties of infancy – feelings of annihilation and fragmentation – have to be dealt with in order for these symbolic functions to develop. She stated, 'The infantile anxiety situations can be regarded as a combination of processes by which anxieties of a psychotic nature are bound, worked through and modified'.

Bion (1962) has considerably deepened our understanding of this highly condensed phrase, 'bound, worked through and modified'. His work with psychotic patients led him to understand what this involves through observing the results of its failure, which he termed observing the remains of 'a psychological catastrophe' (Bion, 1967b).

Bion described how the mother, by taking in and containing the catastrophic anxiety projected into her, transforms it through thinking and thus makes it available to the infant in modified form. The infant acquires the capacity to internalise an object that performs this function – to think about experience and, through thinking, both experience the experience and contain it. He called this function alpha function.

It is this function that binds the psychotic anxieties and, I am suggesting, forms the basis of Freud's protective shield (1920). Bion described ways in which this function can fail. If the mother cannot contain the anxiety but reprojects it, it returns not attenuated, but magnified: it becomes what Bion called 'nameless dread'. The individual then feels constantly on the verge of a catastrophe and defends himself through further violent projection and cutting himself off from

173

experience. I will now present material from a patient who faces this type of catastrophic situation, a patient in whom the failure to acquire an internal object that can contain and think about experience, leaves her on the edge of psychotic fragmentation.

As opposed to Ms B, Ms C, a married Asian woman in her early 40s, has followed a path in which, rather than desperately trying to repair her damaged objects, she denies their existence, and lives out an identification with a triumphant and contemptuous object which pours scorn and contempt on any ordinary human vulnerability, especially if evidenced in herself. She frequently uses words like 'wet', 'whingeing'. Miss B, we could see, lived in a world close to depressive anxieties which were constantly evaded. Miss C's internal world, however, is of a much more paranoid nature. She dreams of being pursued, trapped by insanely violent men.

Since a very early age Ms C has been on a campaign to prove that she is the one on top, usurping the position of her numerous siblings. Any overt display of emotion was felt to be a contemptible loss of control. For example when she received her 'A' level results, she took the envelope up to her room, opened it and came downstairs wearing an expression which did not reveal to her parents, anxiously waiting at the bottom of the stairs, whether she had passed or failed. In this way she triumphed internally over any ordinary emotional reaction, projected it and controlled it in the external parents. As far as I can gather, this represents a particular view of the mother inside her, a rather narrowed one, in which she believes she can only gain mother's love through disowning all vulnerability in herself. In her inner world she was engaged in a collusion with her mother, denigrating the weak and contemptible father. This internal scenario received much support from her external circumstances. Simultaneously, as I will show, she was locked in a battle with this internal father, a battle lived out in the transference, and as I will show, of an intensely sado-masochistic nature. She did well educationally because of her high degree of intelligence but this also supported her omnipotence. She read Sociology at university and during these years she was a member of a gang of young women who had very promiscuous relationships with men. The men were cruelly teased, picked up and then dropped the moment they displayed ordinary human dependence and vulnerability. Her own hated vulnerability and dependence was thus projected into these men representing the father, where it was controlled, mocked and ejected. This way of behaving supported her view of herself as in a superior position alongside mother, looking down on the despised father who has nothing.

This way of living served her needs for some time, though her life offered little in terms of genuine fulfilment and she was never without the threat of catastrophic anxiety. This anxiety came to the fore when her father died after a long and debilitating illness when she was in her late 30s (her mother had died many years before). She said in a rather chilling way, 'I just wanted him to pack his bags and get on with it'. She here shows how she has an internal mother who colludes with her, rather than a figure which can give her support in facing and containing life and death issues. She more recently described how she would get very caught up in excited intellectual arguments with father in which she would try to tie him up in knots. However, when he was so weakened by illness that he couldn't compete, she lost interest. My aim is to convey the chilling, cruel quality of the objects in her inner world. Any display of her own vulnerability is subject to the same chilling cruelty and dismissal.

The death of her father and the delayed effect of the death of her mother resulted in the collapse of her defensive organisation and she was assailed by psycho-somatic symptoms accompanied by the terror of death. She had palpitations and felt her heart would stop at any moment. Desperately she consulted doctors but could never be reassured. She gave up work completely.

Here we see the devastating internal catastrophe with its helpless vulnerability, horrifyingly violent internal persecution further compounded by her own hatred of this state. The death of the parents is not experienced and mourned as the grievous loss that it is, but instead, the parental figures, previously kept far apart, are now set up together inside her combined not in love of each other, but in hatred of her. In phantasy they subject her to a horrifying persecution, murdering her from within, forcing her into the infantile catastrophic state of mind she has previously evaded and projected. Her feeling that she is dying also represents her identification with the dead and dying parents. Like the father in her mind, she is left with no one to support her and help her bear the pain and terror.

The analysis has been characterised by her attempts to regain her original defensive structure. As with many patients of this type, although manifestly they approach the analyst for understanding, there is a deeper aim which is to seek the analyst's help to restore the original defensive structure – and one can see why. The fact that the analysis by its nature is felt to threaten this arrangement, means that the analyst is dreaded. The vulnerability of this patient to the ordinary adverse circumstances of life – having to cope with the real frustration of not possessing the analyst/mother, having to cope with the pain of awareness of separateness with the consequent envy and jealousy – could be dealt with in the only way available to her, namely to identify again with the superior contemptuous object (mother) projecting all vulnerability into the analyst (father). In this process she tears the analytic understanding to bits. This manoeuvre, however, means that she is left, not with internal figures united in love but with retaliating persecuting figures who unite together to force the dreaded dependent feelings into her. During breaks she frequently dreams of being trapped with violent murderous figures.

Early in the analysis she gave accounts of her symptoms, which sounded quite terrifying. These accounts were punctuated by her saying in sarcastic and superior tones, 'how peculiar', 'how odd'. It seemed to me that she was trying to draw me into a collusion with the superior maternal figure, as if the only way she and I could be on friendly terms by my joining her in mocking her 'peculiar' symptoms. At the start of the analysis, she always arrived a bit late for her sessions. She could not bear the idea of sitting in the waiting room and then following me along the corridor 'as your obedient lapdog', as she put it. She desperately tried to maintain that she didn't need me, attempting to make me the one who had to wait, projecting all the hated frustration and dependence into me.

She brought the following dream:

She was being pursued by football hooligans. She comes up against a wall. She looks down and there is a small whining dog at her heels. She picks up the dog, puts it in a plastic bag and lobs it over the wall.

From earlier evidence of the way she treated attempts at understanding, this dream seemed to represent a picture of her analyst who is whining at her ankles trying to get her attention. At another level it also represents part of herself – her hated vulnerability – projected into the analyst where it is mocked, controlled and violently attacked.

Though behaving with apparent superior contempt for me in the session she would occasionally hand me letters just as she was leaving. These were letters written in the middle of the night containing long accounts of her horrifying anxiety and fear of dying. It was as if a vulnerable aspect of herself could only be allowed contact with me if it occurred, so to speak, as a secret message slipped under the door. In this way 'they', the cold mocking figures in her internal world, would know nothing about it.

As one might predict, the patient was much affected by breaks in the analysis. Having murdered the analytic understanding – the analyst's whining – she was left alone with no internal figure to support her against the internal retaliating figures. She felt she was dying, and had attacks of catastrophic anxiety. She, however, experienced interpretations concerning these fears as my attempts to force the hated weakness into her, so that I could be triumphant. She believed that analysts chose their profession to avail themselves of the opportunity of surrounding themselves with weak patients, like whining little puppy dogs, whom they use to bolster their own grandiosity. She often felt that behind my analytic face, she knew what I was really up to, trying to humiliate her.

The patient made some progress. She managed to return to work, eventually full-time, without feeling excessively persecuted. She married a man 10 years her senior who is protective and gives her considerable support. She has become increasingly able to enjoy life – her claustrophobic terrors have lessened and she can go to concerts and operas. This in particular was important as her mother had loved opera but not been able to afford to go. The circumstances of her family in childhood were of considerable deprivation and poverty. They lived in one of London's poorer suburbs which however borders another suburb of considerable wealth. To go to the opera without fear of being persecuted and enviously attacked meant that there was some evidence of a more benign internal figure. Her interests have considerably widened and deepened. However she was still not able to acknowledge that this was achieved with the help of her analyst, for this would imply acknowledgement of her dependency which would then be subject to the contemptuous derision of the inner organisation.

I would now like to bring some material which came shortly after a session in which she had been able to be much freer and had brought a dream and associations which brought a different picture of the parents. They were represented as together and separate from her whilst also making arrangements that she should be cared for. She showed some real regrets at the way the family wasted so much by living in an atmosphere of cruelty and hatred, and also sadness about the loss of her mother.

The recovery of these memories also seemed to convey that she could begin to contemplate that she and I would part, and could attend to our various concerns without its becoming my triumphantly proving to her that I was the boss and she the contemptible weakling, or vice-versa. In

177

other words she could distinguish inner and outer reality and gain some strength and feel supported in her life by the analytic understanding. In the following session she was very preoccupied with gradings at work, a frequent preoccupation for this patient, conveying, I thought, an anxiety that she had been 'downgraded' by recognition of her need for support from her analysis.

In the following week she became increasingly unable to talk to me, now imprisoned in a defensive organisation seducing her into believing that to seek help was to be my whingeing lapdog. (Rosenfeld (1971) described this inner organisation, likening it to an internal Mafia.) She had had a good weekend but couldn't talk about it as she knew I would try to ruin it, suggesting, I thought, that the good weekend was not based on the support of the analysis, but on triumph over it. I had been kicked out: she then has to keep me out as I am felt to be filled with all the hatred of vulnerable dependency that she has projected into me.

She could not talk to me in the next session because she had had a dream. Dreams are naturally linked by her with the analysis: to tell me a dream is to convey that she needs help with understanding something going on inside her. She provokes and withholds, shutting me out, but as this continues, I am felt to be more and more terrifying.

The patient came to the following session and announced that she was going out that night and didn't want it ruined by a session in which she says nothing (she had felt quite ill after the previous session). She then told me about a dream which she produced with a stream of associations and bits and pieces of her current life and her history. The atmosphere was more as if she was telling me these things not to further understanding but to evade it and to keep me away.

In the dream,

> her mother and a friend are in the garden. Then a swarm of bees come and the patient runs in. She closes the door – Mother and friend are trying to get in. She has to keep them locked out and yet they are being attacked by the bees. She can't let them in as the bees will come in too. She feels distantly guilty.

The patient, as I said, produced a host of associations and bits of pieces of history in 'association' to the dream, so much so that I felt I was in a swarm of material coming rapidly from all sides and could not think. She mentioned that her neighbours on both sides, are beekeepers.

I want to emphasise only one aspect of this complicated material. The bees clearly convey a persecutory anxiety of a terrible kind, in which the objects which have been violently fragmented are coming

178

after her. In the context of the session and the previous sessions, in which she has been trying to shut me out, I think one can see that there is a picture of an object (the analyst/mother) which is in a terrible state and yet which she cannot approach or help. Letting the object in will result in her being the target of horrifying attacks (the bees). In her violently locking me out she experiences me as getting into an increasingly bad state, but can do nothing to help. To recognise a helpful mother who is also separate from her, to let her in, and internalise her, also means allowing in all the persecution. Other dreams showed how shutting me out, whilst projecting her own helplessness and vulnerability into me, may be associated with considerable excitement often of a highly sexualised nature.

It is very important to recognise that this material follows a session in which there had been real improvement when she had allowed me in, as a friendly figure. This appears to have stimulated her hatred of her awareness of her need for me.

Though the manifest trauma, the death of the parents, takes place later in life, the difficulties unleashed hark back to the very earliest difficulties of being able to experience a feeding understanding object, to mourn and lose it and so set it up inside as an internal object that can contain anxiety and help her face life and death issues. The unavailability of such an object has led to the construction of a defensive organisation which protects her from psychotic collapse. The patient mentioned that she does have neighbours who keep bees, and these were real adverse circumstances, but the dream shows how adversity becomes horror. Similarly the actual loss of her parents, a major traumatic event, could not be digested and metabolised, in other words worked through, experienced and then learnt from, as such a process, at its inception, is immediately joined up with much more catastrophic internal situations.

To what extent this early failure in acquiring a containing object is due to the mother's incapacity to contain the patient's anxiety and to what extent it is due to the patient's attacking of that function is something that could only be worked out as the analysis developed.

### Conclusion

In this paper I have tried to show how external situations – major losses – produce profoundly different effects in these two patients. The first patient was much nearer the depressive position and so was able to bring situations to do with loss and facing damaged objects. Though she continues to be persecuted by this situation, it is within view and there is a sense of an object whose support she might enlist.

The second patient, however, because of the adverse circumstances of her infancy and childhood has been unable to build up a durable figure in her internal world which can contain and bind psychotic anxieties. To avoid collapse she uses a defensive organisation which supports her wish to disown and project ordinary vulnerability. She projects it and controls it in her objects (the internal father, boyfriends, analyst) where it is violently attacked. She is besieged by anxieties of a much more catastrophic nature, such as the terror of fragmentation (the bees) resulting from her violent attacks on her helpful objects.

Traumatic situations that cannot be faced are constantly re-enacted in ways that are usually deeply unconscious. To quote Freud (1909), '... a thing which has not been understood inevitably reappears; like an unlaid ghost, it cannot rest until the mystery has been solved and the spell broken'. Ms C, in her life, gives life to her worst fears – by triumphing over and destroying helpful objects terrifying persecutors are created.

There is no doubt that early adverse life experiences affect the development of the personality. I think there is also little doubt that severe adversity (such as the early death of parents, or mental illness in one or both parents) has severe effects. There is a paradox, however. Those with the most severe disorders are just those who, because of their fundamental problems in facing internal and external reality, are least able to assess the real nature of their adverse experiences. In many cases it is only after a satisfactory analysis which by securing their relation to internal reality enables them to face external reality, that such patients can decide for themselves the real nature of the external traumas they have suffered.

# Part Five

# Groups

# 12

# The Traumatised Group

*Caroline Garland*

## Introduction

Bion (1952) offers us a powerful schema for understanding the dynamics of the group at work. The tension between the group's relatively sophisticated capacity to work at its primary task, and the powerful regressive pull of the unconscious forces Bion characterised as the basic assumptions, helps make sense of much apparently nonsensical and time-wasting behaviour in any group's functioning. Bion's theory adds an understanding of small group dynamics to Elliot Jacques' (1955) radical approach to the understanding of organisations. Jacques made use of a psychoanalytic view of intra-psychic structures to throw much light on the functioning of multi-body organisations and institutions. Both Bion's and Jacques' work is essential for an understanding of groups in the world of work. However, Foulkes (1964) and his followers take a different line when it comes to groups that meet for primarily therapeutic purposes. Foulkes' model is based on the understanding and therapeutic use of the shared network of communication established over time between members of that group, including the therapist. The focus is on deepening levels of communication between group members, both conscious and unconscious.

Sometimes however, a complex situation arises in which *an entire working group feels itself to be in need of therapy*. In this situation, a combined approach may be helpful and indeed necessary. The work function of the group-as-a-whole has to be kept in mind alongside the individuals' differing needs for comfort and therapeutic understanding. Something of the sort occurs in war. However, traditionally here it is the army that is the primary patient (Hunter, 1946) and the therapeutic task is conceived of in terms of getting the traumatised soldier back into his unit and in fighting form as soon as is possible. Individual sensibilities take second place to the primary task of winning the war. Yet even in peacetime, entire working units can be traumatised, and in need of help. How can the differing needs of both the group, and the individuals within it, be addressed? This chapter is about two separate situations in which a number of people simultaneously found themselves overwhelmed by tragedy, and were seen in a group setting.

As has been described in a number of different ways in this book, when an individual suffers a traumatic event, he is flooded with unmanageable quantities of raw unprocessable 'stuff', and his mental functioning is thrown into disarray. For a while he is overwhelmed, and out of action. When *a collection* of people all feel themselves to be traumatised by a particular event, each will respond in his or her own particular way, but there will also be much experience in common. Can we use our understanding of what happens to the individual, and the ways he begins, with or without help, to recover some sort of working equilibrium, when the group itself, and not only the individual, needs help? Or do we need to start thinking differently?

I am going to describe work done in the last few years with two differing groups. The way in which they differed was fundamental to the work done with them. Some groups may not have considered themselves to be a group at all until the traumatic event took place which united them in the common task of survival – physical, psychological or both. It is the catastrophe that makes a group out of them. These I will call *Adversity Groups*. The passengers in a train which crashes, or the guests in a hotel which catches fire, have only tenuous connections with each other which they might never have needed to notice until they become linked by shared, intense, terrifying experience. Then, at least for a while, disparate individuals get pulled together and become closer, more aware of the bonds between them than they were before the event.

In the second case, the group is already aware of its existence as a group, and knows that it is already joined in some common enterprise, or by some task. For example, the staff and members of a community of disturbed adolescents whose home is destroyed by fire; the social services team in which a team member is murdered; the coach tour that is hijacked by political terrorists – members of these groups are aware of their affiliations, and the reasons for them, before the traumatic event. These I am going to call *Given Groups*, meaning that the existence of the group was a given *before* the traumatic event. In contrast to an Adversity Group, a Given Group can be regarded in certain important ways as already functioning like a single organism, in that although a number of different but related functions are carried out by different parts of that organism, they are done in a way that makes them hang together, aiming towards a common goal, or the achievement of a common task. This might be the manufacture of motor cars, or the rehabilitation of disturbed adolescents, or the care of patients on a long-stay ward.

An Adversity Group on the other hand has no pre-existing task in common. It may be convened by the local medical or social services following a traumatic event, and it may (with luck and considerable local pre-planning) find itself with a therapist trained and experienced in work with groups. Therapeutic work with an Adversity Group must begin with the creation of this loose aggregate of individuals into a single entity, one able to work at the task of considering their individual reactions to the event that obliged them to recognise themselves as a group at all.

## The Adversity Group

Adversity Groups, therefore, are created abruptly by the traumatic event. Survivors find themselves with unanticipated bedfellows, whom they both cleave to and resent. Members ask 'Why should this happen to me?'. This question, often heard in the aftermath of disaster, is not only the voicing of a complaint but also represents a search for meaning, an attempt to make sense of the apparently arbitrary. Each member will eventually have to construct this meaning for himself, but the group begins with a consensus: this was a terrible and wounding event for every one of us; we share this dreadful misfortune. As with a Given Group, the individual's task is to struggle to put into words what has happened, both in the external world and internally – for the therapist, for his fellow survivors, and for himself. This process of communication is both conscious and unconscious, verbal and non-verbal. We hear survivors saying, 'You couldn't know what it was like unless you were there', but perhaps the real burden of what they are saying is, 'You couldn't know what it was like unless you were me'. Thus the conveying of horror and distress through projective identification is inevitable: it is the most powerful way we have of communicating to someone else the particularity and intensity of our own emotional responses. It is part of the strength of a group meeting following a traumatic event that the containment (see Chapter 7) of such powerfully distressing feelings can be done in part by the group itself, rather than by any single individual within it.

The first task of the therapist is to help the members accept and tolerate the fact that they are in fact a group. The members may exhibit a powerful ambivalence to the experience of meeting, in that they cling to each other and to the therapist for some understanding of what happened, but there is also resentment and rage at having to be in this situation at all, at having suffered what they have suffered. If it is not put into words in the session itself, the group may diminish in size very rapidly, and it may never become possible to use the fact of the group as an agent for therapy.

The piece of work I shall describe briefly was carried out with the survivors of a major hotel fire, in which two people died. The first two sessions (each session lasted for one and a half hours) was taken up with accounts of the fire itself and its immediate aftermath. Piecing together the mosaic of different sights, sounds, smells, thoughts, terrors and imaginings eventually built up a complex web of events and feeling in which each person present (there were 15 able and willing to attend the meeting) was able to feel himself part of a shared event, however reluctantly. Other similarities emerged. The most painful of these was the recognition that this event had changed them and their lives irrevocably, however well they might eventually recover. As one member put it, 'Nothing will ever be the same again'. It might be worse, it might even conceivably be better in some respects, but it would never be the same.

By the third session, they found they were moving on from the events of the fire itself and beginning to talk about the difficulties they were having with the reactions of friends, family and colleagues. It seemed as though all of them felt in a generally rattled state where no-one could get it right – neither overt sympathy nor tactful avoidance felt helpful – and they felt relieved, and could even laugh, to hear some of the well-meaning blunders made by each others' sympathisers; and this eventually led to some recognition that it was their own states that made help so unhelpful – and this included my own contribution, which was felt to be keeping the fire alive and still burning in their minds.

This group was unusual because it included the daughter of an older survivor, who had not been in the fire, but who was attending in order to help her father who had been injured. The father and daughter of course exemplified the survivor/relative difficulties, demonstrating *in vivo* the tensions that many of them had experienced with their own friends and relatives. The young daughter wanted to help, but worried in case her help was intrusive or over-concerned, or not enough, or missing the point. The parents on the other hand needed and wanted her help but also worried about taking her away from her own young family, from the things they felt she would really want to be doing. They felt guilt about this, as well as communicating their resentment that they were vulnerable, needing help. She felt their struggle to be independent was rejecting, and she said in an anguished way, 'I want to be *allowed* to help!'. Eventually each was able to say to each other, in the presence of the other group members who were gripped by this dynamic, what neither could have said in the privacy of home – about the immense difficulties of needing, and of giving, help after a life-threatening situation.

It often happens in group treatment that the members working at this process of understanding on behalf of others may have benefited as much if not more as those in the spotlight (Garland, 1982). Taking an active part in understanding and perhaps alleviating another's distress acts to restore an individual's sense of control after a period of acute and sometimes prolonged helplessness, which is the essence of a traumatising situation (Freud, 1926). However, Adversity Groups have a limited span of helpfulness. After four or five sessions, group members may begin to bring in material not directly stemming from the traumatic event and its aftermath. Once a group becomes a general purpose therapy group, and there will always be a pull for it to do so, it can continue indefinitely in a half-cocked way. It is important to end a series of sessions that were convened for a particular purpose at the point that was originally planned. Most members will be relieved to see that the therapist does not believe they need to be in treatment for the rest of their lives as a result of the trauma.

However, a small proportion of individuals will need more work, and one of the functions of an Adversity Group is to provide a chance for the group leader to see who is beginning to recover and who is not. There will be some for whom longer-term treatment, whether group or individual, will be helpful.

## The Given Group

This was a piece of work I shall describe in more detail. I approached it with a single coherent notion which acted as a kind of central organiser of my thoughts in the preparation for the meetings. This focus was the idea that to some extent a Given Group can be thought about and perhaps approached in the same way that we understand and treat an individual patient, but with a crucial difference – namely that that the therapeutic work to be done with a Given Group will centre around the reestablishing of that group's capacity to carry out its primary task.

Therapeutic work with a group is, quite as much as with the individual, also about containment, but the group therapist or group consultant is not in a position to act as container for all the disparate sources of distress, pain, anger, guilt, outrage and confusion he and she may be faced with. When working with a Given Group, we must bear in mind that *the effective carrying out of the primary task is the group's most powerful container*. It is the group's way of holding steady, and of being in a position to think about all the various sources of disturbance that burgeon and eddy about its complex structure, and within its setting.

All Given Groups function around a primary task. It is that bit of work which it has to be carried out successfully if the existence of the group itself is to continue, its *raison d'être*. For instance, members of a hospital work together to cure patients, and alleviate suffering, and perhaps to train new doctors and nurses; the staff in a factory work together to design and make motor cars, or cotton dresses, and to do it well enough for their products to outsell those of their competitors. When too many patients die, or the motor cars fall to bits, or the cotton dresses go out of fashion, the enterprise collapses and the group will eventually disband if it cannot adapt by remedying its approach to the primary task. So the successful carrying out of the primary task, which is the work of the group, is essential to the group's survival. Not necessarily to the survival of the individual members of that group, but to the group itself; and as Bion has pointed out (1961), to take care of the group itself is to take care of the individual members that compose that group. When the members of a Given Group suffer a traumatic event, everything changes suddenly and without warning. Quite suddenly, the primary task has vanished, and another far more immediate task has replaced it – that of survival. If a fire were to break out in, for example, a large teaching hospital, all treatment, all teaching, all lectures, all administration, all eating of sandwiches end immediately as the alarm rings: the job is now for everyone in the building to get out of it at once. *Differentiation* of jobs and roles disappear rapidly: patients and doctors, nurses and occupational therapists, secretaries and managers, cooks and eaters, all are replaced by individuals intent on escape and survival. If it turns out to be a false alarm everyone can get back to work relatively easily, and the disturbance becomes what psychotherapists are ruefully obliged to call *grist to the mill*. But if the fire is real, and people are trapped in the wards, or in the lifts, and there are fatalities, it would be a very long time before anyone could with any semblance of conviction or capacity do any work at all, or before any patient could attend that hospital feeling that this was a competent or safe setting for their treatment. It might take years for any institution to recover from such an event, and certainly it would be much changed by what had happened.

I am therefore saying that although restoring the primary task may be necessary for recovery, it is not sufficient. Barings is not a name that, in our lifetimes, will inspire immediate financial confidence. P & O's makeover of Townsend Thoresen is elaborate, and the roll-on/roll-off cross-channel ferries look and conduct themselves increasingly like the grand old transatlantic liners, but it may be years before those who book an overnight cabin can sleep sweetly. These of course are extreme examples, but the principles are the same whatever the nature and scale of the processes that disrupt and traumatise an institution.

Thus a Given Group that has suddenly and traumatically lost its primary task is, I am suggesting, comparable to the individual whose functioning is overwhelmed by the traumatic event. Each has lost its head. Both become fragmented, dis-integrated, and overwhelmed by unmanageable stimuli from both external and internal sources. Internal communication is lost, and the harmonious, differentiated yet integrated functioning of the whole gives way to something chaotic, as individuals stop carrying out their original functions and turn instead to issues of survival. Intense excitation arises from inside as well as outside the compound organism, as individuals become filled with fear, anger, outrage, or grief, and express or communicate this to each other. Work groupings are replaced by sentient groupings – people turn to those they like and trust, rather than to those they work with (of course there is often overlap). Old leaders are mistrusted – because they are felt to have let this thing happen – and new leaders are thrown up briefly, who are seen to serve different kinds of functions: the switchboard operator rather than the Managing Director, or the Matron rather than the Headmaster, and so on.

The particular Given Group I'm going to talk about was a General Practice in a run-down area of Birmingham. One of the Partners had been killed by a patient with a long history of intermittent psychosis while the Partner was making a home visit to another patient who lived on the same floor of the same block of flats. The request for help from the Trauma Unit did not come directly from the Practice, but arrived in a roundabout way, through a Consultant who was familiar with our work. This meant that when I began to negotiate with them when and how I might come, it was with people who had been *told they needed help* by someone outside the Practice. We might see this as comparable to a frontline worker recognising that someone in the immediate

Understanding Trauma

aftermath of a bad accident is in a state of shock, and needs such and
such kind of help: the patient also knows he needs 'something', without
knowing what that something might be. He simply wants all the
horrible events and feelings to be taken away and for his life to return
to normal, to a pre-disaster state. I told the Consultant we'd be glad to
offer 'something', and within 24 hours I was telephoned by the Practice
Manager. What I had decided to offer was in line with the thinking I
have outlined about the parallels between a Given Group and an
individual: namely four sessions, at intervals to be determined by
progress and need. (See Chapter 4).

The Practice Manager accepted this at once with relief and gratitude.
My impression was she would have accepted whatever I might have
offered at that point, because the very idea that someone had an idea
about some possible kind of intervention was in and of itself the lifting
of a burden. Some of the intense anxiety generated by the desperation
for 'something' to be done, combined with helplessness about what was
the right or the best thing to do, could now be handed over to this
person who was coming, to 'the Tavistock' itself. This projection of
knowledge and expertise must at some point be addressed, because just
as the individual at first imagines you are going to restore him to normal
by taking away the horrible event, the group too turn to you with the
intense dependency and idealised expectations that has its roots in
certain aspects of early mother-infant relations. I felt I was expected not
just to restore the good object, but indeed to *be* that good object, who
was to recreate peace and harmony, and protect them from further
horrors, deal with whoever or whatever had done this terrible thing to
them. I become aware that long before I arrived I was being referred to,
with a blend of irony and intense hope, as 'the expert', and therefore
knew that the disappointment and anger that might develop over the
succeeding weeks as the group discovered that I could not take away
their distress and (in this case) give them back their murdered partner
could become very sharp and painful. These issues become all the
greater if they cannot be addressed by the visiting consultant and
recognised by the group members.

I made two requests, which were more than suggestions but less than
conditions: that the first of our meetings should last for two hours, and
that everyone in the Practice concerned with its running, including the
cleaners and the (voluntary) tea lady should attend. The Practice Manager was dismayed – how on earth could they find two hours in the day
when everyone could be there? Who would offer cover? She was giving
me a glimpse of how overwhelmed they were, and how unable to think

190

about priorities. They were still struggling to carry on with the original Primary Task as originally conceived of: to care for patients (i.e. *others*) and alleviate their suffering. It seemed that what could not be borne was the idea that a change in the Primary Task had now been imposed on them by events outside their control.

If I were to put into words the (one hopes) temporary but absolutely necessary shift in the Primary Task, it would be something like this: *what do we have to do before we can get back to work?* By work, I mean real work that is both bearable for the practitioners and effective for the practice patients. (The two of course are related; we sometimes forget how reassuring it can be for patients to know that their doctors, or social workers or analysts have enough sanity to know how to take proper care of themselves. It is easier to be angry with an analyst who has cancelled a session but is now recovered, than with one who is struggling on bravely coughing and croaking. This is of course is a particular difficulty within the helping professions, where need and distress is habitually attributed to, even projected into the patient, and health, understanding and expertise is retained by the helpers.)

I said on the telephone that they might want to think about actually closing the Practice for a couple of hours. There was dismay in response. How were they going to do that? I repeated her question back to her, saying yes, that was a real question. Well, she thought out loud, perhaps they could put a notice on the door that said that owing to the recent tragedy they were closed until two o'clock ... but ... I said I thought that sounded like rather a good idea.

The second issue was raised when the Senior Partner came on the line and said that he might not be able to attend the meeting, because the relatives of the murdered Partner were travelling down to Birmingham that day and that he'd promised to make himself available to them at any time. This meant he might be with them rather than at the meeting. Perhaps he could ask them to come to the meeting as well; they might find it helpful. This took me aback. He was showing me how his own boundaries, and the Practice boundaries, had been intruded on violently by the killing, and that all the old demarcation lines were lost, as traumatic material flooded back and forth between patients, relatives and professionals. This is the exact equivalent of what happens in the mind of the traumatised individual overwhelmed by horrors. I said that I did not think it was appropriate for the parents to attend the meeting. I recognised that they needed help in their own right, but that I felt my job and his at this point was to help the Practice, and that I felt it was important *he* should attend the meeting and that he should find some way of letting the relatives know when he could be available to them.

There is a fine line between becoming omnipotent, issuing directives (always a temptation in an emergency), and taking care of the boundaries, in this case the Task – *my* Primary Task, and the time and the territory – and one may never know whether one has got it right until much later in the day. But I felt that the Senior Partner had heard what I had said, and been able to make use of it, feeling he had permission to be less endlessly available to everyone.

I approached this first meeting in a state of some anxiety. I had deliberately avoided finding out from the original link, the Psychiatric Consultant, the details of what had happened. It is useful in meetings of this sort if the consultant knows the gist of what has happened, without knowing the details. This is for two reasons. The first is to enable the consultant to hear about the events from the group members without having too many preconceived notions about what happened, and above all without having had the chance to have 'dealt with' the emotional impact of the events beforehand. If the group is going to be helped to reach a point where it can contain its own turbulence, we as consultants must begin by taking it in ourselves, by allowing ourselves to be affected by it *before* beginning to take it in and mull it over, process it in a way that can help them eventually to bear thinking about it themselves.

The second reason is that the effort to communicate the traumatic event to the one person in the room, the consultant, who was not there when it happened, is in itself part of the treatment. The struggle to put into words a vivid and communicable picture of events is part of the processing of the event by the group members, by the group itself. It may not at first be coherent, but over time and with some prompting when events do not make sense, the group itself will arrive at the creation of a total, shared, multiply-layered picture.

There was confusion inside the building when I first arrived. The notice of closure was up, handwritten in a slightly makeshift way. Where were we going to meet? Would I like a cup of tea? I said no thank you, not because I did not want one but because this was to be a working meeting, not a cup-of-tea meeting. Eventually people began to congregate in a large open waiting-room area on the first floor, and chairs were hauled out of various rooms, passed from hand to hand and put down in a rough ellipse, while people ran up and down the stairs and telephones rang constantly and there were frequent rings at the door bell and knockings on the door. It was obvious that this event had disturbed the larger group comprised of the Practice staff *plus* the Practice patients, who had also of course suffered a traumatic loss.

Eventually the room grew quiet. Some people were looking at me expectantly, some with hostility, some were looking at the floor and some were openly crying. I looked all round the room, meeting people's eyes: it seemed important to acknowledge that although this was a group, it was composed of individuals, each of whom had their own role, identity, thoughts and feelings. I said my name and where I was from, and said how many meetings we'd be having, and how we'd then review the situation; that I was with them now because I knew that something terrible had happened within their group, and that I would like them to tell me about it. And in a stumbling and erratic fashion, that is what they began to do, at first through the mouth of the Senior Partner in a formal way, and as they became more engaged, less formally and more personally and painfully.

This group of course had to face, as well as their pain and outrage, the process of mourning, both for the loss of the murdered partner, and as well as for the sort of Practice they had been before the murder happened, which seemed at first in retrospect to have been a Golden Age, a lost Eden. It was not until the second and third sessions that some of the *pre-existing* difficulties could be spoken and thought about.

This first session then was taken up with individual stories and reactions. One of the members (the voluntary tea lady, who seemed to be the representive for the Practice Group as a whole of the sub-group of 'patients', in that she had her arm bandaged and in a sling, and had an unstoppably eccentric quality) seemed to want to foreclose the process of grief by beginning to eulogise the dead Partner at length, saying that she had been too good for this world, and had been taken back by the Lord for his own. I felt that the Partner had represented for her some sort of bulwark against her own deterioration and death. Now that she had lost that protection she was deeply afraid, and angry with the Partner for dying, for leaving her alone and unprotected. I thought she must represent the feelings of many of the patients, for whom Dr Susan had been a very special figure. The constantly reiterated phrase was that 'nothing was too much trouble for her'. She worked a very long day, and was known for her willingness to pop in and see a patient at home long after hours. It began to seem from the way they talked as though they were all endlessly busy and that Dr Susan had been the busiest of them all – so much so that they began to realise how little they had known her as a person, how little they felt any of them had really got to know each other as people; how they only had time to acknowledge one or two essential work issues before they had to dash off once more on the next round of visits or phone calls or surgeries.

A recurring issue in this session was the experience that most of the staff had had with the Press, who'd been felt to be very insensitive and intrusive by surrounding the Practice by mid-morning and trying to interview everyone who went in and out. Some stories were told of how staff had 'dressed like patients', hiding their brief-cases under their coats in order to leave without having a microphone stuffed into their faces. The Press represented the bad intrusive figures, representative of the violent assault that they felt had been done on the Practice as a whole; and I linked this for them with my presence, and my asking them to tell me what had happened, so that I too represented a voyeuristic intrusive figure reminding them over and over again of the terrible thing that had happened, instead of taking it away and letting them go back to normal. One or two members looked politely baffled by this comment, but I thought something of it was taken in because of the way the indignation with the Press began to give way to a weary recognition about 'people only doing their job'.

Most revealingly, one by one most people in the Practice said that for each of them, the first thought when they realised something was wrong – the police cars outside, the grave officials inside – was that each of them had been detected in some serious and probably fatal error: 'Oh my God, I've killed a patient'; 'Oh God I gave the wrong injection', or 'I've let the hard disc crash and lost all the patient data ...' The object most present in the room seemed to be that of a negligent caretaker, a dangerously incompetent or careless caretaker, together with a fiercely judgemental figure coming to exact retribution on behalf of society. I thought that this linked not just with their own individual guilt about having failed to prevent their colleague from dying, but also with important work issues. I chose to take up the work issue (in contrast to work with an Adversity Group where I would have taken up the personal issues). I said something about their experience of how hard it was to feel that they did their jobs well enough, and not to feel they had to kill themselves doing it perfectly. This led to a quite stunned silence for a few moments (perhaps because of my unconscious choice of expression) and eventually to some murmured assent: it felt very hard to go home ever feeling you'd finished your work. It emerged that this Practice never closed, or refused to answer the phone, during the long working day. This led to a series of painful thoughts about the patients themselves, about their demands and their intrusiveness, in spite of the few who'd been sympathetic and understanding. The staff had been at the limit before this terrible event and it had overstretched them to the point where the Practice had broken down, suffered a breakdown, and now they themselves felt like patients, deeply in need of care and understanding.

I raised with them how difficult it seemed to think about how to protect themselves from endless demands, endless requests for accounts of 'what happened'. I wondered what ideas they might have had about how to save themselves from having to make the same statements over and over again. The Second Partner looked at the others and said he had actually thought of writing out a statement which could be pinned up or even handed to people who asked for details – perhaps he should get down to it today. This, fifteen minutes before the end, seemed like a move in the direction of *distributed functioning* again, *differentiated functioning*, characteristic of a working group, as opposed to one still in the grip of a trauma, in which every member is operating independently and autonomously and in multiply-overlapping ways. The others were happy for him to do this on their behalf. The meeting ended, and I, by going away back to London, became the negligent caretaker.

The second meeting came two weeks later, after the funeral. Again, most of the meeting was taken up with deep feelings of anger, outrage and misery, but this time it led eventually to a real sadness. Again in the last 15 minutes they were able to pick up once again their work functioning. How difficult, they said it was, to know when and how it was reasonable to protect themselves, by not going on night visits alone for example, or for asking for help with violent patients. I took up with them their apparent lack of ability to think about protecting themselves not just outside the building, but also inside it – from being over-burdened and over-loaded, endlessly available to their patients at their own expense. They began to talk quite seriously about the possibility of closing at lunch-time on a regular basis. They also discussed the need for a place for the staff to meet privately, as well as a time to meet: it seemed there was no Common Room in the building, no place for staff only. Suddenly one of the women who had not spoken so far burst in quite heatedly, saying to the Second Parter how he was the worst of the lot with patients, he just could not set any limits on his willingness to help them. 'You always say come in', she said. 'It doesn't matter what time of night it is or how long the surgery is supposed to have been closed, you just always tell them to come in and you always make yourself available to them, and I think it is setting a bad habit.' She spoke with a mixture of anger, reproach and affection and I felt it was

195

that precise mixture that made it possible for what she said to be heard, and taken seriously. He said ruefully that it was difficult for him to change his habits because he wanted to be thought perfect and wonderful by all his patients. There was truth even in this piece of self-parody, and I thought it helped the group to consider in what way it might apply to each of them.

In the third meeting, a further three weeks on, there were three major themes: first, should Dr Susan's name be taken off her consulting room door, and should the room be redecorated, ready for a new Partner (appointed even before Dr Susan's death to replace someone who had left). Second, could they now take the decision to close at lunch-time on a regular basis without having to use the murder as an excuse? The notice was still up on the door referring to 'the recent tragedy' – could they take it down and close anyway? I felt that the way in which they were describing patients seemed marginally less persecuted. Patients seemed, as far as I could tell, to resemble ordinary people again and not only predatory creatures prepared to eat them alive. I said something to this effect and they laughed and the Receptionist said that was just the word for patients, they came prowling round the surgery looking for anything they could get out of you, but the laughter offset the note of persecution: patients seemed just about bearable once more, although they were still using locums for night-duty.

In the fourth meeting, by this time three months after the death, they began by saying that they felt things were 'over and done with'; although as the session progressed it was clear that this was far from the case. However, it looked as though some work had been done. The new partner had been helped to move into Dr Susan's old room, and the new name had been put up on the door. Lunch-time closing was now instituted: one out of the four meetings a month was to be a Practice Meeting, and the others were to be time off. The difficulties in the session revolved around the difficult issue of a memorial meeting, and it seemed as though all the sense of being stuck with something unmanageable, acknowledging a loss, a violent death, and that the rest of them were still alive had all been bundled into the thing called a memorial meeting. Which of them would arrange it, and what it should consist of? Neither something wholly religious nor wholly secular would do ... songs? hymns? poems? music? Was it for them, or was it for the patients, or was it for Dr Susan's family? Did they want to do it at all? The disagreements and tensions, ideas and dissatisfactions swung back and forth. I felt I was hearing the group organising itself around the struggle to work out in its group-mind what sort of a person Dr Susan had been, and what sorts of relationships they had had with her, and how they could let her go without feeling they had forgotten her. I said eventually that it seemed as though they felt it had to be a perfect event which would include everything and provide something for everyone, leave nothing and no one out: nothing ordinary could possibly be good enough. They were silent for a while, and then the Second Partner announced he'd do it, he'd just get on with it, and anyone who wanted to join him would be very welcome. There were some volunteers and a small organising committee seemed to appear within a very short time, and I think that both the group and I felt at the end of the session that they were beginning to move again, although slowly and painfully. The issue of night-time locums remained, and in fact stuck fast until the clocks went forward once more, some five months later.

I have summarised the detail of these long and often turbulent and emotional sessions in order to illustrate the point about the work being to do with what had to be said, thought, felt, done and lived through before the original primary task could begin tentatively to reemerge. It is important to recognise that its reemergence is not just the *outcome* of a kind of recovery – a necessary stage on the way to proper functioning, perhaps in an altered form – but is also the *cause* of further recovery, and perhaps even growth, as the group starts to think about itself and its functioning, and to notice how and where and in what way bits of it are still in trouble. Successful primary task functioning is, in my view, the most fundamental container for a Given Group's own disturbance. It provides the structure within which the group can examine and eventually deal with its own problems, both those created by and those revealed by the traumatic event.

## Conclusions

When groups are properly structured and well-run, they can be powerful containers of individual distress, as well as agents of recovery and change. Of the two types of group I have described, the one created by and the other temporarily shattered by adversity, the structure and dynamics of the group itself can be used for therapeutic purposes. Freud (1926) regarded helplessness as central to the experience of trauma. In a group, it is possible to move once more from passivity to activity, through being contained while in a helpless state to being part of the container for others' helplessness. Thus every member is both patient

197

and therapist, in alternating cycles of regression and recovery, until some workable equilibrium is achieved and ordinary life may be taken up once more.

*Since this book was first published in 1998, work at the Trauma Unit has continued weekly. This final chapter, published as an addendum, represents a development of the thinking outlined so far. It concentrates on the complex and reciprocal relationship between thought (the capacity to symbolise) and identification following a traumatic event.*

# Action, Identification and Thought
# in Post-traumatic States

## *Caroline Garland*

This chapter is concerned with three things, intimately connected with each other: first, *trauma*; second, *action*, and in particular the kind of action that is driven by identifications of various kinds. (By 'identification' I mean the process of being, of *becoming* in some important respect, the object as opposed to the self.) Third, I concerned with *thought*, and the connections between trauma, action, and thought. Here I am using 'thought' in the sense of representing action in the mind, without resorting to enaction, the actual carrying out of what has been imagined.

The argument that has already been presented and illustrated in this book is that in a very specific way trauma damages the capacity to think. After a trauma, identification tends to replace thought. There is an enactment of precisely those events which might in other circumstances have been able to be thought about, turned over in the mind, mentalised. Moreover, thought and action about the trauma exist in a reciprocal relation to each other, in that both are attempts to deal with the same specific event, or series of events, involving trouble between the self and the object. Both thought and action can be seen as ways of attempting to depict the nature of this relationship to oneself, and then to deal with it. As far as treatment is concerned, it can be helpful to think about identification following a trauma as *a particular way the patient has of representing a relationship with the object*.

Traumatised patients offer us a clear view of this process. Often in an otherwise workable personality there can be found areas of

199

distinctly concrete thinking, where identifications have replaced the ability to think about something, to symbolise it in such a way that it can be contemplated, considered and not necessarily acted on. On the whole, we can hold things in mind, and think about them, rather than getting rid of them through action. However, patients who have survived a traumatic event demonstrate repeatedly that even a well-developed symbolic/thinking capacity will give way under extreme stress (see Chapter 7). Indeed, *in the area of the trauma* it may never recover its former flexibility, confidence and usefulness for the purposes of *imagining*. This is, I think, what we are talking about when we say someone was 'traumatised.' We mean their mental structures, and their ability to use those structures, have been damaged or impaired in a chronic way. In the area of the traumatic experience, the kind of mental representation employed may never again be able to be fully integrated with the rest of mental functioning (Freud's 'foreign body', 1893) and therefore be available to be thought about coherently. So, whatever the physical damage, ultimately the *trauma* consists of permanent damage to the mental apparatus.

I propose *a description of how* and *a suggestion as to why*, this should happen so regularly and so often permanently in post-traumatic states.

### Three Clinical Vignettes: identification and symbolisation

These three short clinical vignettes illustrate this proposition concerning the reciprocal relationship between thought and action in post-traumatic life. None of these examples involves anything I would think of as lastingly traumatic.

1. The patient, a man in his fifties, was in a five-times a week analysis. He saw himself at the top of his profession, a 'top lawyer'. He was an only child, one of those war babies who met his father for the first time when he was four and a half years old. Neither parent was ever quite forgiven for their reunion, which exposed the boy to an Oedipal anguish that dominated his adult life both with his family and at work – and his analysis was hard put to it to modify this state of affairs. In the early hours of a Thursday morning I had become suddenly and unexpectedly unwell. I had to telephone him at home to cancel his Thursday and his Friday sessions, telling him I would certainly be back at work on Monday. On Monday there was no patient and no message. About 25 minutes after the start of the session, I found a note from him dropped into the letter-box. Written on the

back of the envelope I read the words, 'Please forgive this rather hasty note. . . .' He had had to 'dash into work early for a crucial meeting' and he had just had time to write this note, put it into an envelope and deliver it on his way to his crucial meeting. On Tuesday he was 20 minutes late for his session, and seemed to have forgotten that he had not attended at all the day before. During the half-hour we had left, some work was done on the significance of the 'crucial' meeting's having cropped up when it did, and I thought he understood something about his need to reverse an unpleasant event which he saw as having been done *by* me *to* him. He left the session with many apologetic flourishes. And, not surprisingly in retrospect, he missed the Wednesday session too without warning. Two sessions cancelled at very short notice by me had had to be matched by two sessions cancelled without warning by him. My interpretations after the first missed session had not been able to touch the imperative nature of the urge to equalise the score in an actual, bodily, concrete way.

2.   The second vignette involved a young family. The mother, pregnant with her second child, went away for the first time for a single night when the older child, a little boy, was about 20 months old. The toddler had spent the afternoon of her absence in his own home with his mother's friend and her own child, and they had stayed until the father came home from work to give him supper and put him to bed. The mother returned the following afternoon and was met with a (not unexpected) mixture of welcome and rejection. The next morning, a weekend, both parents were still in bed when the little boy opened the bedroom door and stood just inside it beaming at her. 'Allo, Mama!' he said. Then, once he was sure he had her full and pleased attention, his face darkened and with a fierce scowl he said 'Bye-Bye' very emphatically, and went out slamming the door. This little sequence was repeated more than twenty times over the next half-hour, with very little modification. The mother told me that if she picked up the newspaper, or spoke to her husband, he would raise the volume and intensity of the 'Allo, Mama' until he had her full gaze on him. Eventually the little ritual seemed to have allayed something in him, in that it subsided, giving way to an ordinary weekend day.

3.   The third vignette is Freud's – the 'Fort-Da' game with the cotton-reel, described in 1920 and a long way, as Freud says, from the 'dark and dismal subject of the traumatic neurosis'. He describes a 'good little boy', less than two years old, who although fed and cared for only by his mother, did not cry or protest when this much-loved mother made her occasional sorties from the house. Instead he

invented a game. He repeatedly threw a cotton-reel out over the edge of his cot, saying mournfully to himself as he did so, 'Gone!' Then he hauled it in again on its piece of string, saying joyfully as it bobbed back into sight, 'There!' Why, Freud asked himself as he struggled with this observation which seemed at odds with the idea of the pleasure principle, should the little boy repeat a distressing experience in this way? And as we know (see Chapter 1), Freud went on from this to make some very far-reaching observations about the effects of trauma on the ego.

All three episodes have certain features in common. In each case, a male is left temporarily by a woman, *the mother*, either in actuality or in the transference. In each case the mother was felt to be a central figure, a good object in spite of her absences and the young child's growing struggle with the knowledge of her relationship with father. In each case there is a *reversal* of the direction of the original action. The one who has been left now becomes the one who leaves, or who rejects. This implies that the agent has ceased in some respects to function only as himself, and has divided himself in two. He now presents himself to himself, and to his mother (or mother in the transference), as in some central respect identified with the mother who went away. In a complementary way, the other, the original leaver, has now been identified as the one who is left. Thus there is both an *introjective* identification, and a *projective* identification.

In the first two cases, the introjected object has clearly already had projected into it some complicated feelings. The lawyer behaved as though the absence had been the kind of casual insult that 'top people' habitually inflict on lesser beings. It may reflect the parents' lack of comprehension of and empathy with the terrible shock he endured as his father returned and deprived him quite suddenly of sole possession of his mother. In the second case, the little boy seemed to behave not only as though he himself were angry, but also as though he had attributed his mother's absence to his perceiving *her* as angry with *him*, judging by his darkened brow and fierce demeanour. In the third case, the object identified with is one that goes out worryingly often, even though she also returns. The reasons for mother's absence seem to be puzzling the child. I say this because there is no implicit hypothesis about the causation of the absence contained in the nature of the identification with the object that absents herself (as there was in the case of the lawyer, for instance). Perhaps he is struggling with the idea that mothers are just like that, they go away, and you simply have to put up with it and be 'good' because they don't like upset or protest. In all three cases, it is clear that what is having to be dealt with is the experience of getting stuck with some anxiety-producing event that cannot properly be located in the mind and thought about – and which therefore has to be enacted, or re-enacted, in a concrete or bodily way, as a way of representing it to the self.

However, there are also important ways in which these three incidents differ. In the first, the 'top lawyer' cannot bear to know he has any feelings at all about his analyst's absence. Perhaps that would make him feel small and unimportant, as he did when his big powerful soldier father re-entered the home and took away his mother. Those feelings have to be emptied in their entirety into me, who caused his distress, and this can only be done by enacting the entire procedure in reverse, and, I think, watching carefully the effect on me. In this he differs from the 'Allo-Byebye' child, who is engaged both bodily and mentally in his response. He is well aware of having some painful feelings, but he is also capable of expressing them in a way that is further along the path towards transformation into symbolic representation. The comings and goings have been reduced to a representative opening and closing of a door – and the words *Hello* and *Bye-Bye*, with the accompanying facial expressions, stand for and symbolise those same actions. He too directs his behaviour straight at the offending object, and the reversal seems to contains some fairly openly expressed feelings of revenge, along with the verbal communication. With Freud's child, things have moved further still. In discussing this little fragment of normal activity, Freud thinks that, in part, its function is to provide compensation for the child's 'great cultural achievement' – that is to say his renunciation of instinctual satisfaction through his letting his mother go without protest, accepting her separateness. He is working at dealing with his depressive anxieties. Yet this little boy, young as he is, acts on *a substitute* for the mother, perhaps even a symbol for mother, not mother herself. However concrete the representation of this minor traumatic event, the cotton-reel is a symbol for an actual external object. (I suspect that changes in child-rearing practices over the last hundred years have meant that there is less pressure on today's small boys to have renounced their 'instinctual satisfactions' at such a tender age, and perhaps therefore they have fewer inhibitions about directing their feelings straight at mother.)

Of course a mother's, or even an analyst's, occasional absence is a necessary part of normal development. Yet we can see from the three examples, and the anxious re-enactment of the recipient's version of events, that the absence had presented each of them with something difficult, something provoking considerable anxiety and something that therefore had to be mastered. In all three cases I want to draw attention to the enactment of the identification – *action* rather than *thought* in relation to the object.

I now want to explore the relationship between identification and symbolisation a little further, through two longer clinical examples involving real trauma. I mean by this that they involved events that *could not* be processed, or even in one case begin to be symbolised, formulated as mental events.

### Clinical Material

#### Mr. P

Mr. P. is a man whom, I think, had never had his experiences transformed through maternal containment into a form in which he might gain some distance from them, or begin to objectify them. He could not perform mental operations on his own experience. Symbolic thought seemed to be absent, in part perhaps because his traumas began very early. I saw Mr. P in the prison where he had spent the last twenty years of his life. His index offence, the murder of a child, for which he was given life imprisonment, took place when he was 17 years old.

Mr. P was one of two children, a girl and a boy, born to a woman with a very troubled life of her own. Although Mr P was attached to and dependent on his mother, he was clear that she did not provide physical or emotional affection for either of the children. She worked as a prostitute. He was exposed from a very early age to a constant succession of men through the house, open sexuality, sexual talk and sexual coercion.

The first known assault on Mr P was perpetrated by his mother's partner one weekend, significantly when his mother was away. This was a violent and sexual assault by the adult on an undefended child – and the culmination of many acts of assault masquerading as punishment. His sister was also assaulted and raped (she is now schizophrenic). This assault seemed to confirm what was already a fundamental absence in Mr. P's life, that of any structure in which there was some recognition of a difference between the generations, or the sexes, and in which sexual intercourse was an act of affection rather than of commerce or of brutality. Mr P's behaviour as a child

204

became increasingly delinquent and anti-social, for which he got into trouble, and he began running away from home. At the age of 13 he found himself sleeping rough on the streets of London and he rapidly developed a sort of life as a rent boy, a child prostitute. To some extent this was an identification with his mother. Amongst many other things it was a primitive way of remaining in contact with someone who was needed, but unavailable for a real relationship, very much the situation with Mr P's mother.

Mr. P was picked up by the police soon after he had gained his first real job, which was work in a bowling alley, and was sent to live in a Social Services-run Children's Home. Over the next three years he was exposed to treatment far worse than anything he had so far encountered in his life, all of it done in the name of 'care'. The Director of the Home provided something he called 'regression therapy'. This involved the systematic humiliation and torture of these children until their defences against overwhelming anxiety were obliterated, at which point they were easy prey for the perverse sexual usage to which the Director and his staff subjected them. Most importantly, this total helplessness was induced by the staff's simultaneously restraining the child physically whilst goading it into a tantrum. When Mr P's defences were annihilated through the conviction that he himself was being annihilated, and he lost control both mentally and physically, the torturer became the comforter, with lollipops, sexual abuse, and assurances that this was 'treatment', and good for you.

There are two ways of dealing with extreme helplessness, which, as Freud (1926) pointed out, is the essence of a traumatising situation. One, as we saw with the first three examples, is to identify with an introjected version of the offending object, or with her act. In those particular cases, being left by the mother was short-lived, one of those small, essential but painful, developmental experiences. In Mr P's case, a child from a very different kind of background, the trauma was sustained and devastating. If terrifying experiences, principally those involving the fear of bodily annihilation, cannot be avoided, then to become a terrorizer is one way of feeling less helpless: it is the other that is terrified, not you. Another way is to cease struggling against the fear and horror of near-death, and instead to convert it to excitement, through libidinizing it, infusing it with sexuality, an expression of life, so that what is known to be bad is claimed to be desirable. Perhaps a third is to attack the apparatus for perception and thought itself, and to retreat into psychosis, as Mr. P's sister had done. Mr. P was, like all the children taken into this Home, hungry for some real

care, and thus extremely vulnerable to exploitation by those who pur-
ported to offer experiences that were designated 'good for you.'

When Mr P was 17, he reached the age at which he was considered
to be no longer eligible for Local Authority care, and he was dis-
charged into the community and expected to find work. Chief
amongst his many difficulties was the state of confused and helpless
mindlessness into which he had been driven through prolonged
'regression therapy'. In this state, with no helpful internal object with
which to identify, to leave the Home, live on his own and take a job
as though he had a mind of his own seemed impossible. Nevertheless
Mr. P, aged 17, managed to find a job with a firm of Industrial
Cleaners, and a bed-sitter in which to live.

On the fatal Sunday morning, Mr. P was in a particularly disturbed
state, split between on the one hand the internal pressures of his iso-
lation and inadequacy, and on the other hand the need to become an
adult, earn his living, take part in the world of work and adult relationships. His loneliness and need was aggravated by his mother's
absence with her lesbian lover (and probably therefore by the unconscious link with the weekend 10 years earlier when he had first been
assaulted.) There was a small boy who was playing in the street with
his dog and he seemed easier to relate to than the adults around him.
The boy was persuaded to accompany Mr. P upstairs to his bedsit. We
do not know what happened to cause suddenly and rapidly a fatal
shift in Mr. P's identifications, which was then enacted. Perhaps when
Mr. P. found a vulnerable object, he seized the opportunity to disiden-
tify with the needy, inadequate, regressed and abused aspects of himself through a total projective identification, a total evacuation of
those feelings into the child he had picked up. And at once, into the
gap – almost a vacuum – left by the disidentification, there imploded
the internal version of the murderously sadistic Director of the Home
he had just left. It is striking to note that Mr. P did to the boy precisely and in detail what had so often been done to him.

Mr P had had two primary identifications available to him, both of
them objects installed in place of what might have become his own
mind – the prostitute who was also the abused child; and the murderous abuser. When the first became unworkable (when he had to
leave the Home, live on his own and find employment), all that was
available to him as a way of being an adult male was the second. In
the absence of a mind – a place in which knowledge of the appalling
feelings these circumstances provoked could exist, making it possible
to imagine or day-dream or think about action instead of engaging

directly in it – then total identifications, and their physical enactment, become a solution to urgent internal problems. Mr. P was a man for whom thought, the making of mental connections, was impossible. For the first eight years of his prison sentence, it had never ever occurred to him that there was any link between what had been done to him as a child and what he had done to the child for whose murder he was now imprisoned. His mind, like his body, ran on a single-track line, to and fro, in which all that existed were mutual total projective identifications with the object. There was no possibility of sideways movement, no noticing, no revisiting, no comparing, no recognition – in short, no space. Living was done through the body, and memory and relating were enacted via the body. When the police finally arrested the Director of the Home, they visited Mr. P. in prison in the hope of getting him to give evidence, but what they told him confused him intolerably and he broke down into a state of agitated depression. Much of it was still evident 12 years on, when I saw him. To try to talk to him about the links between the past and the murder was to put him once more into a state of agitation and confusion that amounted to chaos. Certainly I felt, and so did he, that there was something quite helpless about his state of mind, which could only be modified with drink, drugs or other forms of psychic numbing.

In some respects Mr. P., I suggest, is functioning much as the lawyer functioned. The traumatic event could not be formulated and held in the mind, it had to be enacted. In each case, the child was told that what he found so traumatic was in fact 'good for him', to his advantage. In each case the outcome was confusion (between good and bad) and perversion. In each case there had to be found an object who could be made the recipient of all the unwanted vulnerable aspects of the self, leaving the ego free to swell with all the lofty, powerful and dangerous aspects of its other primary identification. The difference between the two of them lies in degree rather than in kind. What existed as a 'foreign body' in the mind of the lawyer occupied the whole of Mr. P's functioning. And ultimately Mr. P himself had to be treated as a 'foreign body' by the society in which he was trying to live.

## Ms. Q

My second case is very different, in that the patient, a young woman of 23, had had a reasonable early life. She had been to University and gained a first class degree in a complex subject. However, she was struggling with only intermittent success to hold on to her mental functioning after a deeply affecting traumatic event. Her mother had very recently been murdered by her husband, the patient's step-father, with repeated hammer-blows to the head. He had then tried and failed to kill himself. At the time of her first meeting with me he was unconscious and still in Intensive Care. In our meetings I felt there was a powerful enactment of the difficult problem this presented her with. The identification with her murdered mother, refusing to lose her by keeping her 'alive' via the identification, meant that she too lost her mind, bludgeoned about the head with a blunt instrument. In this situation she lost her capacity to use words at all. At times she entered a kind of mute, trance-like state which so frightened her boy-friend that twice he had called an ambulance. At other times she would sever meaningful connections with the words she was using and chatter in a manic over-animated way about everything she was managing to sort out for herself since the murder.

In the first meeting, I thought I could see the way she had begun to find of solving this problem. This was to create two mothers, separated from each other by a deep split. There was a secret mother who was still alive and lively, hidden inside her and with whom she could safely be identified in an almost triumphant way. There was also a brutally murdered mother whom she had to get rid of if she was to function at all. I think she did this by talking about the actual moments of the murder extremely tellingly, in such a succinct and vivid way that I found myself shaken, almost for a moment unable to breathe. Eventually I managed to try to describe to her the way in which she got me to feel the horror of the murder, to have as it were the murdered mother inside me, so that she could feel free to keep the live mother all to herself, inside her and away from danger. She got hold of this notion with surprise and a kind of relief. At the beginning of the second session she went straight back to it. She had said to her boyfriend after the session that when she'd told me something about the way her mother had died, I had winced, and she told him that she didn't think I'd winced in an 'oh poor you' kind of way. 'Do you know what I mean?' she said to me. 'There wasn't a kind of cow of a psychotherapist who talked and winced at all the appropriate moments, but actually it was genuine, it made you think, 'Oh God!' and how weird that was in a way for me, because it happened to me but it was you thinking 'Agh'.'

I did not take up that reference to a 'cow of a psychotherapist' because it seemed to me to contain a spark of liveliness. Not all her own aggression to her mother had been projected into the step-father.

I thought in particular it enabled her to express some of her hatred of the mother who had been 'a cow' for leaving her effectively orphaned, and of me for leaving her over the weekend. Yet there remained in this young woman a profound pull towards the literality of an identification and away from the 'mentality' of the thoughts about the murder. For some weeks she was deeply possessed by the need to become pregnant, to keep alive the mother who had had her in her in a very literal way. It also meant she tended to seize on new ideas with tremendous relief, as something to fill and occupy her mind, pushing out the all-too-vivid thoughts of the murder and thus keeping at bay the overwhelming urge to turn to an identification.

Sometimes this switched to an identification with the murdering step-father, whom she was genuinely afraid of killing. A few weeks later, she did in fact perform an act of semi-symbolic murder, which was also a desperate further attempt to rid herself of the sense of being lumbered with the murdered object. She took various bits of her step-father's clothes and pushed them bit by bit through the letter-box of the woman with whom he'd been having an affair, plus a violent letter. In this act she carried out not an actual murder but a token, representative version of the murder. Importantly, it contained both bodily elements (the bits of clothing) and mentalised elements (the letter). Probably both had to be there if the projection of extreme distress was to work. Yet already there was a shift away from the total introjective identification with the murdered mother and toward something alive, if dangerous. (Murder, in this sense, can be seen as a defence against suicide.)

Over 18 months later there was evidence of a further shift away from an enacted identification and towards a recovery of her capacity to symbolise action through thought – through verbalising a wish to do something and allowing the spoken wish to stand for the action. She told me she still had in a bag in her attic the bloodstained dressing-gown her mother had been wearing when she had been struck down, and that stuck to it were fragments of tissue and hair. These physical fragments stood in a concrete way for the last of her physical mother, and she could not bear to relinquish them. She wanted instead, and she spoke about it very vividly, to arrange her hair like her mother's, to put on the dressing gown, and to stalk down the ward in the prison hospital towards her imprisoned step-father, to give him 'the fright of his life.' But, she added, 'I won't do it.' Here the identifications are complex – that with the murdered mother is clear, becoming her vengeful ghost; but also with the murderer, the man who gave her mother the

209

fright of her life. The element of rage in her has an important defensive function, as it must do in all those survivors who suffer from greatly increased irritability (a noticeable post-traumatic symptom) since it has an important organising function as well as being a sign of life in its own right. The broken-down fragments of the ego can reorganise themselves around a convincing state of rage, and give some semblance of coherence to a very damaged personality. (The violent irritability of borderline personalities is probably clung to for this kind of reason.)

A further 18 months later, this young woman, who was by now in a good partnership, gave birth to a healthy baby girl. At first her anxiety about the baby's well-being was overwhelming, going as far as midnight dashes to hospitals with a crying baby. Here the identification that was most terrifying was that of being a failed mother, as in a sense her own was. She had longed for her mother's presence deeply during the pregnancy and had expressed anger with her mother's stupidity for not seeing what 'a dead loss' her husband had been, thus avoiding being murdered. For her, the baby's crying was also her own, and it was unbearable to her. However, after 2 months when the new family had somewhat settled down, and the baby was breast feeding and putting on weight, she and her partner decided to try to help the baby move out of their own bed and into a crib. She decided that she would pick the baby up whenever it cried, and then put it down again in its own crib, instead of taking it once again into their bed. Here we can see the struggle to free herself from the overwhelming identification with the crying baby, and to function instead as the good, alive mother who is able to care for the little girl. Then she told me that whenever the baby cried, she would rush to it saying, 'Mummy's coming, Mummy's coming!' This was one of the only times I ever saw visible tears. She said, 'I'm saying it to her, but I'm also saying it to myself, though I know I'll never see my mother again.' At these moments she seemed able to move out of the pull of some deeply unhelpful identifications and into a position where she could once again think her thoughts instead of having to enact them.

There was a further shift away from the concreteness of the identifications within the next year. She and her partner decided they were now able to sell the mother's house, the one they had been living in since the murder, and buy a new property, one which would be their own. The freezer still contained the last meals that her mother had made and frozen to be eaten later on. She was able to jettison these with a few tears, and eventually as they prepared to move, to put into the skip outside the house a bag containing her mother's unusable clothes. These included the bloodstained dressing-gown, hidden in a plastic bag. As the process of mourning continued, there was increasingly a sense within her of a live mother, one who could breast-feed and care for a baby girl, and she was able to relinquish the remnants of the actual physical mother, along with the old house she had grown up in with her.

Yet for this young woman, the mourning for her murdered mother was a lengthy, complex and painful process. Sometimes she was quite overwhelmed by the sadness, and found mothering her own baby while feeling so unmothered herself very difficult indeed. Much of the eventual success of this mourning must eventually depend on how her life progresses. Some traumatic events are too great, and some are too sustained to allow for a wholly satisfactory recovery, and some degree of dissociation from the physical details of the traumatic event may always remain. This may be a way of dealing with something that is too primitive, too central to the survivor's own being, own identity, to be able to be symbolised. Perhaps the murder of a mother is a case in point.

## Discussion

I go on to describe two particular features of the response to a severe traumatic event which are relevant to this chapter's focus on the relationship between thought and action.

First, it is probably the case that at the moment of impact, psychic organisation is so disrupted that for a few moments the phantasy that ordinarily accompanies perception and sensation, the phantasy that links body and mind, is put out of action. There is then a period of overwhelming confusion, of *dis*-integration, in which pain, ignorance, and the kind of fear that is generated by utter helplessness are dominant. That fear is aggravated by ruptured communication between body and mind. All defences against overwhelming anxiety are lost. Two things follow, more or less simultaneously. The first concerns the body itself. We often remind ourselves, following Freud (1923), that 'the ego is first and foremost a bodily ego'. Yet we only become fully aware of the presence of the body when it is injured or when it goes wrong. The sense of confusion, outrage and agitation that follows damage to the body derives, I am suggesting, in part from the ego's sense that it has, however briefly, lost touch with its normal means of communicating with its own body, namely through phantasy. There is no longer an uninterrupted sense of 'fit'. The ego hunts for information about what has happened to the body, or the bodies of its internal objects, and the outcome can manifest itself as an agitated sense of unidentifiable distress. *Purely mental operations are no longer felt to be credible.* Perhaps some of the more puzzling re-enactments, traumatic repetitions and very insistent and concrete projective identifications that we come across (for example, Ms Q's need to lodge in me the her whose mother had been murdered) are contributed to by this need to work out *through physical experience* what sort of state this post-traumatic body is in, what it can and cannot do, in the hope of reestablishing this essential correspondence between body and mind.

Second is the process that Freud called binding – the attempt to make sense of something that appears meaningless or inexplicable through linking it up with already-existing structures. This is related to the process just described, in that it involves desperate attempts to reforge connections. It has a positive productive aspect, but it is also problematical, particularly in severe trauma, since binding means making links with earlier experiences that are perceived as similar or related. Of course, these are more than likely to be early (even very early) bad experiences, areas of untransformed experience. Thus it is only a few moments before the confusion is added to by an acute sense of personal assault. *Who let this happen? Who failed to prevent this from happening? Who did this to me?* And at the deepest level (see Chapter 7) as Bion, following Klein, spelled out, the object who failed to prevent this pain and confusion is the figure that exposes you to it, and indeed that does it to you: the infant's stomach pain is added to by the terror of a persecuting mother, the bad object, the one that was trusted to protect you from pain, confusion, terror and annihilation. The individual is plunged back into a paranoid-schizoid universe. Segal (1957) has already shown how concrete thinking is dominant in the paranoid-schizoid position. The individual loses touch with depressive-position functioning, in which the object's separateness is known about and tolerated, leaving the mind free to play with ways of representing the relationship with the object.

I want to link this observation with certain aspects of the very earliest forms of identification which involve the body, and bodily movements, gestures, ways of doing things, facial expressions. These begin as imitation, (part of the mechanism of introjection) and proceed in increasingly subtle ways to become identifications, until eventually, in a digested form, they become identity. This early basis of the self in the body links to the recognition that severe trauma involves annihilation anxiety, or the end of the life of the body.

## 13. *Action, Identification and Thought in Post-Traumatic States*

Thus the return to the body is connected with two things. First, the fear for the integrity and the survival of the body, which leads to the preoccupation with physical states; and second the need to repair the correspondence between the physical and the mental, whether that involves the self or the object. The entire system of pre-trauma representation of the body, and the body of the object, has to be reworked before it can be successfully symbolised and thus mourned in a depressive way. And yet of course it cannot be reworked until some rudiments of the capacity to symbolise have been restored. The traumatised individual may become deadlocked in this respect, and then the permanent split – or the creation of the 'foreign body' – is one form of solution. I suggest this deadlock is created by the simultaneous existence of the two facts I have already touched on. First, at times of deep fear and confusion the immediate resort is to turn back to and connect with the body of the primary object (as non-human primates can do so readily). Second, and this what makes the clinging problematical, it is that same primary object that is at best felt to have failed to prevent the catastrophe, at worst to have been its agent. How does this paradox and this problem get resolved?

I am proposing that, in post-traumatic states, the very concrete form of identification with the primary object that is seen again and again in clinical work is a way of getting round the incompatibility of these two facts. In a post-traumatic state, the identifications that are turned to do not, I suggest, really involve a fundamentally different process from that of symbolisation. Both may be seen as part of *a single process* which can be carried out either bodily or mentally, or by some amalgam of the two – as in 'Allo-byebye', or as in the symbolic equation. In post-traumatic states, the move is towards the physical and the bodily, and away from the abstract and the mental. In that it involves 'becoming' the object, or making the object 'be' you, of course it resembles developmental forms of identification, those that Freud recognised as the earliest way we have of relating to our objects. However, it is not identical with them. Post-traumatic identification, I think, includes the recognition that matters may be and can be represented in a variety of ways, but that at this moment the safest way of relating to the primary object is one that involves clinging to it through *being* it, rather than being at a mental distance from it. This way, if the object is perceived as omnipotently powerful and damaging (Mr. P), the ego protects itself by being indistinguishable from it, and therefore shares in its properties. If the object is perceived as vulnerable and damaged (Ms. Q), the ego is equally protected by its

213

identification, avoiding the mental pain of guilt that would have to be endured if it were to continue with its independence and liveliness when the object is dead or mutilated.

Can all traumatic events be processed and made available for thought? Probably not. Some retain their intense and untransformed nature (Bion's 'beta elements') containing all the original affect generated by the event. In part this is because of the intensity of such events. Some experience is not transformable. Some may have to be left as a 'foreign body', in the hope that time and other less dreadful experiences will mitigate its traumatic nature. Second, there is the fact that the good object has already gone bad, become dangerous and is therefore unavailable as a containing object. But also and third, partly because (to use an analogy from *Word for Windows*) the ego has already made a block out of the relevant portion of itself, dragged it with the cursor over onto the body of the internalised primary object, and pressed 'Enter'. It is then installed in an identification with its primary object, one so total it amounts to fusion. That primary object is thus lost to the ego as a container, one which might have otherwise have been able to help with that very process of transformation. Ms. Q's experience makes this problem explicit.

The task of the analyst is to provide a setting in which once again that gradual process of transformation can begin to take place. This means that the distance between the ego and its object can once again be tolerated, triangular space (Britton, 1998) established, and the relationship begin to be formulated mentally, or symbolised. This involves, and is close to saying, that the pre-trauma relations with the object have to be *mourned* (see Chapter 6).

When working with traumatised patients we have to recognise repeatedly that at the centre of the work must lie the recognition of that sense of loss, one so great that it seems to include the whole of the pre-trauma world and existence. It is the loss of the relationship with the good object, whose nature has changed fundamentally. Some new way of relating to this lost good object, and some way of dealing with this very present bad object, has to be achieved. The old symbols standing for the relationship with the good and bad objects (the *pre-catastrophic* symbols) will no longer do to represent the *post-catastrophic* objects. The entire object world has to be reformulated and this is a daunting task. Until this has been achieved, actions will tend to replace the capacity for thought.

Yet when psychoanalysis or psychoanalytic therapy is available, there is the hope of a new working through, and a fresh translation of these identifications and enactments into mental processes – in some cases, perhaps, for the first time. Once the process of mentalisation is set in motion, there is then the potential for thinking, feeling and imagining. And this, for the traumatised patient, is the same as saying that there is the possibility of a personal future once more.

# Understanding Trauma
## Suggestions for Further Reading

Barker, P. (1991) *Regeneration*, London: Viking; repr. Penguin (1992).

Furst, S. (Ed.) (1967) *Psychic Trauma*, New York: Basic Books.

Krystal, H. (Ed.) (1976) *Massive Psychic Trauma*, New York: International Universities Press.

Remarque, E.M. (1929) *All Quiet on the Western Front*, London: Vintage (Random House); repr. (1996).

Rothstein, A. (Ed.) (1986) *The Reconstruction of Trauma*, Madison, CT: Int. Univ. Press.

Shengold, L. (1989) *Soul Murder: the Effects of Childhood Abuse and Deprivation*, New Haven & London: Yale University Press.

Wolfenstein, M. (1957) *Disaster: a Psychological Essay*, London: Routledge & Kegan Paul.

Young, A. (1990) *The Harmony of Illusions: Inventing Post-Traumatic Stress Disorder*, Princeton New Jersey: Princeton University Press.

# Bibliography

Abraham, K. (1907) 'The Experiencing of Sexual Traumas as a Form of Sexual Activity', in *Selected Papers on Psychoanalysis*, London: Maresfield Library, Karnac; repr. (1988).

Ackerman, N.W. (1958) *The Psychodynamics of Family Life*, New York: Basic Books.

Anzieu, D. (1993) 'The Film of the Dream', in *The Dream Discourse Today*, Ed. Flanders, S., London: Routledge, (1993), 137–150.

Balint, M. (1969) 'Trauma and object relationship', *International Journal of Psycho-Analysis*, 50: 429.

Bellow, S. (1953) *The Adventures of Augie March*, London: Penguin Books, (1994).

Bettelheim, B. (1952) 'Trauma and Reintegration', in *Surviving and Other Essays* (1980), New York: Vintage Books.

—— (1960) *The Informed Heart*, Free Press, A Corporation, USA.

Bianchedi, E.T. de (1995) 'Creative Writers and Dream-Work-Alpha', in *On Freud's Creative Writers and Day Dreaming*, Ed. Pesson, E.S., Fonagy, P., Figueira, S.A., Yale University Press: New York and London, (1995), 122–132.

Bick, E. (1968) 'The experience of skin in early object relations', *International Journal of Psycho-Analysis*, 49: 484–6. Also in *Collected Papers of Martha Harris and Esther Bick*, London: Clunie Press, (1987).

Bion, W.R. (1952) 'Group Dynamics: a Re-view', in *Experiences in Groups, and other papers*, London: Tavistock, (1961).

—— (1961) *Experiences in Groups, and other papers*, London: Tavistock.

—— (1962) *Learning from Experience*, London: Heinemann; repr. London: Karnac Books, (1984).

—— (1967a) 'Attacks on Linking', in *Second Thoughts: selected papers on psychoanalysis*, repr. (1984) London: Maresfield Reprints.

—— (1967b) 'A Theory of Thinking', in *Second Thoughts: selected papers on psychoanalysis*, repr. (1984), London: Maresfield Reprints.

Bion, W. (1967c) A theory of thinking. In *Second Thoughts*, reprinted 1984. London: Maresfield Imprints.

Bowlby, J., Miller, E. and Winnicott, D.W. (1939) Letter: 'Evacuation of small children', *British Medical Journal*, 16th December 1939, p. 1202–3.

Bowlby, J. (1944) 'Forty-four juvenile thieves: their characters and home-life', *International Journal of Psycho-Analysis*, 25: 1–57.

Bowlby, J. (1969) *Attachment and Loss. Volume 1: Attachment*, London: Hogarth Press.

Breslau, N.; Davis, G.C.; Andreski, P. and Petersen, E. (1991) 'Traumatic events and post-traumatic stress disorder in an urban population of young adults', *Arch. Gen. Psych.*, Vol. 48: 216–22.

Britton, R.S. (1989) 'The Missing Link: Parental Sexuality in the Oedipus Complex', in *The Oedipus Complex Today*, ed. R.S. Britton et al., London: Karnac Books, pp. 83–101.

Britton, R. (1998) Subjectivity, objectivity and triangular space. In *Belief and Imagination: explorations in psychoanalysis*. New Library of Psychoanalysis. London and New York: Routledge.

Carpy, D. (1987) *Fantasy versus reality in childhood trauma: who's to blame?*, London: Tavistock Clinic Paper no. 645, (1987).

DSM-IV, Diagnostic and Statistical Manual of Mental Disorders, American Psychiatric Association, Washington D.C.

Engdahl, B.; Speed, N.; Eberly, R. and Schwartz, J. (1991) 'Co-morbidity of psychiatric disorders and personality profiles of American World War II prisoners of war', *J. Nerv. Ment. Dis.*, 179: 181–7.

Feldman, M. (1995) *Grievance: The Underlying Oedipal Configuration*, (unpublished manuscript).

Ferenczi, S. (1933) 'Confusions of Tongues Between Adults and the Child', in *Final Contributions to the Problems and Methods of Psychoanalysis*, London: Hogarth Press; repr. (1955).

Fonagy, P. (1995) ' Playing with reality. The development of psychic reality and its malfunction in borderline personalities', *International Journal of Psycho-Analysis*, 96: 39–43, part 1.

Foulkes, S.H. (1964) *Therapeutic Group Analysis*, London: Allen & Unwin.

Freud, A. (1936) *The Ego and the Mechanisms of Defence*, London: Hogarth Press and The Institute of Psycho-Analysis.

Freud, S. (1893) 'On the Psychical Mechanism of Hysterical Phenomena: a Lecture', *Standard Edition*, vol. 3.

—— (1895) 'Studies in Hysteria', *S.E.*, 2, London: Hogarth Press.

—— (1900) 'The Interpretation of Dreams', *S.E.*, 4–5.

—— (1901) 'The Psychopathology of Everyday Life', *S.E.*, 6.

—— (1905) 'Three Essays on the Theory of Sexuality', *S.E.*, 7: 130–253.

—— (1909) 'Analysis of a Phobia in a Five-Year-Old Boy', *S.E.*, 10: 122.

—— (1914a) 'On the History of the Psycho-Analytic Movement', *S.E.*, 14.

—— (1914b) 'Remembering, Repeating and Working Through', *S.E.*, 12: 147.

—— (1915a) 'Thoughts for the Times on War and Death', *S.E.*, 14.

—— (1915b) 'Mourning and Melancholia', *S.E.*, 14: 239–58; rev. (1917).

—— (1915c) 'Introductory Lectures', *S.E.*, 15.

—— (1915d) Thoughts for the times on war and death. Standard Edition, 14: 273.

—— (1916) 'Some Character-types Met with in Psychoanalytic Work: III Criminals from a Sense of Guilt', *S.E.*, 14.

—— (1916) 'Introductory Lectures on Psychoanalysis', *S.E.*, 16: 275.

—— (1917) Mourning and Melancholia. Standard Edition, 14: 237.

—— (1920a) 'Beyond the Pleasure Principle', *S.E.*, 18: 1–64.

—— (1920b) Beyond the Pleasure Principle. Standard Edition, 18: 7.

—— (1921) 'Group Psychology and the Analysis of the Ego', *S.E.*, 18: 69–143.

—— (1923a) 'The Ego and the Id', *S.E.*, 19.

—— (1923b) The Ego and the Id. Standard Edition, 19: 3.

—— (1924) 'Neurosis and Psychosis', *S.E.*, 19.

—— (1926a) 'Inhibitions, Symptoms and Anxiety', *S.E.*, 20.

—— (1926b) Inhibitions, symptoms and anxiety. Standard Edition, 20: 87.

—— (1930) 'Civilizations and its Discontents', *S.E.*, 21: 64–145.

—— (1932) 'New Introductory Lectures on Psycho-Analysis', *S.E.*, 22.

—— (1893) (With Breuer) On the psychical mechanism of hysterical phenomena: preliminary communication. Standard Edition, 2: 1.

Garland, C.B. (1982) 'Taking the non-problem seriously', *Group Analysis*, 15: 1.

—— (1991) 'External Disasters and the Internal World: an approach to psychotherapeutic understanding of survivors', (Chapter 22) in *Textbook of Psychotherapy in Psychiatric Practice*, edited by J. Holmes, London: Churchill Livingstone.

—— (1993) 'The lasting trauma of the concentration camps', (Editorial) *British Medical Journal*, 307: 77–78.

—— (1997) 'From Troubled Families to Corrupt Care: sexual abuse in institutions', in *A Practical Guide to Forensic Psychotherapy*, Welldon and Van Velsen (eds), London and Bristol, Pennsylvania: Jessica Kingsley Publishers.

Green, B.L.; Lindy, J.D.; Grace, M.C. and Leonard, A.C. (1992) 'Chronic post-traumatic stress disorder and diagnostic co-morbidity in a disaster sample', *J. Nerv. Mental Dis.*, 180: 760–6.

Greenacre, P. (1953) *Trauma, Growth and Personality,* London: Maresfield Library, Karnac; repr. (1987).

Greenson, R. (1970) 'The exceptional position of the dream in psychoanalytic practice', *The Psychoanalytic Quarterly*, 39: 519–49, repr. in: *The Dream Discourse Today*, (1993), ed. Sara Flanders, in the New Library of Psycho-Analysis, Routledge.

Hunter, H.D. (1946) 'The work of a corps psychiatrist in the Italian campaign', *Journal of the Royal Army Medical Corps*, 86: 127–30.

ID-10: *Classification of Mental and Behavioural Disorders*, Clinical descriptions and diagnostic guidelines, World Health Organisation, Geneva.

Jacques, E. (1955) 'Social systems as a defence against persecutory and depressive anxiety', repr. (1977) in *New Directions in Psycho-Analysis*, Klein, M., Heimann, P., Money-Kyrle, R. (eds), London: Maresfield Reprints.

Johns, M. (1992) 'Preventable disasters: pride, shame and self blinding', *Psychoanalytic Psychotherapy*, 6: (1) 13–20.

Jucovy, M.E. (1992) 'Psychoanalytic contributions to holocaust studies', *International Journal of Psycho-Analysis*, 73: 267–82.

Keane, T. and Wolf, J. (1990) 'Co-morbidity in Post-traumatic stress disorder: an analysis of community and clinical studies', *J. Appl. Soc. Psychol.*, 20: 1776–88.

Kessler, R.C.; Sonnega, A.; Bromet, E. and Hughes, M. (1995) 'Post-traumatic stress disorder in the National Co-morbidity Survey', *Arch. Gen. Psych.*, 52: 1048–60.

Khan, M.M.R. (1963) 'The Concept of Cumulative Trauma', in *The Privacy of the Self*, London: Hogarth Press, (1974), pp. 42-58; repr. (1996), London: Maresfield Library, Karnac.

—— (1964) 'Ego Distortion, Cumulative Trauma, and the Role of Reconstruction in the Analytic Situation', repr. (1996) in *The Privacy of the Self*, London: Maresfield Library, Karnac.

King, P. (1978) 'Affective response of the analyst to the patient's communications', *International Journal of Psycho-Analysis*, 59: (2–3) 329–34.

Klein, M. (1929a) 'Personification in the Play of the Child', in *Love, Guilt and Reparation and Other Works*, Vol. 1 of the Writings of Melanie Klein, London, Hogarth Press, repr. (1981).

—— (1929b) 'Infantile Anxiety Situations Reflected in a Work of Art and in the Creative Impulse', op. cit.

—— (1935) 'A contribution to the psychogenesis of manic depressive states', *International Journal of Psycho-Analysis*, 16: 145–74. Also in *The Writings of Melanie Klein, Vol. 1*, London: Hogarth Press and the Institute of Psycho-Analysis, (1975).

—— (1940a) 'Mourning and its Relation to Manic Depressive States', *International Journal of Psycho-Analysis*, 21: 125–53. Also in *The Writings of Melanie Klein, Vol. 1*, London: Hogarth Press and the Institute of Psycho-Analysis, (1975), 344–69.

—— (1940b) Mourning and its relation to manic-depressive states. Reprinted in *Love, Guilt and Reparation*, London Hogarth Press (1975).

—— (1945) 'The Oedipus Complex in the Light of Early Anxieties', op. cit.

—— (1946a) 'Notes on some schizoid mechanisms', *International Journal of Psycho-Analysis*, 27: 99–110. Also in *The Writings of Melanie Klein, Vol. III*, (1975).

—— (1946b) Notes on some schizoid mechanisms. In *Envy and Gratitude and Other Works, 1946–1963*. Reprinted 1980, London: Hogarth Press.

—— (1952) 'Some Theoretical Conclusions Regarding the Emotional Life of the Infant', (chapter 6) in *Envy and Gratitude, Vol. 3*, The Writings of Melanie Klein, (1975), London, Hogarth Press.

—— (1975) *Love, Guilt and Reparation and other works (1921–45)*, London: Hogarth.

# Bibliography

Kulka, R.; Schlenger, W.; Fairbank, J.; Hough, R.; Jordan, B.; Marmar, C. and Weis, D. (1990) *Trauma and the Vietnam War Generation*, New York: Bruner/Mazel.

Langer, M. (1989) 'Psychoanalysis without the cough', text of lecture given in Casa de las Americas, La Habana, Cuba (1985); transl. and publ. in *Free Associations*, 15: 60–6, (1989).

Laplanche, J. and Pontalis, J.B. (1973) *The Language of Psycho-Analysis*, London: Hogarth Press.

Menninger, K. (1959) 'The psychiatric diagnosis', *Bull. Menn. Clin.*, 23: 226–40.

Menzies-Lyth, I. (1989) 'The Aftermath of Disaster: Survival and Loss', in *The Dynamics of the Social*, London: Free Association Books.

Milton, J. (1997) 'Why assess? Psychoanalytical psychotherapy in the NHS', *Psychoanalytic Psychotherapy*, 11 (1): 47–58.

O'Shaughnessy, E. (1964) 'The absent object', *Journal of Child Psychotherapy*, 1 (2): 134–43.

Rosenfeld, H. (1949) 'Remarks on the relation of male homosexuality to paranoia, paranoid anxiety and narcissism', *International Journal of Psychoanalysis*, 30: 36–47.

—— (1971) 'A clinical approach to the psycho-analytical theory of the life and death instincts: an investigation into the aggressive aspects of narcissism', *International Journal of Psychoanalysis*, 52: 169–78.

Sandler, J. and Joffe, W. (1967) 'The tendency to persistence in psychological function and development, with special reference to fixation and regression', *Bulletin of Menninger Clinic*, 31: 257–71.

Sandler, J. and Perlow, M. (1987) 'Internalization and Externalization', in *Projection, Identification, Projective Identification*, edited by J. Sandler, Karnac Books.

Schafer, R. (1968) *Aspects of Internalization*, New York: International University Press.

Searles, H. (1963) 'The Place of Neutral Therapist-Responses in Psychotherapy with the Schizophrenic Patient', in *Collected Papers on Schizophrenia and Related Subjects*, 626–653.

Segal, H. (1957) 'Notes on Symbol Formation', in *The Work of Hanna Segal: a Kleinian Approach to Clinical Practice*, New York, London: Jason Aronson; repr. (1981).

—— (1981) 'The Function of Dreams', in *The Work of Hanna Segal: a Kleinian Approach to Clinical Practice*, NY London: Jason Aronson; also in *Do I Dare Disturb the Universe? A Memorial to Wilfred Bion*, (1983), edited by James S. & Grotstein, H.; Karnac Books.

—— (1991) *Dream, Phantasy and Art*, London: Routledge.

Segal, H. (1993) 'On the Clinical Usefulness of the Concept of the Death Instinct', in *Psychoanalysis, Literature and War, Papers 1972–1995*, London: Routledge (The New Library of Psychoanalysis).

Semprun, J. (1997) *Literature of Life*, Viking, USA.

Sodré, I. (1995) 'Who's Who? Notes on pathological identifications', paper delivered at the conference *Understanding Projective Identification: Clinical Advances*, UCL, October 1995.

Steiner, J. (1987) 'Interplay between pathological organization and the paranoid–schizoid and depressive positions', *International Journal of Psycho-Anlaysis*, 68: 69–80.

—— (1996) 'Revenge and resentment in the Oedipal situation', *International Journal of Psycho-Analysis*, 77: 433–43.

Wardi, D. (1992) *Memorial Candles: Children of the Holocaust*, London: Routledge.

Winnicott, D.W. (1952) 'Psychosis and Child Care' in *Through Paediatrics to Psycho-Analysis*, London: Hogarth Press, (1975).

—— (1958) *The Anti-Social Tendency*, London: Tavistock Publications.

—— (1965) *The Maturational Processes and the Facilitating Environment*, London: Hogarth Press (1982).

—— (1966) 'The Ordinary Devoted Mother', in *Babies and Their Mothers*, Free Association Books.

—— (1967) 'The Location of Cultural Experience', in *Playing and Reality*, London: Penguin Books, (1974).

Yorke, C. (1986) 'Reflections on the problem of psychic trauma', *Psychoanalytic Study of the Child*, 41, p. 221.

# Index

## Subjects

223

226

# Index

## Names